WE ONLY KILL EACH OTHER:

THE LIFE AND BAD TIMES OF BUGSY SIEGEL

by Dean Jennings

Prentice-Hall, Inc. Englewood Cliffs, N.J.

THIS IS FOR MARY

Fourth printing . . . . . . February, 1968

 Library of Congress Catalog Card Number: 67–26867 / *Printed in the United States of America* / T95006 / Prentice-Hall International, Inc., *London* / Prentice-Hall of Australia, Pty. Ltd., *Sydney* / Prentice-Hall of Canada, Ltd., *Toronto* / Prentice-Hall of India Private Ltd., *New Delhi* / Prentice-Hall of Japan, Inc., *Tokyo*

BOOKS BY DEAN JENNINGS

The Man Who Killed Hitler

Leg Man

The San Quentin Story
(With Warden Clinton T. Duffy)

Confessions of a Happy Man
(With Art Linkletter)

My First Hundred Years in Hollywood
(With Jack L. Warner)

We Only Kill Each Other

INTRODUCTION AND ACKNOWLEDGMENTS

Herman Melville once wrote: "Even truth itself decays, and lo, from truth's sad ashes pain and falsehood grow."

Two years ago, when I first began stirring the ashes of the Bugsy Siegel-Virginia Hill legend, the truth had decayed indeed, to feed both pain and falsehood.

"So you're going to dig up the bodies in the Bugsy Siegel case?" a newspaperman friend asked.

"I'm going to try," I said.

"Forget it," he advised. "Nobody will talk. There are too many people alive around Las Vegas and L.A. and New York who want to keep the lid on the coffin. The Bug had friends way up in the high places. You'll not only get the fastest brush-off you ever saw, but you might get some knuckles in your teeth, too. Why don't you write a nice, safe book like . . . well, like how to raise orchids or knit sweaters?"

"You're kidding," I said.

"No, I'm not. This was a tough mob, and the guys who are still alive are tough, too. They won't tell you who knocked him off, or what happened to the big dough he had stashed away."

My friend should have known better.

He should have remembered that some people *like* to talk. He might have recalled Shakespeare's lines in King Richard the Third: "My conscience hath a thousand several tongues, and every tongue brings in a several tale." Conscience and people's tongues, plus the official records and the curious recall many people have about a crime are not by themselves the ingredients of a book. But when you put them all together it is possible to reconstruct what happened—and then you have a book.

This is not a book about the Mafia, or the Cosa Nostra or The Syndicate—related subjects so complex and far-flung that the famed Kefauver Commission filled up volumes with testimony in a series of coast to coast hearings, and still did not get below the surface. That story has been written in segments by others, and is still being written as the criminal empire grows.

This is a book about two people who were a sort of branch King and Queen in the western outpost of the crime domain—Bugsy Siegel, the man who invented Las Vegas, and his girl (and secret wife), the remarkable Virginia Hill.

Since I started this project, I have not had any "knuckles in my teeth," perhaps because those involved did not know what I would write. Virginia Hill was the only principal who called me names, and hinted there might be trouble, but I understood the fear and despair in her mind. Also, I never got into her bedroom, where trouble often started, or any other place where she could throw a knife at me, gash my head with the spiked heel of her shoe, or whip me with a pistol butt.

So here is the truth, cleared of decay, and rising from its own sad ashes.

I am indebted first to Art Linkletter and his associate Clyde Vandeburg, who encouraged me in this book from the beginning, and kept me going with moral and financial support.

Likewise, I could not have found the truth without the unselfish help of Virginia's brother, Charles "Chick" Hill, who was with Bugsy Siegel for a long time before that last bloody moment, and who felt from the start that his beautiful sister would never find peace.

Chick Hill and George Raft, both of whom admired the violent and quixotic gangster known as "The Bug," gave me hours of their time in tape-recorded talks, and without them there would have been no book.

The men in law enforcement, to whom Siegel was the enemy, were equal contributors when they began prodding their memories and going through dusty files, and I wish to name them here:

The men of the Intelligence Division of the Internal Revenue Service in Los Angeles, particularly Special Agent Clifford Rice, who wrapped up the Virginia Hill tax case, and has now retired. Captain Daryl F. Gates, then Commander of the Intelligence Division of the Los Angeles Police Department and his predecessor, the late Captain James Hamilton, and the man who was assistant to both of them, Lieutenant M. B. Phillips.

Police Chief Clinton Anderson of Beverly Hills, who submitted to a taped interview, but who would prefer to forget Bugsy Siegel. Lieutenant George Stoner, Chief of the Bureau of Investigation for the District Attorney of Los Angeles, and former Deputy D. A. Eugene Williams, who once flushed The Bug from his hideout.

A. L. Coffey, Chief of the California State Bureau of Criminal Identification and Investigation and his capable aides, Supervising Agent Kenneth Horton, and Special Agent Raymond F. McCarthy, who opened a long-closed file for me. J. Edgar Hoover of the FBI; Virgil M. Peterson, famed director of the Chicago Crime Commission; William J. Durkin of the U.S. Bureau of Narcotics in Mexico City, and U.S. Attorney Manuel Real of Los Angeles.

In Las Vegas, Hank Greenspun, crusading publisher of the *Las Vegas Sun* and his star reporter, Joe McClain, risked their own safety to tell what they knew. So did Paul Price, Siegel's one-time press agent and now a *Sun* columnist; Dick Chappell, assistant manager of the Flamingo Hotel when Siegel's reign ended, and Abe Schiller, the veteran press agent often called "Mr. Las Vegas."

In New York I got valuable information from newspapermen Doug Hearle and Gus Engleman, and from Burton Turkus, lawyer, author, and prosecutor of the Murder Inc. mob. In Los Angeles the late Jim Richardson, former city editor of the *Examiner*, spent hours talking to me about Siegel at a time when I could not foresee this book, and during that same period I also had a memorable interview with the late movie director Rowland Brown.

I am grateful also to Mickey Cohen, the little mobster now in prison, because he enjoyed hearing himself talk, and poured his explosive relationship with Siegel into my microphone.

Jack L. Warner, then President of Warner Bros. Pictures and his former social secretary, Richard Gully, had some unforgettable adventures with Bugsy Siegel, and gave them to me in detail. Author Ovid Demaris, who with Ed Reid first blew the whistle on the underworld control of Las Vegas casinos in *The Green Felt Jungle*, courteously loaned me his personal file on The Bug. The editors of the *Los Angeles Times* and the *Los Angeles Herald-Examiner* let me browse through their extensive morgue of clippings on the Siegel era.

And finally, because there would have been no finished book without them, I want to thank my wife Mary, whose unerring editorial eye checked every line of the story; Gladys Callaway of Los Angeles, who transcribed endless pages of interviews and notes, and Esther Daniels of Mill Valley, who devoted many hours to the typing of final copy.

"We only kill each other," Bugsy Siegel once said.

I hope he was right, and that none of those who guided me to the facts will be penalized for their generous help.

CHAPTER ONE

You live by the gun and knife, and die by the gun and knife.
——JOE VALACHI.

June 20, 1947.

The night wind swept in from the west on Strip 91, the lonely road that ran through the endless desert as a dark vein bearing the sluggish plasma of people and cars that kept Las Vegas alive.

The heat rose from the dry land, and as it flowed into the air currents, the wind picked up speed and sucked up grains of sand and fired them, like shotgun pellets, across the road and the flat land. The tumbleweed broke from its roots, and the gnarled balls sped and bounced with the wind, and the silvery heads of the sagebrush yielded and lay close to the soil.

And in Las Vegas, the old-timers heard the shrieking of the sand-laden wind, closed windows and doors, and canceled whatever plans they had for going out that night.

At exactly ten minutes before midnight, Hank Greenspun, at that time press agent for the new and unique Flamingo Hotel, locked his office door and walked into the casino lobby. The thick glass doors at the front entrance were already trembling from the pressure of the rising wind, and the sand spray was forming little dunes on the outside steps.

Mariano Gissey, the swarthy young *maître d'hôtel*, who had just arrived from Palm Springs to take over the gaudy Flamingo Room, saw Greenspun and greeted him with a frown.

"Hank," he said, "you're not going out on a night like this?"

"The job doesn't say I gotta sleep here," Greenspun said. "I'm going home."

"Listen, kid, you're nuts. I've seen sandstorms before. You hit that highway tonight and you'll be three days digging the sand outa your engine."

"Yeah, I know. See you around."

Greenspun stood there a moment, listening to the droning spiel of the stickmen at the crap table, and the mesmeric sound of the dice, like the rattles of a desert snake. For some of the players the silent strike against the felt was like sudden death. The vast curtained room, forever quarantined against the reality of sunlight, was jammed with the impassive faces of the betters. The castanet click of the chips was a dance without end in a haze of cigarette smoke, performed to the music of the soft crinkling sound of money, folding and unfolding, and stuffed into the table slots. Ben Siegel would be smiling about that when the counting room sheets were turned in. He and his friends had sunk $6,000,000 into his wild dream for the middle of the desert, and it had been tough going. "You're outa your mind, Ben," one hoodlum had said. "You'll have to furnish camels to get the suckers out there."

Hank Greenspun gazed out across the garden terrace where now the wind-borne sand slashed at a quarter of a million dollars worth of trees and shrubs which Ben Siegel had brought in to cover the ugly barren land. Their destruction was swift and cruel —leaves and branches, ribboned and torn by the storm, swirled away into the night.

As he watched, the wind slid under the wrought iron chairs around the enormous pool, and sent them spinning into the water. They rested at the bottom, and the sand covered the blue tile. "Oh, brother," Greenspun remembered saying, "wait till Ben sees that. He's going to blow his stack."

But not that night, anyway.

The penthouse suite, on the fourth floor of the hotel wing across the terrace, was dark. Ben Siegel had flown to Beverly Hills early that morning, leaving his guns and bodyguard behind, and he had said he would be back soon.

"It's getting so I hate to go to L.A., Hank," he said. "I like it right here."

"So why do you go?"

"Because that's where the dough is."

"You got problems?"

Ben Siegel smiled a curious, deceptive smile, like that of a small boy lying without really believing it. "Nothin' I can't handle."

Hank Greenspun would remember that smile.

Now it was midnight, and Greenspun walked quickly to his creaking old Buick convertible, covering his face against the spitting gusts of sand, and started east on the Strip toward his home in Boulder City, twenty-three miles away. Dark clouds of dust spit against the windshield, and the car wobbled and groaned, and now and then he had to stop because he could not see the road. His car crawled through the night, and the headlights drove little yellow tunnels through the storming air. He was angry with himself for his stubbornness. With the speedometer needle flickering at only eight miles an hour, the screaming wind made him weave back and forth across the road.

It was three A.M. when at last he turned into the driveway of his home, eased the car into the garage, and pulled the quaking overhead door down to shut out the terrible night. He switched on the light, and stared incredulously at the car. It was still there all right, but it was naked metal, like the glistening carcass of a skinned deer, for the wind had stripped off all the paint, and even the once-rusted door handles were bright from the sanding. He walked wearily into a quiet, darkened house where his wife and two children had long since gone to sleep, but as he stood in the hall there came a ringing stab of sound from the phone near the door.

He fumbled for the receiver, and said: "Yes?"

"Hank?"

"It's me. Who's this?"

"Dick Chappell. Listen, Hank, get back here to the hotel right away. Come to my office."

"For Christ's sake, Dick—I just got here. The goddamndest ride I ever had in my life."

"Look, Hank—get going. All hell is going to break loose here."

"Somebody stick up the joint?"

"Worse than that. Murder—and I mean murder."

The night air was unusually warm, and George Raft squirmed and perspired and punched the pillow into a lump in the bedroom of his home on Coldwater Canyon in Beverly Hills.

Half-asleep, with asthma making him cough in little spasms, at first he did not hear the telephone. The script of his next picture, a thriller with June Havoc called *Intrigue*, lay half-crumpled on the bedside table alongside a mound of crushed cigarette butts. For a moment he thought the sound was part of a dream.

But it did not stop, and each time it rang, it seemed more shrill.

Now he was awake, and he automatically reached for a cigarette and a match. He found them without turning on the light, and as the match flared, he slowly picked up the phone.

"Hello—"

"George Raft?" The voice was crisp and impersonal.

"Yes," he said.

"This is Tom Slack in the District Attorney's office." The caller hammered out the words. "We want you to come downtown right away."

"What's up?" Raft asked.

"We want to talk to you about Bugsy Siegel."

Raft sucked on his cigarette, and the long drag threw out a glow of light like a little red flare. "You mean *Ben* Siegel?"

"Bugsy or Ben, it's all the same to us."

"Yeah—I know him."

"Sure you know him. Okay, so you're coming down?"

Raft was angry now. He knew it wasn't an arrest, and he knew they couldn't make him come down. He had made too many gangster pictures with scenes like this, and he knew his rights, on or off the screen. "Listen," he said brusquely. "You want to see me, you come out here. You know where I live, and I'm not going anywhere."

"Okay," Slack said. "We'll be out."

Raft was wide awake now, and he slid out of bed. He put on a monogrammed robe over his silk pajamas, pushed his small feet into a pair of slippers, and walked to another bedroom to wake Mack "Killer" Gray, the valet who had been friend and companion for many years.

"Mack," he said. "Put on the outside lights. We're goin' to have some fuzz here any minute."

"Not again? What's the beef now?"

"They wanna talk to me about Ben Siegel."

"No kiddin'. Did he belt somebody in the kisser?"

"I don't know."

Raft went back to his own bedroom suite, carefully combed his black hair, and lit another cigarette. Waiting and glancing down at his watch, he remembered another late evening when Virginia Hill, bringing her own satin sheets, came to the house as a guest because she wanted to stay out of circulation for a few days. She took the second floor suite with her own personal maid, and she stayed there out of sight for more than a week, with all her meals sent in on trays.

Ben Siegel often came to see her late at night, unannounced, but was always gone before daylight. Sometimes he phoned to ask George casually how Virginia was getting along and if there was anything she might need. But Raft knew why he made the call. "He just wants to make sure she isn't two-timing him and lettin' some other guy come in the back door."

Raft then had another and more disturbing thought. He suddenly remembered the hundred grand he had loaned Ben Siegel only a few months ago, and he could still hear Ben saying, flicking that shy and incongruous little smile of his: "Georgie—thanks for the lift. You want a receipt?"

"Not from you I don't," he had said.

"Okay, pal."

One hundred thousand in cash.

Raft heard the gravel skittering in the driveway outside, and footsteps sounded on the brick walk to the front door. He unlocked the night latch. The coach lamp on the white brick wall cast its bright light on the house number, 1218, and he heard a man say: "Yeah, this is the place. He'll be here. He said he would."

Aboard a luxurious houseboat on the Seine in Paris, beneath the long shadows of the Eiffel Tower, a gay and noisy party was going on. The men were sleek and handsome, the women lovely and chic. Off in one corner, a man was humming "How Are Things in Glocca Morra," the hit song from a new musical in New York, and in another part of the salon the young Americans were talking about the spectacular debut of Jackie Robinson of the Dodgers, the first Negro to play in the major leagues.

Virginia Hill was there in a stunning Howard Greer dinner gown, and because the New York columnists had often identified her as "the Alabama heiress," she was hemmed in by the schemers and the one-night lovers and the hunters ready for the challenge.

It was then that a young woman, being introduced to her for the first time, looked at her in obvious surprise.

"Virginia Hill?" she said. "Well, I must say you're covering up pretty well. I guess the show must go on."

"What do you mean?" Virginia snapped.

"You mean you haven't heard?"

"Heard *what*?"

The woman looked at her, suddenly embarrassed. "I'm sorry," she said. "I thought surely—well—I'm not going to be the one to tell. You better get a newspaper right now."

In Rome, on a sultry summer day when the hot sun bathed the seven dusty hills, and the Tiber was merely a brown and sluggish stream, the Countess Dorothy Taylor DiFrasso was summoned to the telephone for an overseas call.

"Who is it?" she said testily when the connection was made.

"*The Journal-American* in New York. We'd like to ask you about Bugsy Siegel."

"I don't know any Bugsy Siegel," she said. "Unless you mean Mr. Benjamin Siegel."

"We understand he was once your—well, your sweetheart."

"Ridiculous! I was very fond of him but—now see here, you didn't call me from New York just to ask a silly question like that. What's going on?"

She listened stiffly for an instant, and then, as the words jumped over the humming wire, the news hit her like a punch in the stomach, violent, sickening. She swayed, and almost dropped the phone, and her mind ran backwards to the day nine long years before when Ben Siegel came to the Eternal City with her, as lovers had come there together before and would again.

The image dissolved back to 1947, and she whispered into the phone: "Oh, no—no—no."

"Are you all right, Countess?" New York asked. "Hello, hello—"

The Super Chief, luxury train of the Santa Fe, was a ribbon of soft light snaking through the canyons of rocky hillside in eastern Nevada.

Sweeping across the lonely desert, the sandstorm spread grit on the shining rails and coated the Pullman windows with dust, and the long beam of the engine headlight shimmered on spangles of sand.

Walking through one of the long cars, the Pullman conductor rapped on a compartment door and stood there until it was opened a crack. A young girl's voice spoke softly. "Yes, who is it?"

"The conductor," he said. "Sorry to bother you, but are you the Misses Barbara and Millicent Siegel?"

"Yes, we are."

"Ah—well, I have a message from Mr. Chappell of the Flamingo Hotel in Las Vegas. He has asked us to stop the train at a station outside the city, and he says he'll meet you there. I'll let you know when we get near there in the morning."

"But why can't we get off at Las Vegas?"

"I don't know, Miss."

The two girls exchanged puzzled glances, and one of them closed the compartment door. The train whistle sounded its mournful bleat, like a coyote crying in the night, and the wind carried the echo away.

It takes all kinds of people to make a city—and a policeman's memoirs.——CLINTON H. ANDERSON, Chief of Police in Beverly Hills (*Beverly Hills is My Beat*, Prentice-Hall, Inc.)

June 20, 1947.

In the city of Beverly Hills, all kinds of people were following their daily routines and customs, none knowing he would be a name in a policeman's memoirs.

On North Maple Drive, Louella Parsons had a fleeting thought about Benjamin "Bugsy" Siegel, remembering how he had come to her box at the Santa Anita racetrack. "Hello, Louella," he had said, "here are some tickets for you on the next race. Have a winner—with my compliments."

"No, thanks, Ben," she said with dignity. "I prefer to pick my own losers."

In another home not far away, comedian Joe E. Lewis fiddled with the tuning knob on his radio set. Two hours before, Swifty Morgan had phoned and said: "Joe, Art Cohn and I are going over to Ben Siegel's place and he wants you to come along." And Joe had said he couldn't make it, not tonight of all nights, because he wanted to listen to his favorite radio program. "Tell Benny for me I'll catch up with him later tonight." "I'll tell him," Swifty said. "But Joe—what is your favorite radio program?" Joe grinned. "Gangbusters," he said. So Joe stayed home and listened to "Gangbusters," and he didn't go to Ben Siegel's place on North Linden Drive, and that was lucky for him.

Later, when Swifty woke him in the middle of the night and told him, Joe said wryly: "What do you know. Just like they say on 'Gangbusters'—crime doesn't pay—well, not like it used to."

In the Lou Costello Youth Foundation office on East Olympic Boulevard, the plump little movie comic was riffling through the batch of mail that came to the charity organization he and his partner, Bud Abbott, had founded to keep youngsters out of trouble.

"Hey!" Costello cried joyfully in his squeaky little voice. "Here's a twenty-five hundred dollar check from Ben Siegel. What a sweet guy. I'll get him on the phone right now and thank him."

"I don't think he'll talk to you, Lou," one office worker said.

"Of course he will," Costello said. "He always talks to me."

"I guess you haven't been listening to the radio, Lou. Ben Siegel isn't talking to anybody."

Mickey Cohen, sound asleep in his Moreno Avenue home, jumped like a scared chicken when the doorbell rang. He fumbled for his gun, but it wasn't within reach. He ran aimlessly from room to room, peering out the windows, and the scar on his face was drained of blood. And then it suddenly occurred to him—he knew from experience—that killers rarely ring doorbells. They simply walk up to you, or catch you in a car, and blast. He switched on the floodlights that bathed the front entrance, and through a one-way mirror peephole he saw uniforms.

"Goddam cops!" he muttered to himself.

He opened the door wide and snarled, "Well, what's the roust this time?"

"Take it easy, Mick," one policeman said. "They want to see you downtown."

"Downtown?" he growled. "What's the phony rap this time?"

"A murder, Mick. They just want to know where you were tonight."

The frown suddenly left his face, and he smiled at them, catlike, as the tenseness flowed away from his jutting chin. "Oh—only a murder? Hell, that's a breeze. I'll be right with you."

June 20, 1947. 10:20 P.M.

Charles "Chick" Hill, nineteen years old and girl-crazy, was in an upstairs bedroom at 810 North Linden Drive in Beverly Hills, waiting for Miss Jerri Mason to take off her clothes.

It seemed to him, as he said in retrospect long afterward, that he spent endless evening hours watching girls undress, or helping them with fumbling hands when they were shy about it. He remembered how his sister Virginia helped him find a chorus girl when he was only 12 years old, and her motherly advice: "If you want to sleep with them, fine, Chick, but don't go marrying anybody."

And so he slept with them—in Chicago and Mexico City and Hollywood and even back home in Alabama—and Virginia got girls for him when he couldn't find one himself. But occasionally, when one of these fleeting loves became serious and he mentioned marriage, Virginia would tongue-lash him in her fury. She would suddenly move to another house or another city, and the girl of the moment was automatically removed from the scene. Virginia would find a new face and body for him.

But now, though they were in Virginia's house, she was away in France, and Jerri Mason was out of her reach. He was going to marry Jerri, and the hell with Virginia. Let her scream and curse afterward. Let Ben Siegel tell him he was a horse's ass for marrying this little broad. He had said to himself: "I'm nuts about this cute little redheaded babe, and I'll do what I damn please." And so it was understood between them. Any day now.

They were alone in the bedroom on this evening, and Ben Siegel was downstairs with his pal, Al Smiley (Smiley the Russian). Chick touched Jerri, and she drew away, saying softly: "Chick—Ben might come up here any minute."

"Honey—he won't be coming to our room. He's got his own room."

"Well—I—Chick—What was *that*?"

He had heard it at that instant, too. A muffled burst of sound, like distant gunfire. And suddenly he thought of Virginia's jewels—a hundred thousand dollars worth—hidden in a wall safe in her bedroom down the hall. The guns were there, too—his and Ben's.

He made the hallway in one jump. "Ben!" he called. "Ben!"

And then came the cry of terror. "Chick—for Christ's sake!" That was Smiley's voice. "Chick—douse the lights, Jesus!"

Chick reached for the wall switch at the head of the stairs. But before the living room and the stairs were blacked out he had already seen the blood, and now there was no sound anywhere in the house.

CHAPTER TWO

The sun was aflame in the June sky, and the air moved in trembling waves over the hot pavement.

It was a day for life, rather than death, and the sounds of the city were the voices and sounds of living, moving things. On the sidewalk outside the Groman Mortuary on West Washington Boulevard, with their backs turned toward the blinding yellow light from the sky, a group of men wiped the perspiration from their faces and waited. Some were mere curbstone idlers, drawn to this grim place because they heard it was the day of interment for Benjamin "Bugsy" Siegel, king of the underworld.

Others were plainclothesmen from the Intelligence Division of the Los Angeles Police, and they wore their kind of uniforms—plain sport jackets and slacks. They talked to one another in subdued tones, and smoked cigarettes; their eyes were on every passing car and every man or woman who walked along the street.

The hoods from the Siegel mob would surely be there, saying good-bye to The Bug. The wanted killer himself might show. The cops had mug shots in their pockets, at which they glanced now and then, and checked the numbered faces against the faces of strangers passing by.

Inside the mortuary only five mourners posed stonily beside Ben Siegel's box. It was a handsome coffin made of scrolled silver and bronze and lined with silk. It cost $5000—Ben Siegel could have made that with one pass of the dice at the Flamingo—and in candelabras at the head and foot wax lights flickered. "Light breaks where no sun shines," said Dylan Thomas, "and death shall have no dominion."

And as the candles shed their fluttering light, the mourners, stiff and silent, could watch the casket without seeing a face that had once been handsome and alive. The cover was hermetically sealed so that no living eye would see him again.

In retrospect it seems significantly strange that none of Siegel's courtiers came. Not Mickey Cohen, Siegel's hired muscle. Not Smiley the Russian or Chick Hill who saw him die. Not Virginia Hill, whose body had been his when he wanted it. Not Lawyer Jerry Giesler, who had once saved him from execution, nor his ever-loving pal George Raft, nor Meyer Lansky, who crawled up from the gutter with him. And not one man from the Flamingo, his castle in the Nevada sand.

What did the family think, standing in that empty room of death by the silver shell?

Esta Siegel, the slender Brooklyn blonde he had married long years before? They had been divorced when the Flamingo was still a skeleton in the desert, and now she would never get the million dollars he had promised to pay in alimony for pushing her out of his life.

Dr. Maurice Siegel, the respected Beverly Hills physician who knew what his brother was, and loved him just the same?

Bessie Soloway, Ben's favorite sister, quietly sobbing as the candles burned?

Millicent and Barbara Siegel, the teen-age daughters he had tried to shield from the kind of life that paid for their expensive finishing school and their beautiful clothes?

There was no one there to know or ask what they thought. They wanted no eulogies, even if there had been men with courage enough to defend a ruthless life. They wanted only prayers and the Twenty-third Psalm.

And Rabbi Kert began: "The Lord is my shepherd; I shall not want. . . ."

When I was with Ben he bought me everything I wanted.
—Virginia Hill

THE LIFE AND BAD TIMES OF BUGSY SIEGEL

"He maketh me lie down in green pastures; He leadeth me beside the still waters. He restoreth my soul . . ."

> *The circumstances surrounding Bugsy Siegel's career in crime tell the story better than words. Here was an individual whose life was a constant challenge to common decency. Yet he and his criminal scum were lionized and their favors sought after in so-called respectable social circles.*——J. Edgar Hoover

"He leadeth me in the paths of righteousness for His name's sake . . ."

> *Siegel was a brainy guy who might have made it big on the right side of the law.*——Walter Winchell

"Yea, though I walk through the valley of the shadow of death, I will fear no evil: for thou art with me. . . ."

> *He told me he had personally killed twelve men, but then he must have noticed my face, because he laughed. "There's no chance that you'll get killed," he said. "We only kill each other."*——Del Webb

"Thy rod and thy staff they comfort me. Thou preparest a table before me in the presence of mine enemies. . . ."

> *Sure, Ben always carried a rod. So did I when I come close to killing him once. But just because he wanted to have dinner with me that last night and I didn't go they figured I must have done it.*——Mickey Cohen

"Thou anointest my head with oil. . . ."

> *Bugsy Siegel was officially an aristocrat of the new underworld . . . he had become one of the most formidable criminals of our time.*——Westbrook Pegler

"My cup runneth over. . . ."

Maybe he did kill people. Maybe he had to. But he was like a father to me, and the best friend I ever had.——Chick Hill

"Surely goodness and mercy shall follow me . . ."

I didn't want Bugsy Siegel in my house. I wasn't going to wake up some morning and see the front page saying "Movie Tycoon Machine-Gunned by Opposition Mob," and then I wouldn't be able to read the paper anyway. But he got in.——Jack L. Warner

"All the days of my life. . . ."

Countess Dorothy DiFrasso naively believed Bugsy was an innocent overgrown boy, but he had a weird assortment of grifters, cutthroats, and confederates.——Elsa Maxwell

"And I will dwell in the house of the Lord forever."

Rabbi Kert whispered a final prayer, the candles were snuffed out, and the coffin was wheeled to a waiting hearse.

The mourners filed out into the sunlight, blinking in the glare from the cloudless sky. They climbed into a limousine, and the cops shrugged and walked slowly to their unmarked cars a block away. The family limousine drove east on Washington Boulevard, a lonely island in the rushing tide of traffic, and the cops let it go without a tail. The car swung over to Sunset, turned at North Gower, and entered the gate to the high-walled Beth Olam Cemetery. Number 900 North Gower. City of the dead.

There was a gaping square opening in Section M-2 of the mausoleum, three rows up from the floor. Like an enormous filing cabinet, crypts were arranged from floor to ceiling. File and forget. Stick him in the drawer, secure it with a slab of marble. Fasten a bronze plaque so no one will have to guess where he went. "In Loving Memory from the Family. Benjamin Siegel—February 28, 1906–June 20, 1947."

The brass table lamp in the Beverly Hills apartment was not

designed to soften the worn planes of his face—like the studio lights when he was a star—and George Raft looked old and tired. His once glossy black hair was gray and stringy, like a worn rug, and no makeup hid the knife wound behind his left ear or the thin tracks of time on his skin. In a bedroom drawer, like some dead thing in a vault, was the toupee he refused to wear around home, and when he breathed the sucking sound of asthma was heard.

"Memory is my worst enemy," he said. "The damn asthma killed my mother, and it'll kill me. So I'm on the sleeping pill routine."

The telephone in the living room, which clanged like a streetcar bell in the old days, was silent now, hour after hour, and the neighborhood postman no longer dumped sacks of fan mail at the door. Not that that mattered. George never learned to read very well, and he could barely write his own name. The studio answered the mail and the mash notes, and handled the assembly line business of sending out shiny prints of the famous face with the scrawled signature, "Sincerely yours, George Raft." It took him months of laborious practice to learn that simple bit with the pen. But at least the letters came.

We were working together on his life story, in the apartment on Charlesville Boulevard, a block from the busy Wilshire artery, and it was like digging in a tomb. Memories are sad and dusty fragments, and that's all he had.

One of those memories, more vivid than most, was of Benjamin "Bugsy" Siegel, his friend.

"Of course, you know I never called him "Bugsy," he said. "He hated it, and nobody in his right mind ever called him that to his face."

"But he got the name from the mob."

"Oh, sure, back in the old days in New York. They called him 'Bugs' because he was hotheaded, and it stuck. Even when he and Meyer Lansky formed their Jewish gang, the cops and the newspapers called it the Bug-Meyer mob."

George fished in a pile of faded newspaper clippings and brought up a tear sheet from the *Los Angeles Examiner*. It showed George with his arm around Siegel, and they were smiling at some secret joke. They looked sharp in their $175 suits, with monogrammed handkerchiefs and shirts.

"He don't look like a hoodlum there, does he?" George grinned.

"No," I said.

"Why, you know every time I saw him at the racetrack or around town he was always with the big names. Georgie Jessel, Cary Grant, Mark Hellinger, Jimmy Durante, guys like that. I always figured that if he was good enough for them, he was good enough for me. I never knew anybody who didn't like him."

"Except J. Edgar Hoover."

"Well—of course he's a nice guy, too. I see him at the races now and then. But you can't expect Hoover to—well, what I mean is, I don't think he ever met Ben Siegel face to face, and he didn't really know him."

"And you?"

George was thoughtful for a moment, idly fingering the clipping. "Yes," he said. "Like my right hand, I knew him when he was a tough kid on the Lower East Side in New York. He was gutty and he was ambitious.

"He came out here because he wanted to be somebody. Damn few people knew what made him tick, but I did. I thought he was a great guy. I was crazy about a lot of these guys they called gangsters—Joey Adonis, Willie Moretti, Frank Costello. Maybe that's why I was such a good screen gangster. I used to copy their little mannerisms in pictures.

"I remembered the way Ben used to comb his hair, and so I did it the same way when I was playing a gangster. He got a kick out of it. Funny thing, he was losing his hair even before he was forty, and it bugged him. He tried all kinds of lotions and treatments but it kept falling out anyway. One Christmas just for a gag I gave him a toupee. Cost me two and a half bills."

"Did he ever wear it?"

"Hell, no. He was too vain for that. He used to go to bed at night with a chin strap to keep his profile looking good, and he wore those shades over his eyes."

"You don't mind talking about Ben?"

"No, because nobody ever bothered with the truth about the guy. There's been a lot of phony stuff printed. I can tell you plenty, but I won't knock him. But listen—Hollywood is full of people who knew him. Why don't you talk to them?"

"Who are they, George?"

"The cream of the town," he said. "Like Jack Warner. See Rowland Brown; he's the director who discovered me. Find out about Wendy Barrie and Marie McDonald. Too bad the Countess DiFrasso's dead—she could give you an earful. And Virginia Hill. I hear she's on the lam somewhere in Europe. There isn't anybody from coast to coast who didn't know Ben Siegel."

"That's quite a cast, George."

"I almost forgot Mickey Cohen. He damn near killed Siegel one time. Oh—it's quite a story, believe me. And it's all there."

But it was not all there.

"Time's glory is to calm contending kings, to unmask falsehood and bring truth to light"—so said Shakespeare. But Time has not unmasked the falsehoods in the dossier of Benjamin Siegel or brought the truth to light. It has only told new lies. And there are men living who do not want the story told.

CHAPTER THREE

"In Loving Memory from the Family. Benjamin Siegel—February 28, 1906. . . ."

In the Williamsburg district of Brooklyn, a labyrinth of crowded tenements, dirty delicatessens, pushcart peddlers, and struggling synagogues, Jennie Siegel gave birth to her first son.

Happy Jennie Siegel, twenty-six years old. She would live long enough to see him die.

No scientist has ever solved the mystery in the strange linkage of the genes that makes one son a killer, another a respected physician. James D. C. Murray, the noted defense counsel, once said: "Juvenile delinquency starts in the high chair and ends in the death chair," but few people know who or what put the mark of Cain on Ben Siegel.

It was not the maligned environment of Brooklyn, for Brooklyn also spawned Danny Kaye, Barbara Stanwyck, Clifton Fadiman, Mae West, Robert Merrill, and a dozen other respected and successful people, many of whose families also knew poverty and despair. It was not competition with siblings, because Ethel, Bessie, and Maurice Siegel had not been born, and there was only sister Esther, who was a year older than Bugsy.

Even though Williamsburg was infested with bookies, con men, and fast buck boys, Siegel once admitted that he committed his first major crime on the Lower East Side in Manhattan. He was the youngest of three thieves in that caper—a stickup in a loan company office—and when he related the experience to Chick Hill one day he said: "I had to run like hell for about ten blocks, carrying two bags full of small change, before the guy chasing us ran out of breath and quit. It might have been better if they'd caught me because after that I was game for anything."

Bugsy Siegel left home without finishing grammar school, and thereafter he prowled the dusty warrens of the East Side—a night creature in a band of tough, ruthless teen-age boys. He rolled drunks, burglarized lofts, and learned to be fast with the gun and knife.

Occasionally they invaded rival territories, and it was on one of those forays to the Hell's Kitchen district that Siegel met a handsome, swarthy older boy named George Ranft. George, who had been born and raised in a sleazy cold water flat on West 41st Street near Tenth Avenue, was already showing the footwork that later took him to Hollywood and dancing stardom under his new name of Raft.

Young George's footwork was especially fast when it came to eluding the cops.

The fear-flight mechanism he shared with Ben Siegel and the other delinquents of his youth was so much a part of the family crises that many years later, when four policemen gave him an honor escort into a New York theater for his newest picture, his aging mother did what came naturally. "Run, Georgie, run!" she screamed. "Don't let the cops get you."

And because the cop on the beat was always the symbol of trouble and oppression, Ben Siegel, too, learned to hate him.

Like his friend George Raft, Siegel always had weapons handy. If they couldn't get blackjacks, a roll of nickels in the fist or a stolen gaspipe coupling would do the job. They stole anything that could be carried away, and they showed their contempt for the police by bombing them from rooftops with bricks, milk bottles, flowerpots, or paper bags filled with water.

Ben Siegel clung to this sometimes dangerous horseplay; when already a name in the big mob, he often dropped bags of water on the police from windows of the country's best hotels. Albert Anastasia, Lucky Luciano, and other gangsters in the syndicate frowned on this habit, and when one dripping cop stormed into Siegel's hotel looking for the villain, Anastasia snarled: "For Christ's sake, Ben. Why in hell you keep pulling this kid stuff?"

"Because I get a kick out of it," Siegel replied.

Another time, making a social call at the late Polly Adler's lavish brothel in New York with gangsters Terry McGurn and Lucky Luciano, Siegel could not resist the horseplay. "Terry and Bugsy decided to give me a lesson in interior decorating," Polly later wrote in her book *A House Is Not a Home* (Holt, Rinehart and Winston, Inc.), "and they began by hauling the sofa into the kitchen, and the stove into the living room.

"They got the stove about halfway through the door when they noticed Charlie Lucky looking at them—not saying anything, just looking. In two seconds flat the furniture was back in place."

There are few men living who know exactly when and how Bugsy Siegel made the transition from a punk robber to a swaggering gangster who knew exactly where he wanted to go. Maurice Siegel and Meyer Lansky probably know.

One is trying to forget. The other, in the tradition of the underworld, has never talked and never will. But the fragments of Siegel's early days, culled from the records and the statements of friends and hoodlums alike, establish the pattern.

During the early days of Prohibition—the bloody decade euphemistically known as the "gay twenties"—two ruthless mobs controlled the Lower East Side in New York. One was composed of homicidal Italians, who were responsible for most of the thousand gang killings of the time, and their roster included such dreaded men as Lucky Luciano, Joey Adonis, Vito Genovese, and Albert Anastasia. The other gang was an all-Jewish group, first headed by Louis "Lepke" Buchalter and Jacob "Gurrah" Shapiro, known as "the Gold Dust Twins." Meyer Lansky and Ben Siegel were in the gang originally, but soon formed their own outfit. It was known as the Bug-Meyer mob and in the history of crime it remains an infamous name.

The lesser goons, who sometimes lived only as long as they were useful, included Harry "Big Greenie" Greenberg, a slugger and stink bomb expert; Allie Tannenbaum, who was paid up to $75 a week for strong-arm work; Phil "Farvel" Cohen; Sholem Bernstein, who would kill for a round-trip ticket to anywhere and a $500 fee; and Abe "Kid Twist" Reles, a monkey-faced moron who liked to murder just for the hell of it.

There was one other diminutive monster who was destined to survive innumerable purges and die a rich man. His name was Morris Sedwitz, alias Sedway, known to the mob and police alike as "Little Moe." A skilled burglar in his youth, he worshipped Bugsy Siegel, ran errands and did the dirty work for his hero. In turn, he was scorned by Siegel and, as the years passed, finally hated by the man who pulled him out of the ratholes of New York and brought him to the promised land of Las Vegas.

Little Moe knew the hatred was there, but he never had the guts to admit it. When Senator Charles Tobey of New Hampshire had him squirming at the Kefauver hearings in 1951, he mentioned Siegel to Sedway and snapped: "He was a rat, wasn't he?"

"A rap?" Sedway stalled.

Senator Tobey spelled it out. "R-a-t."

"Maybe—I don't know."

"He got what was coming to him, didn't he?" the senator persisted. "Good thing, wasn't it?"

Sedway fidgeted in his chair. "I wouldn't comment on it," he said.

Little Moe, Lansky, Big Greenie, Willie Moretti, Kid Twist, Lepke, Joey A., and the others were the soiled lumps of clay in the kiln with young Ben Siegel. Each of them played their part in the synthesis that made Jennie Siegel's firstborn son a heartache and a legend.

Siegel first felt the bone-cracking fingers of a cop when he was twenty years old. He was picked up in Brooklyn when one of the neighborhood girls, whose name never made police records, charged him with rape. Siegel was booked and fingerprinted, and thus won the first entry on his police record—now No. 190586 in the swollen file of the Federal Bureau of Investigation.

By the time Bennie Siegel, as he was booked, came to court, some unknown emissary had dissuaded the complaining witness and the case was dismissed.

The Bennie Siegel file, covering the case of rape and his every other arrest in New York, seems to have vanished from the New York Police Department. Deputy Police Commissioner Joseph

Martin admits (at the time of this writing) that he is nonplused by the fact that there is no official record of one Bennie Siegel.

The only police memento remaining in New York of Siegel's criminal activities is a small full-face mug shot which came from Philadelphia when Siegel was arrested there in April 1928, on a charge of carrying a concealed weapon. The picture shows Siegel at twenty-two—a pouting, contemptuous youth with baleful eyes under a snapbrim hat with a wide black band. Siegel beat that rap, too.

There is another curiously blank page in the record. On November 11, 1931, when Siegel was the unopposed leader of the east side mobsters, he summoned the eight handpicked scoundrels who handled shakedowns, the muscle deals where they talked with fists, and murders for his assorted rackets.

The eight men who gathered in a luxurious suite at the Hotel Franconia on West 72nd Street, included Lepke and Shapiro, who even then were organizing Murder Inc.; Philip "Little Farvel" Kovalick also known as Cohen; Hyman "Curly" Holtz, Harry Teitelbaum, Louis "Shadows" Kravitz, Joseph "Doc" Stacher (deported to Israel, he is now the only member of the group living), and Harry "Big Greenie" Greenberg, whose association with Siegel eventually killed him.

Not long after the meeting was called to order Captain Michael McDermott of the New York police alien squad arrived uninvited with his men, and carted all nine off to headquarters. Admittedly the arrest was nothing more than a roust, an underworld term applied to a raid made when the police want merely to aggravate. Nevertheless, the nine were lined up and photographed in their snap-brim hats, gaudy neckties, and double-breasted chesterfield coats.

No charges were brought, and Siegel, who never stopped griping about this roundup, was later successful in having his face blocked out of the picture. The police had no choice. Under Section 516 of the New York Penal Law, all photographs and fingerprints must be returned to a dismissed defendant—including all copies and duplicates—unless he has a prior conviction. Moreover, it is a misdemeanor to refuse such a demand.

Ironically, while the early files on Siegel have evaporated into thin air or have been deliberately withheld, this damning photograph still exists in many newspaper libraries.

When he was still in his twenties, Siegel had a suite in the Waldorf-Astoria, where Lucky Luciano was already living in luxury two floors above him. Siegel married Esta Krakower, who has called herself his childhood sweetheart, and bought her a country home at 46 Braden Road in fashionable Scarsdale. He had already made one trip to California, and another to Hot Springs, Arkansas, where Owney Madden, former chief of the West Side mob, eventually retired to avoid almost certain execution.

Siegel also went to Miami Beach for a vacation and there, to his embarrassment, was grabbed in a gambling raid. In court, pleading guilty, he said his name was Harry Rosen, and he paid a $100 fine. It was to be the first and last conviction on a long and bloody record.

Florabel Muir, the noted Los Angeles newspaperwoman who started her career on the New York *Daily News*, once recalled seeing Ben Siegel with some of the hoods in a speakeasy on Forsythe Street in Lower East Side Manhattan. Frank Hause, then managing editor of the *News*, whispered to her: "There's a young fellow coming up in the mobs. He's the enforcing member of the Bug-Meyer Mob."

Siegel was then wearing the standard livery for gangsters—a tight coat with a velvet collar and a derby hat. His pointed shoes had a high gloss, and his handmade shirt was monogrammed. The derby addiction was short-lived, and he soon switched to snap-brim hats, a style made popular by his friend, Broadway columnist Mark Hellinger. It was almost impossible, as the crime historians know, to distinguish between the big-name hoodlums and the legitimate celebrities in the Broadway crowd.

Politicians, criminals, columnists, and stars of the entertainment world all moved in the same social set. They gathered in the same restaurants and nightclubs, often used the same barbers and masseurs, retained the same lawyers. They dressed alike, talked alike, and almost thought alike. Collectively they could fix almost anything but murder. And occasionally they did that, too, especially if the victim was a hoodlum who would not be missed.

It was the time of the great abortion—Prohibition.

The liquor flowed from boats, trucks, cars, and bars. It came from bathtubs, dirty stills, backroom vats, and hijacking legitimate shipments from overseas.

Folding money counted in the hundreds, thousands, millions. The passwords in New York were Hines, Dwyer, Rothstein, Madden, Fay, Fallon, and Walker. And clinging to them, like pilot fish to the shark, were the creatures of the shadow world—Lepke and Zwillman, Shapiro and Siegel, Adonis and Schultz, Waxey Gordon and Lansky, Costello and Moretti, and hundreds more. They never had it so good. Blood colored booze and the folding green. Bury one gun and spawn another. The law was sick and dying, and no one cared.

Ben Siegel's New York, when he was growing up, was the New York so artfully disguised in the fables of Damon Runyon. As Runyon saw it with his wry humor and his love-everybody approach, it was the place of *Guys and Dolls* who all had hearts of gold. The good guys were all the hoodlums and grifters and con men, and the bad guys were the cops who made life tough. Crime was just a harmless little game, and its heroes in almost every conflict were the gangsters who could outwit the villainous men with the badges.

George Raft, who began his long association with the mob under the sponsorship of killer Owney Madden and who was shipped off to Hollywood with Madden's money, was hanging around poolrooms and sleeping in the subways when Prohibition began.

He graduated to thievery (he once told me he was a bad pickpocket but a good shoplifter) and was a "stand-in" shooter at the floating crap games in the Club Durante. That is, when the players were tipped off about an impending raid, Raft and other unemployed men took over the dice from the big-name gamblers like Arnold Rothstein. They would submit to arrest, pay a small fine, and get a five-dollar bill for their services. Shortly afterward the game would resume. "At that time," Raft told me not long ago, "I felt there was no difference between a detective and a gangster. They had the same methods of working, and were just trying to outsmart each other."

This was also the New York of brassy Texas Guinan, who has since been immortalized as a sort of fairy godmother, even though she contributed the phrase "Hello, sucker" to the language, and would happily rob the customers of everything they had. It was the New York under the strong-arm rule of Owney Madden and big Frenchie DeMange. It was the New York of a Broadway thug called Al Brown who later moved to Chicago and became Al Capone.

It is not surprising that both George Raft and Mark Hellinger, who frankly and openly admired the mob, would one day be called upon to testify in court that Ben Siegel was a sterling character.

"When I became a movie star and was asked about the tough guys I knew," Raft told me, "I said: 'I think they're the greatest guys in the world.' These fellows (Siegel, Costello, Adonis, Luciano, and Madden) were gods to me. They all had Duesenbergs and sixteen-cylinder Cadillacs and, like somebody said, when there was money around you might step on some of it. Wherever they went there were police captains and politicians bowing to them, and I thought these fellows can't really be doing anything wrong. Why shouldn't I be like them, and I wanted to follow them."

"Just as the twig is bent," Alexander Pope said, so was Ben Siegel formed. He was a boy when he learned the power of money, and when he became a man the system had not changed. Young, handsome, and ruthless, Siegel made his mark during those incredible years that the Eighteenth Amendment was enforced.

There was a time in later years, when with tongue in cheek, he told Los Angeles police officers that he earned his huge income from a string of twenty-five garages with offices on Delancey Street called the C. & G. Corporation. He also said there were regular crap games in some of these garages in which the players included Charlie "The Bug" Workman, who was eventually killed on orders from Lepke and Abe Reles. Siegel was not joking about the crap games, as his private account books revealed, but his ownership of garages was purely fictitious. Actually, as the FBI files show, most of Siegel's money came from bootleg liquor.

The Bug-Meyer mob not only hauled liquor and supplied armed convoys for other groups trucking it between Philadelphia and New York, but they also had a wholesale liquor business of their own. They operated warehouses, illicit stills, a smuggling network in Canada, and boats running offshore along the Atlantic coast.

At one point, when the City of New York was loading garbage into barges and dumping it in the ocean, Siegel made a deal with the barge skipper to pick up whisky shipments at sea and deliver them to the city's sanitation pier. For months he paid the skipper four dollars a case, but when Prohibition agents planned to raid the pier and ruin this operation, Siegel was tipped off in advance. The skipper was the only man arrested.

There were also hijackings, shakedowns, and murders which, though they did not always contribute revenue, had the net effect of eliminating trespassing competitors.

As was the custom among the wealthy gangsters, Siegel had hidden away his wife and two baby daughters, Millicent and Barbara, in an expensive home in Scarsdale. Esta Siegel, who subsequently testified that Ben was "a fine husband and a thoughtful father," lived a quiet life in her fashionable suburb, and it is likely that unsuspecting neighbors believed the fable that her wealthy husband was a traveling man who rarely had time to come home.

There was some truth to the story. Siegel was constantly traveling—from an apartment at 85th Street and Broadway or the Waldorf to his headquarters on Grand Street near Lewis Street on the Lower East Side; to the City Democratic Club of Brooklyn, where Albert Anastasia held court; to Joey A.'s office at 4th Avenue and Carroll Street in Brooklyn; and to the Riviera Hotel in Newark where Abe "Longy" Zwillman ran the Jersey mob.

Being an underworld leader was a hazardous profession during Prohibition—traitors and toughs were knocked off so often that the gravediggers worked overtime—and every mobster of any stature had a personal bodyguard. Siegel's private torpedo—handpicked by Anastasia, was Abe "Kid Twist" Reles, an undersized animal with cold eyes and long hairy arms. Reles was tough, cool, and quick with the cannon, and his mere shadow in Siegel's presence was enough to discourage a rival killer's gun.

Nevertheless there were some who tried, and the instigator, in each instance, was Irving "Waxey" Gordon, so named because of the waxlike smoothness of his fingers when he picked pockets in the early days.

Waxey was not only hungry for underworld power, but also he yearned for the affection of the Broadway show business crowd. With the money he piled up in bootlegging and Manhattan real estate investments, Waxey put up the cash for two Broadway musicals *Forward March* and *Strike Me Pink*, which helped Jimmy Durante along the road to fame.

Waxey "should of stood in bed," as his pal Joe Jacobs once moaned when he lost a World's Series bet. Instead he chose to take on the opposition in general and Bugsy Siegel in particular, and the resulting war was a busy period for morticians. Siegel knew he was threatened. He never went out unless Reles was along, and most of the time they traveled in a bulletproof car.

One day while Siegel was in his office there was a phone call from a hoodlum who said he was Charles "Chink" Sherman, a onetime narcotics peddler who had defected from the Gordon mob and joined the Bug-Meyer gang.

"Why didn't he come here instead of phoning?" Siegel asked.

"I don't know, Ben," one of his men said. "He just said he had to see you about a big deal, then he hung up."

"Where is he?"

"Broadway and Thirty-fourth."

Siegel, Reles, and another bodyguard named Farvel Cohen went out, climbed into the big armored sedan, and drove up Broadway. They had only crawled a few blocks when another car slid alongside and a machine gun suddenly stitched a line of holes on the driver's side of Siegel's sedan.

"The bastards suckered us," Siegel cried. "Get moving!"

The big car leaped and picked up speed, but the assassins did not wheel around for another try. Instead, they shot down the first side street at full throttle, lost control, and smashed into a pillar of the Third Avenue El. Four men scrambled out of the battered machine, and the last one was out of sight when Siegel caught up.

"Any other time," Siegel breathed, "and any other car, and they would have taken us."

"I got hit, Ben," Cohen spoke up quietly.

"What do you mean you got hit?" Siegel exclaimed. "This car's bulletproof."

"No, it ain't," Cohen said. "I got a slug right in the ass."

Cohen slid over a foot, and Siegel saw the spreading blood on the seat. "Well, I'll be damned!" he said. "Here—I'll drive and we'll get to a doctor."

Twenty minutes later, in the Anastasia home in Brooklyn, a doctor extracted a big chunk of lead from Cohen's wound (Siegel recognized it as a powerful bullet called a "401") and a close examination of the sedan showed that at least four other slugs had pierced the steel.

In November of 1932, Siegel called a war meeting of his personal mob in the Grand Street headquarters. The conference had just started, and bodyguards were on hand, when a bomb was lowered down the chimney. The plotters had overlooked a right-angled offset between the hearth and the mouth of the chimney so the main force of the blast was confined. But the long flue was shattered with a thunderous rumble, scattering bricks, hot coals and lumber around the room.

Siegel was struck on the head by something—a piece of wood or perhaps a brick. His solicitous friends took him in an ambulance to the nearby Gouverneur Hospital on South Street, and he was given emergency treatment for his injuries. Newspaper reports at that time said Siegel's ambulance was tailed to the hospital by a car full of rivals who wanted to make sure The Bug wouldn't walk out alive. One of these gentlemen—he was probably there to administer a *coup de grace*—was apparently one Francis Anthony "Tony" Fabrizzo, a tough gunman whose two brothers, Louis and Andy Fabrizzo, had already been executed in the gang wars.

Siegel's men, not underestimating the caliber of the men hovering outside, smuggled Siegel out another door and got him home.

Today there seems to be some conflict about the facts of this episode. A contradictory version came in a report from Burton B. Turkus, the Assistant District Attorney of Brooklyn who earned the nickname "Mr. Arsenic" when he broke up the Murder Inc. gang and sent seven thugs—including the notorious Lepke—to the electric chair.

Turkus says Siegel was taken to a Catholic hospital ("I couldn't identify it because it was a touchy subject," he told me recently) and given a private room. On the third night of his stay there, Turkus said, Siegel quickly dressed, sneaked downstairs, and was met outside by two confederates.

They drove to a house on Fort Hamilton Parkway in southwest Brooklyn where Tony Fabrizzo was staying with his father, and posing as detectives, tricked him into coming out. He was greeted with three gunshots, and the bombing was avenged.

Turkus adds that Siegel immediately returned to the hospital, regained his room without being seen, and thus established a perfect alibi.

The records of this nocturnal killing have disappeared or been withheld from me along with the rest of the Siegel dossier in New York. Siegel was never arrested for the Fabrizzo murder, nor even questioned about it. Moreover, even in his most garrulous lapses, Siegel never discussed the Fabrizzo affair with any intimate friends.

In any case, when it became clear to both sides that their best men were being killed without any appreciable gain, the so-called Big Six arrived at a compromise with Waxey Gordon, and the deadly war came to an end. One of Reles's last vivid recollections, before he went to prison in 1934 on an assault charge, was of an evening in the Riviera Hotel in Newark.

Siegel was there with Longy Zwillman, and after a couple of drinks, Longy confessed he was losing sleep over Jean Harlow.

"You know *her*?" Reles said with a whistle.

"Yeah. A long time."

"You'll never make it," Siegel said. "There's too many big guys out there with more dough than you've got."

"Then they're not givin' it to her," Zwillman said defensively. "I've been sending her money right along. I sent her another hundred last week, and she isn't sending it back."

"She'll drive you nuts," Siegel laughed.

"She'd drive you nuts, too," Zwillman snapped. "She even drives her old man nuts. Well—he isn't really her father. And come to think of it—that makes it a nice kosher setup for him. Next time we're on the coast I'll introduce you to the whole family. The old lady, too. She's hell on wheels."

"Thanks," Siegel grunted. "I don't need 'em."

Siegel was wrong. He did need them when the time came, and it was to be one of the strangest associations of his life.

CHAPTER FOUR

The smell of death enveloped Joey Amberg. When Ben Siegel gave the order to take him, the mob knew Joey was as good as embalmed. The Bug was judge and jury, and when he "fingered" a man, there was no appeal. Not even to Anastasia or Luciano or Adonis. If Joey had had any sense he would have left town.

Joey and his brother, Louis "Pretty" Amberg, were Brownsville punks skilled in usury, shakedowns, and drug peddling. Sometime during 1933 there was a cafeteria strike in Brownsville and Abe Reles, who had already murdered half a dozen men because he got physical pleasure from killing, was picked to work out a settlement. By a simple formula, someone paid Reles and the strike was magically settled. Resisting only brought risk of a plague of impromptu funerals. In this instance, Reles asked a fee of $8500, and the strike ended.

Then came Joey Amberg claiming that he was entitled to half the money because the cafeteria union was his business. Reles refused. As was customary in these disputes, Ben Siegel called a hearing in Joey Adonis's restaurant on Fourth Avenue in Brooklyn.

Siegel presided, with Charlie Lucky, Albert Anastasia, Reles, and Louis Capone around the table, and Joey Amberg alone arguing his case. The session was brief, and Siegel decided: "Give him the money, Abe." Amberg took the cash and went his way, but Reles was angry and baffled by Siegel's ruling.

"Why'd you do that, Ben?" he asked. "He didn't do nothin' to make that dough."

"I'm just giving him rope," Siegel said bluntly. "He'll hang himself one of these days."

A year or more later one of Siegel's men, a goon named Hymie Kazner, floated into the Canarsie River from a sewer duct. Kazner had had friction with Joey Amberg, and two of Siegel's men, Louis Capone and Harry Strauss, immediately concluded Joey had done the job. Amberg was brought to Siegel's office and there, under the chief's merciless cross-examination, he wilted and confessed he had killed Kazner and stuffed the body into the sewer line.

On September 30, 1935, Joey was shot by Siegel's firing squad in front of a Brooklyn warehouse. Shortly afterward his brother, Pretty Amberg, was chopped up with an axe and his car set afire near the Brooklyn Navy Yard. It was Ben Siegel's valedictory on the eastern murder front for quite a while.

When Prohibition came to an end, there was a temporary panic in the underworld. Bootlegging was one of the few crimes in history condoned by the people, ignored by the law, and guaranteed to yield fabulous profit with a minimum of grief. It made millionaires out of illiterates, heroes out of homicidal Robin Hoods, and corrupt public figures out of honest men.

Now it was over; the golden vein had petered out.

The Big Six syndicate, acutely aware of the staggering drop in revenue, naturally considered expansion in what were then minor channels—prostitution, gambling, narcotics, extortion in industry and labor, and wholesale murder for appropriate fees. The mob was also looking into untapped lodes—Florida, California, Texas, Louisiana.

Most experts on crime, along with writers who specialized in that field, have asserted that Bugsy Siegel first abandoned New York and moved to California in 1936 or 1937. There is an apochryphal story—and it is virtually indestructible—about why Siegel went west. The mob leaders were supposed to have taken a discerning look at Ben Siegel—urbane, handsome as a movie star, and with an Adolphe Menjou flair for clothes—and unanimously voted to send him west as the manager of a branch office. Even Burton Turkus, who knew almost as much about organized crime in New York as J. Edgar Hoover, helped perpetuate this bit of fancy, and said that Siegel left in 1937, financed by Lepke and Luciano.

There never was such a conclave; the decision to move to California was Siegel's own. Actually, Siegel had been making regular visits to Los Angeles for many years, and had rented a house on Arden Drive in Beverly Hills as early as 1933. Two years later, introducing himself as a "sportsman" to Lawrence Tibbett, he rented the famed singer's luxurious home at 326 McCarthy Drive.

Moreover, Siegel needed no financing from Lepke, Luciano, or anyone else, as was confirmed in a delinquent tax return, prepared by a Boston accountant. It shows that from 1929 to 1935 Siegel had a net income of $381,194.50. At one point, he told a friend that he had made a million dollars before the end of 1933, but had lost a considerable part of it in the stock market. "If I had kept that million," he said, "I'd have been out of the rackets right then. But I took a big licking, and I couldn't go legit."

Siegel's talk of intended reform must be taken with reservations, because at the time Bugsy's talents were limited to larceny, murder, and shakedowns, and he had no training for honest work. Also, there is evidence that, rather than being short of cash, Siegel had enormous reserves he neglected to mention in his tax returns.

For instance, on December 9, 1936, Mr. Charles Ward strolled into the Continental Illinois National Bank in Chicago with a briefcase stuffed with $100,000 in currency. He asked to have the money credited to his personal account in the Midway Bank of St. Paul, Minnesota, and then walked out. Charles Ward, as it happens, was an exconvict who became president of the huge Brown & Bigelow advertising firm in St. Paul. He was also an intimate friend of Siegel's, and airline and hotel records proved that Bugsy was a frequent, though sometimes incognito, visitor in St. Paul.

When investigators later took a close look at Siegel's remarkable financial pyramid, Ward admitted that the $100,000 he had deposited in Chicago was a loan from his dear friend. Ten months later, when Siegel was making distinctly unfriendly demands for the money, Ward sent him this note:

Dear Ben: Inclosed find two Liberty Bonds for $20,000. Sorry I couldn't make it $25,000, but as you know I am short of cash on account of my stock deals. Am lucky to have enough to eat on. Hope this will help you, I am,

Sincerely yours,
Charles Ward.

Ward repaid the rest of the loan in December, but this time without any personal greeting. He had his bankers send Siegel a draft for $80,000, drawn on the Guaranty Trust Company of New York. That same month, Ward's assistant, William Marzolf, shipped to Siegel a painting called *The Sea Captain's Daughter* in Beverly Hills. Marzolf's letter said the painting was worth $4000 and was "the highest valued picture in the Brown & Bigelow collection. Charlie wanted you to have it."

Ward, who often wrote sweet little notes to Siegel's teen-aged daughter, Millicent, and signed them "Uncle Charlie," died without ever revealing details of his mysterious association with Siegel, or explaining how, without any security, he could borrow $100,000 from a gangster. There is no record of what happened to the painting. As far as anyone knows, Ward never paid Siegel any interest on the loan, but if the painting was really worth $4000 it could have been considered a sort of loan fee, and at 4 percent that was a modest rate indeed.

Just once, when Ward was asked in St. Paul about Siegel, he made it very clear why he didn't want to talk. He was afraid he would be killed.

If Ben Siegel was not sent westward on an official decision by the syndicate board of directors—and there is naturally no record of such action—why did he give up the security of his familiar jungle in New York for a distant outpost where he was a total stranger?

Unquestionably, Siegel's mind was prodded by a nameless emotional turbulence. He cringed from the sordid compound in which he was raised, and he was repelled by the illiterate and uncouth creatures who executed his commands. He killed because he had to kill. But he also knew that in the power struggle of the underworld he would be a target himself, sooner or later. He hated the name Bugsy because it put him in the same low class as Kid Twist and Three-Fingered Brown and Little Ziggy and Kid Dropper Kaplan. He hungered for the other side of the fence, and wanted to mingle with the so-called respectable people without the constant threat of an embarrassing roust. Going to California would slam the cover on the dirty sewer from which he crawled.

Also there was a girl. Her name was Ketti Gallian, a diminutive French actress with long blonde hair and a saucy heart-shaped face. She had been discovered in Paris by Winfield Sheehan, the shrewd mastermind of the movies, and brought to New York. Ketti was in Manhattan undergoing the apprentice training of a starlet when she met Ben Siegel, and the concussion was audible up and down Broadway. George Raft, who saw them together often, recalls that Siegel spent $50,000 in one way or another to help his imported Gallic delight. When Ketti was shipped out to California —to take English lessons and screen tests at Fox—Siegel went along. He was living in the Lawrence Tibbett house when her star fell and she was sent home to France. He never saw her again.

The transmutation of Bugsy Siegel, hoodlum, into Benjamin Siegel, Esq., sportsman and *bon vivant*, was achieved without the touch of a Frankenstein.

The usual expensive props were available, and he used them all. His chic address was the rented mansion on McCarthy Drive. He took membership in the Hillcrest Country Club. A fashionable girls' school was selected for Millicent and Barbara, plus daily lessons for them at the exclusive DuBrock Riding Academy. A rubdown or a steam bath was available in Director Eddie Sutherland's private health club on Rexford Drive. He rubbed shoulders with George Raft, Jean Harlow, Clark Gable, Bruce Cabot, and other reigning stars.

It was during Siegel's preliminary explorations in Beverly Hills that Longy Zwillman kept his promise and took him to meet Jean Harlow, her mother, and Marino Bello, her stepfather. In his book, *Harlow* (Bernard Geis, Assoc.), Irving Shulman mentions that Bello had connections with gangsters, and that Jean Harlow resented having Siegel and others in her home. Nevertheless, Jean liked Siegel, was one of his sponsors when he started captivating the Hollywood snobs, and was often identified as godmother for Millicent Siegel. Even after Jean died in 1937, there were affectionately-autographed pictures of her in Millicent's room.

Marino Bello and Siegel had an instant rapport. Both had piracy in their soul, both understood the gullibility of the average man, and they had a common admiration for the big names of the underworld. Bello was no killer or overt thief, but he had a talent for double-talk and con games that involved raising substantial amounts of money. He lived for the big dream—a lost gold mine, a buried treasure, a Rube Goldberg invention that would make him outrageously rich. He and Ben Siegel would soon join forces in two grandiose schemes that even Munchausen would have thought preposterous.

Siegel's deposits in his checking account at the staunch Union Bank & Trust Company were never less than $10,000 a month and in some thirty-day periods they exceeded $80,000. About half these deposits were cash, although Siegel had no business or visible source of income.

And then there was the Countess Dorothy Dendice Taylor DiFrasso. Hedda Hopper once said sagely: "Crooks as well as shady ladies like to mingle with celebrities. Bugsy loved to socialize. He'd turn up dressed to the nines, to take a drink or play poker as the guest of all kinds of people." Inversely, Hedda might have added, the big names liked to mingle with the hoods—and did. Mickey Cohen once had goggle-eyed natives lining up for his autograph and ignoring surrounding celebrities.

Dorothy DiFrasso, a dark-haired, buxom woman with frosty blue eyes, who was then credited with having a multimillion dollar fortune, was the daughter of Bertrand L. Taylor. He had made millions manufacturing leather goods in Watertown, New York, and when he died, the estate was divided between Dorothy and her brother, Bertrand L. Taylor, Jr., a member of the Board of Governors of the New York Stock Exchange.

Dorothy had had an unhappy marriage with an adventurous British pilot named Claude Graham White, and on the rebound married Count Carlo DiFrasso, a distinguished but relatively penniless Roman nobleman. She went to Italy with him and bought the Villa Madama, an ancient palace whose thick walls were covered with priceless frescoes by Raphael. "I'm telling you," Ben Siegel once said reminiscently, "this joint was bigger than Grand Central Station, and half the guys she had hanging around were Counts or Dukes or Kings out of a job."

The Countess often traveled to Beverly Hills, usually without her husband, and for the first two or three years she was a guest at Pickfair, the Mary Pickford-Douglas Fairbanks estate. Then she bought a house, a homey hacienda of thirty rooms or so, at 913 North Bedford Drive, and the celebrants who came there were the great names of the screen.

For her first major party, a boxing ring was set up in her garden and her guests were "entertained" with three bloody bouts in which the gladiators were battered pros. The onlookers for this curious form of amusement included Marlene Dietrich, Loretta Young, Charles Boyer, Fred Astaire, Dolores del Rio, Frederic March, and Clark Gable.

Elsa Maxwell, who may have been the most audacious free-loader of all time, mentioned this offbeat affair in an intimate newspaper biography of the Countess. Elsa added that people were willing to overlook Dorothy's oddities because she had "a racy wit, did the most outrageous things," and apparently had a vocabulary that could burn holes in asbestos.

This remarkable woman, bored with the same jaded faces of Hollywood and newly jilted by Gary Cooper, was on the prowl when she met Ben Siegel. "The thrill was the emotion that ruled her," said Elsa Maxwell, "this—and love."

The Countess was in her box at the Santa Anita Racetrack one day with James McKinley Bryant, a prominent New York hotel man, and Richard Gully, a cousin of England's Sir Anthony Eden. Bryant saw Siegel heading for the betting windows, called him over and introduced him to the wide-eyed Countess. That first encounter was brief and seemingly perfunctory. Siegel left her and joined George Raft, who also had a box. Shortly afterward, Florabel Muir went to an evening formal affair and was dumbfounded to see the young New York gangster in the receiving line alongside the Countess DiFrasso.

"Hello, Benny," she said.

He said nothing, bowed to her with a self-conscious grin, and turned to greet the next arrival. Bugsy Siegel, the semiliterate mobster from the Lower East Side, had made society. He was not only in the receiving line with the stars and the doyenne of the glittering international set—he was in her bedroom, too.

One still evening in Beverly Hills, when there was no cooling current of air from the sea a few miles to the west, George Raft drove his black Cadillac convertible from Coldwater Canyon to Romanoff's Restaurant just off Wilshire Boulevard. He stepped out of the car, leaving the engine running for the parking attendant, brushed some cigarette ash from his coat, and made a slow and studied entrance through the gilded doors.

He was a marqueé name then, earning more than $5000 a week, and the casual walk into the crowded restaurant—as though the camera was turning—was *de rigeur* for stars of the highest galaxies. His Highness, Michael Romanoff, Hollywood's phony prince, already advised that Raft was coming, met him in the foyer.

"Hello, George," he said.

"Hello, Mike. Hope you have room for me."

"We're very busy tonight, but for you. . . ." Mike could play games, too. "The usual booth?"

"Thanks."

Raft moved sinuously across the crowded room, like a sleek black reptile threading a path around a series of obstacles. "Some of my friends used to call me Black Snake," he told me once. "I guess it was the way I walked." The walk-on had to be done with care, because every head would turn, and Louella or Louis B. Mayer or Jack Warner might be there. They always saw you coming in, never when you were going out. He sat down, lit a cigarette and leaned back.

He gazed at the menu card, but he was not seeing the print. The food was unimportant, only the faces mattered. His eyes traveled around the room, as all other eyes were doing, probing like searchlight beams to spot who was there.

Raft recognized a man in another booth whose graying hair was flat and combed straight back, as though fixed by a spray; thick dark eyebrows were an accent on his broad, smooth face, and long earlobes lay flat against a neck that was beginning to show loose fat. The man in the booth, unrecognized by most of the diners, was Mr. Joseph Doto of New York, better known as Joe Adonis, or Joey A. if you really knew your mob. There was a girl with him, a new face in town, and Raft examined her as a connoisseur examines a work of art. He put down the menu, slid out from under the table and walked to the booth.

"Hello, Joey," he said.

"Why, hello, Snake," Adonis smiled.

"What's up?"

"Just here for a few hours. Nothing special. You seen Ben Siegel lately?"

"Yeah," Raft nodded. "He's building a house. Quite a place."

"Oh say, George—" Adonis suddenly realized they were not alone. "I'd like you to meet a friend of mine. Honey, this is George Raft, as if you didn't know."

Raft smiled at her with his eyes. He had learned long ago that he should never smile with his lips parted because, inexplicably, it made him look less mysterious.

"George, meet Virginia Hill."

"Glad to know you, Virginia. You from out of town?" He knew she was from out of town. She had to be. There wasn't a good-looking woman within fifty miles whose name and talents he didn't know.

"I'm from Chicago," she said softly. "But I'll be living here, too."

"That's fine. Maybe we'll be seeing you around."

"Maybe."

Raft shook hands with Joey and went back to his table. He wondered where Joey had found this girl and whether she belonged to him. She was a beauty, he thought. She had it, whatever it was, and there weren't too many in town. He would be seeing her again. Oh, yes.

It took Ben Siegel only a few months to find the places where he could plant the juice in Los Angeles. For a token payment of $500 he bought a one-quarter interest in a company called Redondo Beach Properties, and it immediately began yielding enough to support a new girl now and then. The company neither owned buildings nor sold lots, but did have the gambling concession in sleazy beach front bars and restaurants.

He also had a 15 percent piece of a dog-racing track in Culver City, the once graft-rotten community which was the home of Metro-Goldwyn-Mayer.

In Brooklyn, as a sort of sentimental remaining root, he operated an insurance business which one hoodlum's macabre sense of humor described as "insurance against getting bumped off." In Chicago at the same time, Siegel and Longy Zwillman were partners in a hot dog business which, had it not been for one unique aspect, would have been a very prosaic enterprise indeed for such a pair. The gimmick was a little machine that cooked hot dogs by electrocuting them. Siegel, who was occasionally capable of wry laughter, once described it as the only hot seat in existence which Lepke and seven other executed killers would have traded for the one in Sing Sing.

For one other business in the works, Siegel could foresee an enormous profit. Among the picturesque villains of southern California when Siegel moved west was Anthony Cornero Stralla, a stubby man with the rolling gait of an old salt, chilly slate-colored eyes, and the purpling cheeks of the hypertensive. He habitually wore a ten-gallon hat (a Prohibition agent once said he could almost hide that much booze in it) and he was tougher than a suit of mail. He was known around Los Angeles as Tony Cornero, and it was no secret that he had made a fortune on the high seas robbing bootleg liquor from rum-runners operating between the Mexican and Canadian borders.

When the Prohibition law died, Tony was suddenly unemployed, like most of his underworld contemporaries. He had done a brief stretch at McNeil Island Penitentiary for the only time he was caught smuggling liquor, and when he came out he was eager for action, preferably at sea. He considered legitimate shipping for a while, but was pessimistic about profits. Then he conceived the daring idea of running a gambling ship anchored off the Santa Monica shore.

Ben Siegel heard about this piquant plan one day, and immediately hurried to George Raft's home.

"Georgie," he said, "I need twenty grand in a hurry."

"Who doesn't?" Raft said. "What's it for?"

"Tony Cornero's got a million dollar idea, and I want in on it."

"I've heard about it—the gambling ship."

"It's terrific," Siegel said eagerly. "You lend me the dough, and we'll all make something."

Raft avoided Siegel's probing eyes and looked away. "I haven't got that much cash, Ben," he said.

"But you can get it."

The meaning was clear. *Get it!* "Okay, pal," Raft said. "I'll try."

The next morning Raft drove 140 miles to Arrowhead Springs, a summer resort southeast of Hollywood, and borrowed the money as an advance against future pictures from a friend, the late producer Myron Selznick. He wasted no time, but turned around immediately and barreled back to Los Angeles. He gave Siegel the cash, and the gangster threw it into Tony Cornero's pot.

Though Raft knew nothing about it, Siegel also went to the Union Bank & Trust Company, borrowed $15,000, and gave it to a hoodlum pal, Whitey Krakower, to make a similar investment in Cornero's scheme.

When Tony had raised enough money (it was estimated at the time that the stockholders had invested about $500,000) the steamship *Rex* sailed out of port on its first cruise under Captain Cornero. He dropped the hook three miles off the Santa Monica shore, bought a fleet of sturdy water taxis, and began transporting the suckers to his floating Monte Carlo.

The vessel was promptly raided by a posse of deputy sheriffs, since those waters were under the jurisdiction of Los Angeles County. But because they were not quite sure of their authority, the deputies arrested only the customers, and it was said cries could be heard all the way to lawyers' row in downtown Los Angeles.

Cornero stifled his rage, hauled anchor, and steamed to a point twelve miles out in the ocean. And there he stayed, adding two more ships to the gambling fleet. It was remarkable in a day when Dramamine was not generally available—and I saw it myself on two trips to the *Rex*—how many greenhorns paid large sums for the privilege of having their stomachs churned by bumpy seas.

Ben Siegel had called it right. It was the sweetest little racket since the invention of shaved dice.

George Raft heard about the whole Navy of suckers and how they braved *mal de mer* to lose their money, and he naturally began looking for some dividends on his twenty grand. Raft had a staggering overhead, what with courting Betty Grable and Norma Shearer, among others, and he was chronically broke. He told me he was constantly feuding with Jack Warner and other studio heads, and he was suspended so many times he looked like part of a puppet act.

When Siegel adroitly evaded Raft's hints about repayment of the loan, the actor wrote him as follows:

> Dear Ben: Between the Federal government, studios, and several other personal transactions, I've really been hard pressed for cash. I will surely greatly appreciate whatever you can possibly afford and spare for me, and I honestly trust that you fully understand this request.
>
> Again I'd like to remind you, Ben, that if my finances weren't as bad as they actually are, under no circumstances would I have ever asked you.
>
> Your friend and pal,
> George

Not long after he mailed this obsequious dun, Raft was driving down Sunset Boulevard toward the Paramount studios when Siegel came along behind him, and motioned him toward the curb. He got out of his car, and silently handed Raft a check for $2000.

"What's this for?" Raft asked.

"Well—I had an argument with Cornero," Siegel replied. "I'm getting out of the *Rex* deal, and I want to pay you back. Here's two on account."

"Gee—thanks, Ben."

"Okay, pal. I'll get the rest soon as I can."

Raft recalls that it took Siegel months to square the entire loan in payments that never exceeded $500 at any one time. Fortunately, Raft could not get a peek at Siegel's account book in which he meticulously noted the bets he was making every day. Though he was slow about paying Raft, Siegel was betting from $2000 to $5000 a day on horse races, football games, baseball games, and prize fights—and winning most of the time.

With Siegel's acumen as a gambler, it is unlikely he invested money with Cornero only to withdraw when business was in the black. Perhaps he lied to Raft. He was not above swindling his friend, as Raft later learned, and perhaps he had not invested in the gaming ship at all. In any case, Tony Cornero's enterprise only survived a year.

Earl Warren, then Attorney General of California, organized a massive assault on Tony's ships. The raiders dumped $100,000 worth of equipment into the sea—120 slot machines, 25 blackjack tables, 20 roulette wheels, and countless dice tables—and the big dream went down with the fish.

Cornero was allowed to keep the *Rex*, but he soon lost the ship, too, to three high rollers in a crap game. Tony was later shot down at his own doorstep by an unknown enemy, for the second time, but he survived the wound. He was at Las Vegas one evening, negotiating an astronomic deal to build a multimillion dollar hotel and casino. During a lull in the conference, Tony strolled heavily to the nearest crap table, laid down a bet, and tossed the dice against the green felted backstop.

"Snake eyes, the loser," the stickman intoned. Tony dropped dead.

The moment Ben Siegel saw the lush vacant lot on Delfern Avenue, he knew he had to have it. He had decided, now that he was identified with the exclusive Dorothy DiFrasso crowd, that the Lawrence Tibbett house was not compatible with the "wealthy sportsman" tag. It was not what the realtors advertise as a showplace. It was adequate as a part-time home for an opera singer, but it was not the kind of house likely to be singled out by the guide on a tourist sightseeing bus.

Delfern Avenue was in Holmby Hills, a name to delight the tax collector and the genteel rich. It started just off Sunset Boulevard and ran north along with Baroda, Beverly Glen, North Faring, and St. Pierre, where, at one time or another, lived Fanny Brice, Claudette Colbert, Buddy DeSylva, and Vincent Price. A parallel block away was Mapleton Drive, with a fabulous constellation that included Art Linkletter, Bing Crosby, Judy Garland, Humphrey Bogart, and Alan Ladd.

Siegel's lot at 250 Delfern was on the same street with the

homes of Sonja Henie, Bonita Granville, Anita Louise, and Director Norman Taurog. "Nice classy neighbors," Siegel once said. The feeling was not mutual.

The plans for Siegel's house called for a total cost, excluding furniture and decorating, of $150,000. The house, which was to crown a wooded knoll with an enchanting view, was built of snow white brick. Bulldozers gouged a hole in the earth behind the house for an Olympic-sized swimming pool, and beside it was a pool house large enough to house the average family of five.

Ben Siegel, more impatient than a bridegroom, was at the building site almost every day, badgering the contractors and trailing carpenters and plumbers to make sure they were following the blueprints. He often went there after dark, occasionally coaxing George Raft to go along, and together they would stumble through the various rooms, lighting wooden matches so they could see.

"Why in hell don't you bring a flashlight?" Raft asked.

"Well," Siegel said, "I keep forgetting the damn thing."

At one stage, when the house was almost finished, Siegel took Raft to the master bedroom on the second floor and showed him a sliding panel controlled by a concealed button.

"What's that for?" Raft asked.

"It's a trap door, what else? Why don't you put one in your house?"

"Who needs it?"

Siegel gave him a wistful smile. "I do," he said. "I got two others in the house. Maybe some day I gotta get outa here in a hurry."

Ben Siegel's conception of homey elegance, rococo as it was, was compatible with the frustrations of a man whose early years were spent dodging in and out of ratholes in New York. His personal bathroom was walled with red marble, and Esta Siegel's dressing room, almost within walking distance of their king-sized bed on its two-foot platform, was a splash of light from mirrors on both walls and ceilings.

In the library was another hidden wall repository, reached by pulling out bookcases that hung on ball-bearing hinges. Siegel had filing cabinets there, and a large safe in which he kept all his jewelry, account books, and two guns—a Smith & Wesson .38 revolver and a .38 Colt automatic.

The bar and lounge room, also on the first floor, was early Cecil B. DeMille, with two eighteen-foot carved divans flanking the walk-in fireplace and display cabinets with soft indirect lighting. The liquor cabinets were stocked with rare rums, whiskies, and cordials, and in the lounge—smuggled into the house at night and installed by the master himself—was a battery of slot machines.

There were six so-called "vanity" rooms for the ladies, equipped with crystal bottles containing exotic perfumes and comb and brush sets trimmed with turquoise, amethyst, silver, and gold. The dining room table was custom-made of inlaid woods and large enough to serve thirty people without extension leaves. The wall-to-wall carpeting was so expensive that all of Siegel's servants—and he never had less than three—were ordered to remove their shoes before going in to do the daily dusting.

He had two unlisted telephones—BR 2-1989 and CR 1-0360—with many extensions on both floors, and some were equipped with devices that could muffle his voice when others were within earshot.

The layout, as Siegel said more than once, was quite a triumph for a boy who started his professional life dropping flower pots on policemen. (In later years, when experts weighed the flaws and errors that destroyed Bugsy Siegel, it was generally agreed that an inordinate vanity, neutralizing his natural caution, was a large contributing factor.)

He was a fanatic on the subject of health and virility, and few could have endured his program for physical fitness. He smoked an occasional cigar, and he liked a snifter of brandy but he drank very little of that. He was a skilled boxer, and was constantly coaxing Champ Segal, George Raft, and a gas station operator named Joe Moll to go a few rounds.

He swam in his own pool, or in the Raft pool almost every day, and he kept many business appointments at the Hollywood Y.M.C.A. where he spent every afternoon either in the steam room or working out in the big gym. At bedtime—and only his most intimate friends had the nerve to tease him about it—Siegel rubbed skin cream over his handsome face and donned an elastic chin strap to keep his profile from sagging. He went to bed early, struggling with the "It Pays to Increase Your Word Power" section in

Reader's Digest or reading other self-help articles, and at ten P.M. —which was often taps in his house—(unless he was out for the evening) he turned off the lights and covered his eyes with a sleep shade.

He had a pathological fear of losing his hair, and at Drucker's Barbershop in Beverly Hills the diplomatic barbers ritually assured him they could see new growths here and there. There was a wordless understanding among his friends that they would tell him white lies about his hair, because they all knew it was falling out, and it would only be a matter of time before baldness set in.

Raft recalls that he and his so-called bodyguard, Mack "Killer" Gray, were with Siegel one evening in a gambling joint at Lodi, New Jersey. Standing at the bar, enviously gazing at Gray's luxuriant head of hair, Siegel blurted out: "Hey, Killer, how do you keep your hair like that?"

"I don't know," Gray replied. "I don't do anything special. It just grows like that."

"I'll give you twenty-five hundred bucks if you let me cut off a hunk," Siegel snapped.

"You're kidding!"

"No, I'm not."

Gray glanced at Raft, and the actor nodded. "Okay, Ben," Gray said with resignation.

Siegel borrowed a pair of scissors from the bartender, snipped off a thick lock, and stuffed it into an envelope he had in his pocket. He peeled off twenty-five one-hundred dollar bills from the fat roll in his pocket, silently handed them to Mack Gray, and stormed out of the place. Later, when he was back home in California, he took the hair threw it into the fireplace flames like a witch doctor exorcising an evil spirit. Unhappily, Mack Gray's hair grew as fast as ever, but the Siegel scalp was thinner than before.

It was fairly obvious, though, that Bugsy Siegel could achieve his goals with or without hair. He knew what he was doing in the papier-mâché world of Hollywood where he needed neither guns nor mob, and his daily log reflected a planned and determined march.

He kept a meticulous record, not only of expenditures and bets, but also of names and numbers of people he had already met or wanted to know. Thus, some of the early phone call notations in the green memo book read like this:

Du Brock's Riding Academy—N. Hollywood 3343
Millie Factor—HE 0967
Charlie Einfeld (Publicity Director Warner Bros.)
Mark Hellinger—HE 7614
Sol Wurtzel (movie executive) West LA 39405
Harold Lloyd Jr.
Bobby Breen (singer)

Jean Harlow met her sordid death on June 7, 1937, and thereafter, presumably because there was no longer any pressure on her stepfather to keep gangsters out of her home, this notation began to appear regularly in Siegel's personal ledger: "Call Marino Bello. WH 2266."

The two men were often seen together in public—Bello with his needle-sharp moustache and white spats, and Siegel in his custom-made dark blue suits, and an occasional finger wave to disguise the thin areas of his dark hair. They had a daring project in process and many times Ben Siegel had said to his friends: "If this one pays off, I won't have to work another day the rest of my life."

In the meantime, as though the dream had already come true, Siegel was making some remarkable bets through the Robert B. Greene Co., a commission house at 80 Wall Street in New York.

Cash payable memoranda from the Greene Co. in the fall of 1937 included the following:

Oct. 11. You had Giants to finish ahead of Cubs for season $3000 to 2500.
By cash: $2500.00

Nov. 2. You had LaGuardia to win by 400,000 votes. $3600 to 3000.
You had LaGuardia to be elected Mayor 8000 to 2000.
You had Dewey to be elected D.A. by 75,000. $5000 to 2500.
You had Dewey to be elected D.A. by 75,000. $2500 to 2500.
By cash herewith: $10,000.

Nov. 20 You had Harvard over Yale 1000 to 1500.
You had Purdue over Indiana 500 to 1100.
By cash: $2600.00

It seemed as though he couldn't lose. But that was before the luck started to change. It would have been much better, when he wanted to lie with a woman, to have stayed away from the Countess Dorothy DiFrasso.

CHAPTER FIVE

"The Bug," a New York gambler once said, "was always a sucker for an exciting long shot bet." This gentleman, who prefers to be nameless, recalled that Siegel once bet on the same long-shot horse four times in less than a month. The nag, aptly named Bulwark, won three times, and Siegel's gross profit was about $10,000.

But the long shot in the summer of 1938 had nothing to do with horses. The big bet his friends were worried about involved $90,000,000, and the odds against Siegel and the Countess Dorothy DiFrasso were so astronomical that even Longy Zwillman, who was kept *au courant* in Jersey, said he would rather bet six, two and even that the sun wouldn't rise again.

There was in New York, it seems, a bibulous old man named Bill Bowbeer. Like Billy Bones in the Robert Louis Stevenson tale, Bowbeer had a map with the location of a fabulous buried treasure. It was crudely drawn on a tablecloth—or so Siegel learned—and, lacking a sea chest, Bowbeer carried it in the frayed inside pocket of his coat. He pulled it out in smoky taverns from time to time, and offered a piece of the treasure to any drinking companion willing to finance a search.

But no Squire Trelawney turned up to take the risk, and Bowbeer was glumly considering turning the tablecloth into a shirt when, in an encounter so improbable that it might have been cleverly arranged, he met the Countess DiFrasso and her checkbook.

Ben Siegel never explained how or why Dorothy happened to be in a sawdust *boîte de nuit* hobnobbing with riffraff. In any case,

Bowbeer showed her the map, and in no time at all she was in Michigan chartering the *Metha Nelson*, a three-masted schooner of some 460 tons, then tied up in the Los Angeles harbor at San Pedro, but owned by a Detroit bank.

On a foggy morning in September, the *Metha Nelson* creaked away from her berth and sailed south to Ensenada, just across the border in Mexico. There she was boarded by most of the crew and passengers (some were later described as looking like San Quentin's class of '38) and the vessel promptly put to sea again.

The passengers on this odd voyage—they might have been handpicked by a Hollywood script writer for a stock plot—included the following:

The Countess DiFrasso, *the Angel*
Ben Siegel, *the mastermind*
Miss Philomena Renzi, *personal maid to the Countess*
Marino Bello, *stepfather of the late Jean Harlow, and production manager aboard*
Miss Evelyn Husby, *Bello's private nurse*
Richard Gully, Esq., *English bon vivant, later social secretary and protocol interpreter for Jack Warner*
Dr. Benjamin Blank, *official physician for the Los Angeles County Jail*
Harry "Champ" Segal, *member of the prominent Segal lock family, exfighter, racetrack tout, ring manager and, at the time, in charge of physical education for his longtime friend, Siegel*
Captain Bob Hoffman, *German navigator and master of the vessel*
Bill Bowbeer, *holder of the map*

There were some twenty men in the crew, many recruited from bookie joints in Hollywood and equipped with six-shooters just in case any of the Long John Silvers rebelled, or pirates appeared. Richard Gully, Champ Segal, and Dr. Blank are the only living survivors of the expedition, and Champ says he went along only to keep an eye on the Countess. "Three days before the vessel sailed," he says, "Dorothy's brother, Bert Taylor, phoned me from New York and begged me to go so she'd have some protection. He was suspicious as hell about the whole thing and scared stiff to have Dorothy going off with all these strange characters."

Gully went aboard frankly apprehensive. He had never been a bodyguard for so much as a poodle, and his experience with weapons was confined to throwing darts. He hoped, knowing that Siegel and Dorothy were partners in more than a treasure hunt, that the gangster would be a gallant saviour if things got tough. Gully need not have worried. For Ben Siegel this assignment was far less complicated than planning the murder of a two-timer.

The vessel was off the coast of Baja, California, when Siegel, who up to that moment had been mysteriously noncommittal, revealed their destination. The *Metha Nelson,* he said, was headed for bleak Cocos Island, a slip of land on the vast Pacific some 300 miles off the mainland of Costa Rica. The island, only four miles long and two miles wide, belonged to Costa Rica, but was uninhabited. Somewhere on the tiny rectangle of jungle, he said, perhaps hidden in a deep cave, was ninety million dollars worth of gold and jewelry.

"We're gonna grab the stuff," Siegel said with blazing eyes, "and we're all gonna go home rich."

It seems incredible that Ben Siegel and Dorothy DiFrasso, neither of whom were idiots in a business deal, could have been so thoroughly credulous about this legend that ranks with the Abominable Snowman and the Loch Ness Monster. Any schoolboy can go to the nearest public library and find references to the Cocos Island treasure. Yet seagoing adventurers, including in recent years such solid citizens as Sir Malcolm Campbell and Vincent Astor, have been going to Cocos for more than a century, searching for the gems and the bullion supposedly stashed away there by the evil captain and crew of the English merchant ship *Mary Deere.*

"In my wildest dreams," Gully says now, "I never believed we'd find a dollar's worth of gold. I was out of a job at the time, and for me it was just a pleasant cruise to a desert island. But these other jokers believed the treasure was there and that they'd all be rich."

Siegel, as Dorothy's field general on the trip, had overlooked nothing. The vessel had dories and motor launches on deck for ferrying equipment ashore. There was dynamite for blasting, gasoline power units for operating rock drills, and enough spades and shovels to dig another Forest Lawn. Siegel and his Countess were not interested in Spartan cuisine, and had brought cases of expensive canned meats, sauces, soups, caviar, and other delicacies, as well as fine wines, liqueurs, and brandy.

Because she had an innate sense of propriety with strangers, the Countess and her personal maid occupied the most luxurious stateroom alone. When Siegel visited Dorothy, Philomena Renzi discreetly withdrew to the lounge.

Dr. Blank, who had been a medical school classmate of Ben's brother, Dr. Maurice Siegel, shared a stateroom with Siegel, and Bello had a smaller cabin for himself. Richard Gully slept in the lounge, and does not remember where Evelyn Husby, Champ Segal, and Bowbeer stayed.

In any case, Miss Husby stopped sleeping alone on the fourth day out. Bello, who suffered from coronary heart disease and openly credited Evelyn with nursing him back to health, summoned Captain Hoffman one sultry evening and said he wanted to marry the girl. The skipper performed the ceremony on the bridge, with crew and passengers as happy witnesses, and there was a gay reception and supper in the main lounge.

"We were all there, of course," Gully says drily. "Where else could we go?"

No one knows what wistful thoughts ran through Dorothy DiFrasso's mind as she stood alongside the petite and radiant bride. Gully believes that if she and Siegel had been legally free to marry, the Countess might have tried to talk him into a shipboard ceremony, too. Siegel probably loved the eccentric countess as much as he could love anyone in the period before he knew Virginia Hill. But he was far too calculating to get deeply involved with Dorothy. He had no intention of divorcing Esta—not then, anyway—and, unfaithful as he was, he was proud of his home and family.

The long voyage southward, through emerald waters that were fluorescent at night, was a pleasant trip.

Siegel was up at dawn every day, trotting around the deck, or boxing a few rounds with Champ. Knowing something of Siegel's hoodlum days, Gully was surprised to find himself yielding to the man's undeniable charm. Moreover, it was obvious that Siegel was a leader of men, and had the respect of every person aboard.

"I often thought later how tragic it was the way he wasted his life," Gully told me. "I don't like to praise a man with a record like his—and it's pretty frightening when you get into it—but on that trip he never got out of line once. He had authority, he was pleasant. He carried a gun, but he didn't make a show-off of himself."

Siegel was extremely reticent about his underworld connections, and said nothing to Gully or anyone else about his activities with the mob. But he did mention Meyer Lansky, his former partner in the Bug-Meyer mob, and reminisced about their wild adventures during prohibition. "There is a guy," Siegel said, "who has a brilliant mind and for my money is one of the great organizers of his time. I don't see him much any more, and that's too bad."

In the evenings, when the Countess turned on her console phonograph and chose a record from an imposing collection, they all sat around the lounge and talked about the treasure.

Occasionally Siegel and Champ started a poker game, and Gully, whose impeccable Continental manners and clipped British accent made him a natural target for jokes, inevitably became their pigeon. Skilled in sleight-of-hand, they slyly dealt him a full house or four of a kind, and when Gully showed his hand, Champ, Bello, or Siegel would lay down a straight flush. Gully's despair on these losing hands was always a signal for explosive laughter, but when Siegel later confessed to Gully that they had stacked the deck, he returned all the money and suggested that tennis might be a safer and less expensive game.

The lure of gold kept all of them in a state of exhilaration as the *Metha Nelson*, her single diesel throbbing, pushed southward. None of them remembered (if they had ever known) the words of St. Matthew: "Lay not up for yourselves treasures upon earth, where moth and rust corrupt, and thieves break through and steal."

Late in September, they reached the Costa Rican harbor of Puntarenas and there, by prearrangement, the *Metha Nelson* was boarded by an Army colonel named Siegfried Campos, and six soldiers who carried Tommy guns. The Costa Rican government was willing to indulge these eccentric American explorers, but if by some miracle they stumbled on anything valuable, Costa Rica wanted its share. Any sensible speculator would have realized that Costa Ricans themselves had already turned over every foot of ground, perhaps for a hundred years, without finding the fabled wealth. It was always possible, though, that earlier searchers may have been off, and so Siegel was compelled to sign an agreement giving Costa Rica one third of anything they found. "That's okay with me," he said with a shrug. "We'll still have sixty million left."

Captain Hoffman turned his ship seaward again, and some days later—the island must have looked like the phoenix rising from its fiery bed—the lookout cried: "Land ho!" Hoffman dropped anchor a mile offshore from a small inlet called Waver Bay, just below the 2788-foot summit of Mt. Iglesias. Siegel and Hoffman went ashore in a small boat, landing on a sandy beach which was not more than a hundred yards long.

It was immediately apparent that this was no magic island like Tahiti, and they could understand why even the Costa Rican natives did not want to live there. The shore was rocky and buttressed with steep cliffs; the jungle grass thrust its sharp blades shoulder-high, and the trees were tangled growths, chained together by thick vines. There was almost no level land, and in the little canyons, where other men had sought the gold, they found the rotting remains of crude shacks.

In subsequent trips with men from the crew, Siegel and Bello set up tents and campsites. They brought tools and food and weapons. And they set up watches around the clock, because there was evidence that they were spied upon by the animal eyes of wildcats, boars, snakes, and rats.

Gully calls it "the ten terrible days": cruel sun in repeated waves of 85° heat; warm rains of the season, hour after hour, drenching clothes and spirits; the stench of decaying plants and animal feces; sweat and swearing; the moist corrosive air, coating clothes and food with green.

But they searched frantically for the gold.

"Did we dig?" Gully says. "Christ, did we dig! We drilled through rocks and shale. The climate was murderous but we couldn't stop. We dynamited whole cliffs."

For ten days and nights they slaved, and Ben Siegel fumed

and cursed. The rain dripped down over his long lashes and blurred his vision. The rain splotched the makeup on the Countess Di-Frasso's tired face when she came ashore once; she was taken back to the *Metha Nelson* and there she stayed. The rain seeped into their brains, and some of the hoodlums cracked: "Hey, Pete, let's climb up and get us a coconut."

"Climb, hell," said one hoodlum known only as Pete. He grabbed a Tommy gun from a startled Costa Rican private, and a tattoo of slugs ripped across the soggy fronds drooping against the sky. The coconuts dropped like dead birds, and pale white liquid oozed from their shells.

"You dumb son of a bitch!" Siegel screamed. "Put that down! You want one of these grease balls to get the wrong idea and blast you in the belly?"

Pete sheepishly handed back the gun. He stumbled over the rocks and went down to the sea where he sat in numbed silence.

The ten terrible days. It was not the heat and the bugs and the smell that finally discouraged them. It was the moment of truth: the treasure was a nightmare. It was not there; perhaps it had never been there. They could tear up the whole eight square miles in ten days, ten months, ten years, maybe. Ben Siegel knew he was licked.

Angry and sickened by the indigestible facts, Siegel abruptly ordered Captain Hoffman to round up the crew and hoist anchor. In a somewhat garbled version given to his brother Hyman years later, and recorded in *They Called Him Champ*, by Hyman R. Segal (Citadel), Champ Segal said that Siegel quit because he had received reports that the stock market was unsteady and wanted to communicate with his brokers to protect his holdings. Champ added that Siegel left the *Metha Nelson* at San Jose in Guatemala.

But at the time Siegel had no sizeable investments on Wall Street, and he was far more concerned with his gambling interests in Los Angeles. Actually he told Hoffman to take the ship directly to Panama, and there he abandoned the Countess and the rest of the guests. His diary shows the following entries:

Tues. Nov. 1. Cash taken out of our savings account and sent to me for b.t. bus. [buried treasure business] in Panama by E. S. [Esta Siegel] $3000.

Nov. 9.	Cash taken out of our savings account to pay for plane ticket for me to come back home from b.t. bus. in Panama. $350.
Nov. 11.	Day of my return from b.t. bus. trip, and fixed all my records up and everything.

As a further indication that Siegel was more anxious about his regular wagers than in the market fluctuations, the diary also shows that, on the same day Esta had to withdraw $3000 from the savings account, he had a bet riding on the great horse Seabiscuit in Los Angeles, and won $2200.

He flew home alone from Panama, and Champ Segal later reported that the Countess was so miffed about being deserted that she made a pass at him aboard the ship. Champ said she asked him for "a little loving," but that he gallantly resisted with the excuse that he couldn't betray his best friend, Ben Siegel. Richard Gully's reaction to Champ's claim was bitter and succinct. "How pathetic!" he said. "Champ wasn't such a bad guy but he certainly didn't appeal to Dorothy. I don't blame him for trying to justify all the things that happened on the way home."

Gully says that Champ Segal and a crewman named Abe Kappelner began quarreling with Captain Hoffman. The feud had almost reached open fighting when a typhoon hit the *Metha Nelson* in the Gulf of Tehuantepec. The screaming winds and mountainous seas slammed the ship around like a cork, swept gear off the decks, and injured half a dozen crewmen. The diesel engine was jarred loose and was so badly damaged that it became useless.

The *Metha Nelson* was wallowing helplessly in the boiling ocean when an S.O.S. brought help from the *Cellini*, an Italian motor vessel heading northward on the same course. The *Cellini* towed Captain Hoffman's battered ship into Acapulco, and she lay there for almost a month waiting for a new engine from the United States. The Countess DiFrasso grew impatient—she had lost all interest in the cruise anyway—and flew with Gully to Mexico City. Bello and Champ Segal were entrusted with the responsibility of getting the *Metha Nelson* back to Los Angeles.

When the vessel limped into Los Angeles, Captain Hoffman, to the consternation of all concerned, had Segal and Kappelner arrested on a charge of mutiny, and demanded a Federal Grand Jury investigation and indictment. Imaginative editors on the Los Angeles newspapers promptly labeled the *Metha Nelson* a "hell ship," and for a day or two they dusted off all the available, but old, pictures of the Countess DiFrasso with Cary Grant, Gary Cooper, Mary Pickford, and other movie star friends; of Marino Bello, smiling covetously at his beautiful stepdaughter, Jean Harlow; and assorted poses of Champ Segal at sporting events here and there. There were no such photos of the true boss of the cruise, Mr. Benjamin Siegel, wealthy sportsman, nor was his real identity revealed at the time.

The men and women on that Grand Jury must have been more perceptive than most; after they heard testimony from Gully and the others, they refused to indict, and thus the story died.

But one item would not stay buried—the anonymity of Bugsy Siegel.

In the city room of the *Los Angeles Examiner*, Jim Richardson, the gangling, scowling city editor, swore every time he saw a society item coupling the Countess Dorothy DiFrasso with Mr. Benjamin Siegel.

Not long before Richardson died, I sat in his home in Arcadia —this was about 1958—and we talked about crime and about Bugsy Siegel. He remembered the day the phone rang on the city desk and a guttural voice said: "Why don't you investigate this Mr. Benjamin Siegel you're writin' about all the time?"

"Why should I?"

"Because he's a killer. That's why."

Richardson also remembered how Johnny Klein, chief investigator for District Attorney Buron Fitts, had gone east to do a little graduate work at New York Police headquarters. He was running through a batch of mug shots, just to check names and numbers, when a fellow detective plucked one and said: "Now there's an outstanding citizen named Bugsy Siegel."

"Never heard of him," Klein said.

"You never heard of him? Why, Johnny, this guy is one of the worst killers in the country and he's living right in your backyard."

So Jim Richardson, one of the great information purse seiners of his time, went fishing. "I decided to blast this bum," Richardson said. And presently the *Los Angeles Examiner* came out with a blunt story in which Benjamin Siegel, wealthy sportsman, was unmasked as Bugsy Siegel, gangster.

In Beverly Hills, pacing the wall-to-wall carpet, Ben Siegel considered his gaudy mansion, and his oversize swimming pool and all the money he had in a respectable bank—and he burned. Among other things, the exposé had wafted into the clubhouse of the Hillcrest Country Club and, as those respectable members held their noses, Siegel was compelled to resign.

He didn't understand it. No osmosis could filter the hard cold facts through his thick skin. Then and later, Siegel felt that if he had laid his guns aside, and could get a Dun and Bradstreet rating and socialize with George Raft and the Countess DiFrasso, it didn't matter whether he had killed one or a dozen men. His fury turned to thoughts of editor Jim Richardson.

It is the fond belief of many substantial citizens who are sprayed with wet newsprint, that the offending editor or reporter can be fired by applying heat to the owner or publisher. The pressure usually comes from social quarters—the victim belongs to the same club as the publisher and they have mutual friends—or the dollar threat is imposed. "This man gets fired off your paper," the standard phrase goes, "or I withdraw my million bucks of advertising."

Occasionally it works; more often it backfires.

Richardson said he was reading copy one day when in came Harry Crocker, popular society columnist for the *Examiner*.

"Jim," he said, "I was at a Hollywood party the other night, and the Countess DiFrasso grabbed me. She's fit to be tied because of that story on Ben Siegel."

"Oh—he's Ben Siegel to you, too? Around here we call him Bugsy. Are you scared of this hoodlum?"

"Sure I am," Crocker replied. "This guy is bad news. Nobody calls him Bugsy. I've heard he'd just as soon kill you for using that name."

"Relax, Harry. He's not going to fool around with a newspaperman."

Crocker was shocked at Richardson's attitude, and told him

that the Countess, on the strength of a long and close friendship with William Randolph Hearst, had promised to get Richardson fired.

"No man or woman alive goes to the Chief with stuff like that," Richardson said.

"But she will," Crocker said.

And she did. Puffing like a steam engine on an upgrade, the Countess drove to San Simeon and there, because Hearst learned why she had come, was purposely kept outside the control gate. She returned to Los Angeles, tear-stained and frustrated, but she was not ready to quit. She would be at San Simeon again, and her performance the second time would be ugly.

Not long after the Hearst episode, Richardson had a surprise visit from Mark Hellinger, the former Broadway columnist who had been lured away from his New York beat to make pictures for Jack Warner. Richardson had long admired Hellinger's work, and they had a warm, mutual friend in Damon Runyon. But to Richardson's bitter disappointment, Hellinger had not come to reminisce or even bring a greeting from Runyon. It was obvious that he was there for one purpose—to find out what new indignities, if any, the *Examiner* was planning for Bugsy Siegel.

It grieved Richardson to find a man of Hellinger's stature stooping to this kind of subterfuge, but he had no way of knowing that Hellinger and Siegel had been friends for years, and that eventually Hellinger would publicly endorse the underworld king.

"At the time I thought that Mark should have been on my side," Richardson said. "But my God, there he was, fronting for this bum. I never talked to Mark again about it, and he's gone now, but I always hoped he realized he was wrong."

As it happens, Richardson had something definite in mind: he wanted Bugsy Siegel in jail. And to put him there he'd have to get inside the gangster's private safe at the Delfern Avenue house. He had a man who could do it.

CHAPTER SIX

One morning at ten o'clock, the quiet time in the city room of the *Examiner,* Jim Richardson came in early to write some letters. He was absorbed in the job when a copyboy crossed the room and said: "Mr. Richardson, there's a guy outside says he got something for you about Bugsy Siegel."

"Is he sober?"

"Yes, sir."

"Send him in."

The stranger came in, hatless and wearing sports clothes, and he looked like a pro. "How'd you like to have a man inside Bugsy Siegel's house?" he said bluntly.

"I'd like it fine," Richardson said. "What's the proposition?"

"The proposition is that I'm going to work in the house as a butler. Anything I dig up goes to you, and if it's good stuff you give me a job on the paper."

"You got a deal, boy," Richardson grinned. "What's your name?"

"Huie. Bill Huie."

Huie actually moved into the Delfern Avenue house where, calling himself Robert LaSalle, he served meals, made the beds, waxed floors, and performed other household chores. He was relieved to note that Siegel himself was absent from home, and apparently he established a happy rapport with other members of the family. One of Siegel's sisters (Huie described her as "a fat little girl in her early twenties") was living at the house temporarily, as was the gangster's father, "a portly, moustached old gentleman who had worked hard peddling suits all his life."

Huie seems to have spent considerable time babysitting the two Siegel daughters—reading aloud, taking them to the movies, or accompanying them to the DuBrock Riding Academy. He also snooped around the house, a bumbling sort of Dick Tracy, peeking into closets, cabinets, filing cabinets, and Bugsy's bedroom.

It has never been clearly established exactly what Richardson and/or Huie gained by this dangerous espionage. Bill Huie, boy reporter of 1938, has since achieved national fame as William Bradford Huie, novelist. His best-selling works include *The Execution of Private Slovik*, *The Americanization of Emily*, and *The Revolt of Mamie Stover*. But the only Huie literature which mentions his adventure in the Siegel house is a reminiscence called "My Christmas with Bugsy Siegel," which was published in *The American Mercury* in 1951 when Huie was the editor of the magazine.

Huie's version of the affair does not agree with Jim Richardson's account. Huie recalls a hair-raising moment or two, for instance, after he had inspected Siegel's personal files, when he thought Bugsy had penetrated his masquerade, and was about to let him have it. "Bugsy!" Huie wrote. "He was coming to stop me! I flattened against the wall and prepared to shoot him." Huie said he had photographed incriminating papers in Siegel's files, had turned this evidence over to "proper authorities," and sworn out a warrant for Siegel's arrest.

Richardson did not mention any of this excitement. He simply said that Huie's most damaging discovery, in the basement of Bugsy's home, was a stack of gallon cans of what smelled like Chanel No. 5. "I was sure this was smuggled perfume," Richardson said, "and, if you'll excuse the expression, this could have raised a beautiful stink."

Richardson tipped off Art Hansen, a Federal Customs officer, and a raiding party was organized on January 18, 1939. When Hansen and his posse reached the house—without Huie, needless to say—Siegel was waiting at the front door with a roguish smile. He even suggested that Hansen start his search in the basement.

"You'll find some excellent fig preserves there," he said. "Take some. They're very good. And be sure the *Examiner* reporter with you gets a jar, and gives it to Mr. Richardson with my compliments."

Hansen's men gave the place a thorough shakedown, but there was no contraband perfume, nor anything else illegal. Only figs, which Richardson ate happily.

And so there was no big story for Jim Richardson or Huie or anyone else. Huie never reappeared at the *Examiner* to claim the promised job, and Richardson said: "You could hardly blame him for running away. Bugsy might have sent one of his boys after him."

(What really happened in the Siegel house when Huie was working there? I wonder, for instance, what happened to the "evidence" he photographed, and how did Siegel know Huie was an *Examiner* spy? I was also intrigued by the mysterious prowlings in the Siegel filing cabinets and the cliff-hanger incidents when Huie said he might have to kill Siegel. During the research for this book, I wrote two letters to William Bradford Huie—one in care of his New York publisher, another to his home in Hartselle, Alabama—and I asked him if he would fill in the blanks. I never got a reply. I suspect he would like to forget the article he wrote.)

Early in 1939, with Dorothy DiFrasso choosing the points of interest and arranging the proper stopovers, Bugsy Siegel's timetable was getting the results he had planned.

"Bugsy had a list of important people he wanted as friends," Hedda Hopper said, "and Dorothy DiFrasso was the front for this campaign. She conned some of the biggest names in our town to take this hoodlum into their homes."

One of the names on Siegel's list was Jack L. Warner, chief executive of the vast Warner Bros. picture empire. The Warner home, whose portico looks like a scaled-down version of the White House, was and still is at 1801 Angelo Drive in Beverly Hills. The costly structure sits on a knoll in the middle of a fourteen-acre estate. The land in this private kingdom, only a few blocks from Beverly Hills Hotel, is probably the most expensive residential soil in the world. There is a high wall around it, a twelve-foot-high gate at the main entrance, and an armed guard with a huge Great

Dane stands there to repel unauthorized visitors. To this mansion, with its priceless collection of jade, china, and paintings, came the great names of the world to be entertained by the master of the movies, and Dorothy DiFrasso was determined to have Ben Siegel among the regulars.

One day, shortly after the *Metha Nelson* cruise, Ann Warner casually mentioned she thought it would be nice to have the Countess DiFrasso for dinner some evening.

"You mean Dorothy and her friend Bugsy Siegel, the gangster," Warner said.

"Oh, Jack, he's not a gangster," she protested.

"Listen to me, dear," Warner replied. "Mr. Ben Siegel is never coming into my house. And if he ever does get in here—and I think you're starting to work me into letting him in—it won't be an hour before some cop comes and takes him away."

"You're just imagining things," Ann Warner said.

"No," he said.

"You're being dramatic."

"Oh, no I'm not. Why should I take a chance? I don't want to find myself in the papers with a lot of lead in me, and I wouldn't be able to read about it anyway."

Warner recalls with a wry smile that the subject was not dropped, and that Dorothy DiFrasso, as he puts it, "was busy with every trick in the book, working on me and my wife to get Bugsy Siegel into my house."

Presently there came a formal invitation to a dinner party, with the Countess DiFrasso as the hostess. The Countess had rented Mary Pickford's mansion, on a large estate adjoining the Warner property, and her soirées there (almost never with less than forty guests) were the talk of the Hollywood social set. The Warners accepted, and J.L., as he is known around the studio, went to the dinner unaware that he was being played for a sucker.

"Sure enough, when I get to the Pickford house," Warner said, "the first person I meet is Bugsy Siegel. And Dorothy, who was a smart cookie, worked on me during the dinner and there was nothing I could do."

Mrs. Warner, it seems, had invited everyone on the guest list to come to the Warner house after dinner and see the latest Warner Bros. picture in J.L.'s private projection room. Just before the group started for the Warner house—they had to drive or walk around the block because there was no way to get over or through the stone wall—Warner nudged his wife and said: "Honey, I don't like it. I don't want to frighten anybody, but I'm sure the coppers will be around."

"Jack, you're making it up."

"I am not. Just wait."

The guests that evening included Gary Cooper, Clark Gable, and Cary Grant, all of whom had either entertained Ben Siegel in their own homes, or had met him with the Countess at other parties.

It probably never occurred to any of these stars that Siegel was using them. They liked him. They said as much more than once. They did not know the details of Siegel's criminal history in New York. He was no vulgar, cigar-waving thug like Al Capone. He wasn't compromising his friends, he had no risky stocks to sell, and if there was a gimmick in his ambitions it wasn't visible yet.

But Jack Warner, who had an uncanny radar sense about crooks, had already met most of the world's charming villains and he had no need for Ben Siegel and his talents. He remembers that he was extremely irritated and uneasy because the gangster was actually inside his house.

He was in the library, controlling the sound for the picture his guests were watching, when he heard footsteps on the staircase, and a man ran past him in the gloom. Warner jumped up just as the intruder, unable to see in the darkened room, collided with a large couch. Warner helped him up, and guided him into the billiard room adjoining the library. There he recognized the uninvited stranger as Mickey Black, a prominent criminal lawyer who was then representing Siegel.

"Sorry to crash your shindig," Black said, "but I had no choice."

"What goes, Mickey?" Warner asked.

"The cops are upstairs and they want Ben."

"I knew it!" Warner exploded. "Who'd he bump off this week?"

Black grimaced. "He hasn't bumped off anybody. That stuff is out. They just want to talk to him."

"Okay, Mickey. He's in there. When your eyes get used to the dark I'll show you where he's sitting, and you can get him out without any fuss."

Warner's guests were only vaguely aware that someone had tapped Ben Siegel on the shoulder, and that he had left his seat. With Mickey Black leading the way, Siegel went upstairs to the main floor of the house where he was coldly greeted by Lieutenant Lefty James, then considered by some hoodlums to be the toughest cop in Los Angeles. They left immediately. Dorothy DiFrasso later said heatedly that she should have been told what was happening, but Warner chose to say nothing. He was acutely allergic to unpleasant newspaper publicity, and fortunately the press never knew what took place in the house.

That night, Siegel was questioned again about the real purposes of the *Metha Nelson* voyage. The Los Angeles police and Federal agents, especially those concerned with narcotics, found it difficult to believe that Siegel had actually gone on a treasure hunt. Some of them suspected, and they never quite abandoned that suspicion, that Siegel had gone to the Cocos Islands to pick up a drop. Heroin perhaps, morphine, or even crude opium.

The notion that Siegel was one of the world's major drug dealers persisted through all the years he lived in and around Los Angeles. As late as 1963, in her book *The Whole Truth and Nothing But* (Doubleday), the late Hedda Hopper stated: "Siegel had set up a milk route, as he called it, for running raw opium . . . to cookers in Tijuana . . . and across the border for distribution and sale in Los Angeles."

When I asked Hedda for the source of this scoop, she replied: "I got it in Las Vegas."

"From whom in Las Vegas?" I persisted.

"Oh, you know," she said. "The Mafia."

Gangster and killer he was, and that has never been denied. But many of the wiser cops and top level agents who tailed Siegel for years don't believe that he was involved in narcotics. Chick Hill, who had a father-son relationship with Siegel, remembers one incident in particular when they were interviewing prospective employees for the Flamingo Hotel. Chick was quite taken with one applicant until Siegel said: "The guy's a junkie. And I wouldn't have a junkie working for me under any conditions. They'll plug their own mother if they need the dough for a fix."

In any case, Ben Siegel never got inside the Warner house again, and the Countess DiFrasso looked elsewhere for prominent men and women who could help her man. It was really no problem. They couldn't get in line fast enough.

It was the neighborhood kids who first became aware of the strange, ugly man in the apartment house on West Eighth Street in Los Angeles.

They saw him there—a fearsome, simian creature with a broken nose and a twitching scar under his left eye—long before he was noticed by the cops, and they backed away from him every day when he appeared at the door to glance up and down the street, warily, before he jumped into his car. They knew he was Jewish, because one boy had spotted a gold mezuzah dangling from his waist, and some thought he was a fighter because they had occasionally seen him poised on the balls of his small feet, shadow boxing with an imaginary foe. But none of them ever saw his gun.

The newcomer's name was Mickey Cohen, and he was a "heist guy." He had come back to Los Angeles after years of warfare in the jungles of New York, Cleveland, and Chicago, and around his belly and chest were the knife cuts and bullet scars of skirmishes in alleys and poolrooms and cheap nightclubs. "In those days," one top-ranking cop said later, "Mickey was nothing but a gun-toting punk, but he had guts and he was tougher than a hungry tiger."

This was 1939, and Mickey had taken a fast powder out of Chicago after splitting a hoodlum's skull with his pistol butt. He was told to get lost—or else—and had chosen to go back to California where his record showed nothing worse than an arrest for vagrancy. It was a good place for a rod man to work.

One hot summer day, Mickey moved away from the somewhat isolated West Eighth Street apartment, and took a flat in Hollywood where he could be closer to the action. Shortly afterward, he and a couple of his friends walked into a bookie joint on Franklin Avenue. It had a thirty-phone book with a fix, and the first time Mickey cased it he knew it could be a big heist.

The three men pulled guns, and Mickey growled: "The first guy that moves gets it."

The mysterious babble of voices at the phones was suddenly stilled. The cashier sneaked a look at the gun in his drawer, but when he saw Mickey's cold eyes, he reconsidered, and his hands went up.

"Smart boy," Mickey said.

At that moment—and unfortunate timing it was—there arrived a short, ratty thug known around town as Little Joe. He was a bagman and messenger for Ben Siegel and Jack Dragna and he had wandered into the joint, with $22,000 in cash in his pocket, merely to get a race result.

Mickey knew about Little Joe—a thief trusted by Siegel only because he had neither the brains nor the guts to cheat—and he said: "Okay, pal, let's have it."

Little Joe's mouth began to twitch. "I ain't got nuthin'," he said. "I just come here to lay a bet."

Mickey cocked the trigger of his gun. "Don't gimme that crap," he said. "You want it in the head, quick, or slow in the belly?"

Little Joe wet his lips, reached into his coat pocket for a thick brown envelope, and gave it to Mickey with a trembling hand. "Ben Siegel will kill you for this," he said in a whisper.

"Well, what do ya know," Mickey said. "So the dough belongs to the big mob man. Ain't that too damn bad."

"You're askin' for it, mister."

"Shut up."

Mickey frisked the rest of the customers, picking up a couple of 4-carat rocks in the process, and then he and his men scrammed. Two days later Mickey had a social call from Harry "Champ" Segal. Champ, who has been called "a character right out of a Damon Runyon piece," was not in the rackets himself, but knew all the big shots and the little guys on the fringe.

"Mick," he said, "Ben Siegel wants to see you."

"Yeah? What for?"

"Look, Mick," Champ said, "I'm one of the few guys in town who knows all about you, where you live and what you're doing here. Do me a favor. Ben told me to get you."

"The hell with him."

"Mick, you know who Siegel is."

Mickey sneered and the words came up out of his throat. "Sure I know. The big mob from New York. Mr. Bug from the Bug-Meyer gang. Champ, Ben Siegel can be in the Big Six all he wants, and I can work for Mickey Cohen all I want, but I ain't buttin' into his business and I expect the same from him."

Champ nodded, and he was smiling. "He's a real nice guy, Mick. Use your head and go see him. He said to meet you at the Hollywood Y. He works out there every day. And if you figure that's not protection enough, take a pal with you."

"I don't need anybody. I'll go alone."

The next afternoon, Mickey put on a pair of tight-waisted pants, stuck a .38 at his belt, and slipped a .45 into a sling hanging under his left armpit. He washed his hands three or four times, as was his custom after touching objects that might be covered with germs, and jammed a huge Stetson hat down to his ears. It was one of his best $50 numbers with a very broad brim, and the color matched his silk necktie with the embroidered initials M.C. He trotted out to the street looking like a giant mushroom in motion. The skin of his face was dark and taut.

He parked near the Y.M.C.A., and went quickly down to the locker room with his pointed shoes rapping a tattoo on the wood floor. Ben Siegel and Champ were waiting.

Siegel was smiling, and the surge died down in Mickey's blood. He had anticipated a scowling face and a sneering wisecrack from the notorious Bug, and he was disconcerted by the sweetness and light. Siegel was slipping into a blue shirt, and Mickey noticed he was wearing blue boxer shorts and blue socks, and a dark blue tie hung over his shoulders, ready to knot. *For Christ's sake,* Mickey thought, *he's almost pretty.* The eyes were baby blue beneath long dark lashes, the dark hair showed finger waves, and the mouth and chin were soft and feminine.

"Hello, Ben," he said.

"Hello, Mickey. Thanks for coming. I hear you're opening up out here and you're scoring pretty good."

Mickey stiffened. "What do you mean?" he asked.

"You got too much moxie for your own good, is what I mean."

"Yeah? What do you want?"

Siegel slipped the tie around his neck, and glanced into a mirror to measure it for the proper length. The smile was still there, like a flicker of light touching the shadows of his lips. "I want you to do me a favor, Mickey," he said.

"What favor?"

"I want you to kick back the dough you heisted from Little Joe. And the jewelry, too."

Mickey felt the hot current running again, and it came out through his tongue. "I never got no money, and I never got no jewelry. So there ain't nothin' to kick back."

Siegel gave him an impatient glance, like a teacher trying to explain to a dull-witted child. "Now, look, Mickey," he said quietly, "let's not kid each other. I'm just asking you for this little favor for me and Jack Dragna."

Mickey's eyes smouldered and his right hand strayed to his waist. "Goddamit," he snarled, "Let me tell you one thing. I wouldn't kick back to my own mother. When I put my life on the line, I don't kick nothin' back. And in the second place I don't know what in hell you're talkin' about."

"You're dumber than I thought," Siegel said, "and I'm not going to argue with you. I want that stuff back."

Mickey spat profanity, spun around on his little feet, bounded up the stairs out into the sunlight so bursting with rage that he could barely breathe. Champ Segal, eyes wide with shock, came running after him, and grabbed Mickey's shoulder so hard he almost fell backwards.

"Get your hands off me, Champ!" Mickey cried.

"Are you crazy?" Segal panted.

"Listen, Champ," Mickey said. "If the son of a bitch makes one move I'll kill him right now. I don't care who he is. Just tell him to lay off me."

Mickey stalked off with his right hand closed around the .38, and he kept the Y.M.C.A. entrance in sight as he headed for his car. But Ben Siegel stayed in the locker room, and Mickey went home, vaguely nettled because his adversary had let him go without a fight. He was ready to kill. He knew he was not in Ben Siegel's class, and it made the hate run through his brain. He knew he would see Siegel again. Soon. He fingered the gun, and it felt good.

CHAPTER SEVEN

Ben Siegel discovered in 1938 on the *Metha Nelson* cruise that Dorothy DiFrasso had a persistent weakness for investments which, though they stirred the imagination, were too often losing long shots. She had dropped a formidable sum, for instance, in the manufacture of soya bean foods, a gustatory nightmare of which Elsa Maxwell once said: "She caused us the agony of having to taste these horrible concoctions." The Countess drew out too soon from zipper enterprises. "Imagine the money she could have made," Elsa said, "if she had retained her interest in this all-important feature for women's clothes."

But at last, as Siegel and Marino Bello thought when once again they joined forces, she finally had a winner. The bonanza was a new explosive with the awesome name Atomite. The two chemists who perfected the formula, and they must be nameless here because they may still be dealing with classified material, staged a demonstration in the Imperial Valley desert for Siegel, Bello, and the Countess. They not only pulverized a couple of small mountains, but blew the lining out of every gila monster and rattlesnake within miles.

"Oh, brother," Siegel exulted, "if I'd only had some of this stuff in the old days."

Dorothy DiFrasso was sufficiently bowled over by the shock waves to sign a notarized contract and put up $50,000 for a percentage of the profit. She immediately got off a cablegram to Count DiFrasso in Rome, urging him to grab the next boat for California, and when the Count witnessed what Atomite could do, he was sure that Mussolini, busy preparing for war, would pay a bonus price for it.

There are some conflicting versions of what happened next. Probably the most reliable account, relayed by the Countess herself to Jack Warner, says that Mussolini sent the Bello-Siegel-DiFrasso combine a cash advance of $40,000 and requested they all come to Italy for a sample detonation.

On the steamer traveling to Europe, there was some strange nocturnal stalking from deck to deck, with the result that the investors accused Siegel of trying to steal their secret ingredient. Siegel in turn suspected the blast engineers of dickering with a rival foreign power and planning to cheat the Countess.

Consequently, there was considerable chilliness in the group when it reached Rome. The Countess also had a perplexing little problem of her own. Since she was accustomed to mingling with people of wealth and social standing, she now found herself in an awkward position, traveling with a notorious gangster who had no rating at all.

Unquestionably, she was in love with Ben Siegel. Once, in a wistful and soul-baring chat with the young Englishman, Richard Gully, she said: "I don't care what others think, but to me Ben is a kind of knight. If he had been living in the time of King Arthur, he would have been a gallant member of the Round Table." This was a pretty sentiment—and I can only conclude she knew very little about either King Arthur or Bugsy Siegel—but it did not solve the dilemma.

However, in daydreaming about Sir Siegel, the Countess somehow remembered that in England the abbreviation for baronet is bart. According to the ancient custom, a knighthood is valid only for the subject's lifetime, whereas a baronetcy is inherited. Impulsively, she decided to rename Bugsy. In Europe he would be Bart Siegel. And if anyone thought Bart really meant Baronet she would not deny it.

And that's how Bugsy Siegel, late of the Lower East Side, traveled through the rarified atmosphere of the spas in Italy and France—but not in England, of course. Benito Mussolini, exiled King Umberto II, Count Ciano, and other distinguished Italians all thought that Siegel was a baronet who came from an old English family, and all the available information indicates that Siegel wore his new title and mantle with unshakeable aplomb.

Long after World War II, when Elsa Maxwell lunched with King Umberto in France, they reminisced about Bugsy's trip to Rome, and Elsa confessed that the fake baron was really—as she put it—"a big shot in Murder Inc." Elsa patiently explained the syndicate to His Majesty (as reported in her book *RSVP* [Little-Brown & Co.]), and told him how Siegel and the other gangsters controlled gambling and other rackets by using hired killers.

"It is impossible to believe your government permits such an organization to exist!" King Umberto said.

"Unfortunately it did," Elsa replied, "and your countrymen from Sicily started the whole thing."

Elsa recalled that the former monarch burst out laughing after he thought it over, and realized how the Countess DiFrasso had conned them all.

Actually, Siegel's temporary elevation was useless when the time came for the explosive test. No one really knows what went wrong. Perhaps Siegel's hunch was right and the inventors had either been sabotaged or had peddled the formula to another country. In any case, when all the war ministry dignitaries had gathered for the demonstration, and the detonating button was pushed, there was a little wisp of smoke, and the only thing that disintegrated was the $40,000 the Countess had taken as an advance—and had already spent.

Mussolini gave the word. Repay the money—or try his new jail. The Countess paid. She not only had to give back the money, but she and her titled husband were further punished when Il Duce expropriated the Villa Madama. Siegel, Bello, and Dorothy had to move out of the main house and live in the stable, which, while sumptuous enough for people as well as the horses, was not up to her standards.

Mussolini then further insulted her by installing a couple of unpleasant house guests—Herr Joseph Paul Goebbels, Hitler's Minister of Propaganda, and General Hermann Goering, the heavily upholstered leader of the German Air Force. Ben Siegel, Jewish and violently anti-Nazi, knew Goebbels' evil reputation, and was apoplectic every time he saw the German rolling up the Villa driveway in his bulletproof Mercedes.

"Look, Dottie," he said to his love one evening. "I saw you talking to that fat bastard Goering. Why do you let him come to our building?"

"Oh, I've known him for quite a while. I can't really tell him to stay away if he wants to come down here on a social call."

"I'm gonna kill him, and that dirty Goebbels, too!" Siegel growled.

The Countess blanched. "Ben!" she cried. "You can't do that!"

"Sure, I can. It's an easy setup the way they're walking around here."

"That's not what I meant," she said breathlessly. "If anything happens to these men while they're Mussolini's guests, you know what they'll do to Carlo."

"Yeah," he said. "Yeah—you might be right."

Siegel abandoned his homicidal inspiration, and that was too bad in view of the crimes Goebbels and Goering committed later when the Nazi machine rolled over Europe. Siegel always regretted that he had not killed Goebbels, especially, but he lived long enough to see Count DiFrasso die a natural death in bed instead of being knocked off by a firing squad.

The unpleasantness in Rome canceled what Siegel and the Countess had planned as an extended visit, and they moved north to the resorts of the French Riviera.

George Raft and Norma Shearer—he was courting her at the time and says he cannot remember the exact date—were in the Sporting Club at Deauville one evening. Raft was sitting at a *chemin de fer* table when a chip came over his shoulder and plopped on the table; when he looked up, Ben Siegel was there grinning at him.

"Hey, Georgie!" he laughed, "What are you doing here with all these blue bloods?"

"Well—I'm the guy that's courting Norma Shearer," Raft said, "and this is as good a place as any."

"Yeah, I been watching you. You look like a toothpaste ad, showing your teeth every time you look at her."

Raft glanced across the room where the Countess DiFrasso was hemmed in by the customary circle of parasites. "You're in high society yourself, Ben," he said. "How long you gonna stick around?"

"Until Dottie wants to go home, I guess."

"You just might never get back."

"I'm in no hurry, Georgie."

Two days later, when a cablegram came from New York, Ben Siegel was suddenly morose and restless. He began packing immediately, and he was gone when Raft looked for him around the French resort. Siegel never explained his abrupt change of plans to his Hollywood friends, but the men in the mob knew why he was coming home, and what had to be done. One of the New York hoods, Harry "Big Greenie" Greenberg, was threatening to sing. Siegel knew it could be a very discordant tune, so Big Greenie had to be taken. Right now.

CHAPTER EIGHT

Mickey Cohen had made a sucker out of the great Ben Siegel, and the word was around town about how the brave little fighter had told off The Bug. Some were saying that Mickey would eventually kill Siegel, and others were saying that Mickey was a dead pigeon.

Not long after that first confrontation in the Y.M.C.A., Mickey got a message that Siegel wanted another meeting. Accompanied by Joe Sica, a Jersey roughneck with a long record for assault, robbery, and other violent crimes, Mickey went to an office building half a block from the intersection of Hollywood and Vine. On the first floor, directly above a pawnshop owned by a petty Hollywood mob man, was a shabby office whose door was guarded by two musclemen, one on each side, sitting on plain wooden chairs. Inside, with his handsome face twisted into a scowl, was Ben Siegel. Next to him, behind a massive desk, sat Jack Dragna, the *capo mafioso* of Los Angeles, who had long represented the syndicate on the West Coast.

The brief conversation that morning was like the first one. Anger and four-letter words. Nervous fingering of gun butts. Clenched fists and threats. Mickey again refused to kick back either money or jewels, and when he and Joe Sica stalked out, Jack Dragna was talking to them about sudden death. But nothing happened.

Mickey was "steaming," as he later put it. He had two loaded guns in his pocket, and was aching for a draw. But when Siegel backed down for the second time, obviously unwilling to fight,

Mickey naturally concluded he was a coward. Mickey should have known that Siegel was too smart to get involved in a brawl that might make news or bring the police. If Mickey himself had realized that too much publicity is the kiss of death for men in the rackets, he would not be behind bars today. At the time, Ben Siegel did not know Mickey's weakness for wanting to see his name in print. He saw only that Mickey was a nervy little guy who was not apt to quit under pressure, and he needed men like that in his California plans.

One key to underworld wealth and power, as Ben Siegel and others had known for some time, was in the race wire service. No bookie anywhere—and there were thousands tucked away in the back rooms of cigar and other small stores and bars—could function without getting entries, odds, results, and other pari-mutuel payoffs.

The No. 1 race news service when Siegel moved West was the Continental Press Service, owned and operated by James Ragen, Sr., in Chicago. With bookies from Chicago to Los Angeles paying from $100 to $1200 a week for the service, there was a golden river flowing into Ragen's headquarters, and the Capone mob watched it with envy.

They couldn't knock it, but they could set up a rival wire. Thus was born the Trans-America Service, with Siegel and Dragna directing western operations and gnomish little Moe Sedway as chief salesman.

There is no existing record that shows how many cracked skulls or how many unsolved murders were a direct result of Siegel's western war on Continental Press. But one incident alone —told to me with a twisted sort of pride by Mickey Cohen—is a clue to Siegel's eventual success.

Mickey said Siegel came to see him one day. He was alone, unarmed, and in a jovial mood. He told Mickey about the growth of Trans-America Service in Nevada, Arizona, and other western states, but admitted he was having problems in the rich Los Angeles market. Continental's manager there was a man named Russell Leonard Brophy, a tough character with strong connections at City Hall.

Siegel had offered Brophy a deal, and Brophy, who had

courage, had said: "No dice. No deal. And you can tell the Capone mob I said so." In New York Siegel would have put a bullet through a man for cracks like that, or sent him to the hospital with a pistol-whipping. But this was Los Angeles and the setup was not the same. So he had come to Mickey, because Mickey was muscle, and Brophy's resistance called for muscle work that would stop just short of the morgue.

One morning when the wires were throbbing in Brophy's downtown headquarters, Mickey Cohen and Joe Sica shoved a receptionist out of the way, and marched into the telegraph room. They coolly ripped out one wire after another, and when Brophy rushed out of his private office to halt the damage, Mickey struck him with a pistol butt. Mickey and Sica clubbed Brophy until he was bloody and semiconscious, and then they walked out.

Later, when the two thugs were arrested and brought to trial, they were given suspended jail terms and fined. Sica paid $200, but Mickey was only charged $100. Long afterward, when I was investigating Mickey's illegal activities for a magazine assignment, I asked him why there had been a difference in the two fines.

"Well—" Mickey said with a sly grin, "I guess I only hit him a hunnert dollars' worth."

"But it was enough to put Brophy out of business?"

"Oh, yeah," Mickey laughed.

"And after that you went to work for Siegel?"

"Yeah, I did. I had a piece of everything. It wasn't exactly like working for him. Ben was the boss, sure, but he never gave me no orders. I had to stay under cover most of the time, but I done the work."

No one knows whether Mickey did any killing for Siegel. He would never confess a murder, of course. But he had the know-how, Chicago style or any other method, and because he was always asking for trouble, he had had the personal experience of being an intended victim in half a dozen murder attempts.

When the time came to handle the problem of Mr. Harry "Big Greenie" Greenberg, Siegel naturally thought of Mickey Cohen.

"Listen, Ben," one of the mob said, "I wouldn't fool around with Cohen on any big hits. Especially in L.A."

"Why not?"

"Because he ain't got the sense to keep his mouth shut."

And Ben Siegel knew the man had a point. The hired gun would have to come out of the East.

Any horoscope would have shown that all the wrong stars were working against Harry Greenberg. A semiliterate Polish immigrant, fat and sloppy, Greenberg had jumped ship to get into the United States and, because he was wanted by immigration authorities, had a limited usefulness to the mob.

Greenberg—directly employed by the infamous Louis "Lepke" Buchalter—was handy with his clublike fists and an expert on stink bombs and was often summoned when a labor dispute got out of hand. He worked for Lepke almost ten years before government agents found him in Brooklyn, and put him aboard a freighter for deportation.

Greenberg never arrived back in his native Poland. He escaped his guards before the vessel docked in France, swam ashore, and remained in hiding for months somewhere on the Continent. He eventually turned up in a German seaport, got a job as a deckhand on a freighter bound for Canada, and somehow managed to get into Montreal. And there, when the last of his cash vanished in a gambling house, Greenberg wrote a letter to a friend in New York. He needed money, and he said he expected Lepke to send him a bundle. A big bundle. And if the bundle did not come—well, Big Greenie was a bird in a cage, ready to sing to the cops about the mob.

Lepke and the other hoods knew Greenberg wasn't joking, and the vote to knock him off was unanimous. Lepke and Mendy Weiss assigned Albert "Allie" Tannenbaum and Jack "Cuppie" Migden to handle the execution, and the two went to Montreal by train, and registered at the Windsor Hotel. Less than an hour later, casing the Ford Hotel, where Greenberg had stayed, they discovered he had already checked out.

Months later, Big Greenie turned up in a rooming house at 1804 Vista Del Mar in Hollywood, and his arrival there was immediately reported to Ben Siegel by underworld stool pigeons. Siegel promptly went east for a series of meetings with Lepke, Anastasia, and Longy Zwillman. Using the name Berish Siegel, or

Berish Sanger (Berish is the Yiddish for Benjamin), Siegel moved around from one hotel and one area to another. He was at the Pennsylvania and the Commodore in New York, and twice at the Robert Treat Hotel in Newark.

The decision on Greenberg remained unchanged. Siegel asked Zwillman to get a couple of guns, and bring one of the young hoods to Los Angeles. Allie Tannenbaum got the assignment. One morning in November, Tannenbaum was picked up at his house on Linden Boulevard in Brooklyn, and driven to Newark Airport by Sidney "Shimmy" Salles, one of Zwillman's errand boys. Zwillman was waiting for him, and climbed into Shimmy's car.

"The deal is all set, Allie," Zwillman said. "Ben Siegel has Big Greenie stashed away, and you'll be met out there. And here —take this with you."

"What is it?" Tannenbaum asked, hefting the package.

"Two guns. Shimmy will drive you to Philadelphia. You buy bullets there, and you get on the plane there. Here's two hundred and fifty bucks for the fare. If it's more, we'll make up the difference."

Shimmy drove to Philadelphia, and Tannenbaum bought two boxes of shells, one for a .38 revolver, the other for a .45 Colt automatic in the sporting goods section of Wanamaker's. Shortly afterward, he boarded a United Air Lines plane for Los Angeles.

Tannenbaum was met at the Burbank airport by Frankie Carbo, a young gangster who was already beginning to show the ruthless qualities that would later make him powerful in the crooked fight racket. Carbo drove Tannenbaum to his apartment in the Villa d'Italia, and presently Siegel appeared there.

"You got the pistols, Allie?" he asked.

"Give 'em to me," Siegel said. "I'll try them out."

Tannenbaum handed the package to Siegel with the two boxes of bullets.

"When do I take him, Ben?"

"I don't know," Siegel replied. "I might handle it myself."

On November 22, when most of Hollywood was preparing to celebrate Thanksgiving the next day, Siegel and Carbo asked a young tough named Whitey Krakower to steal a getaway car. Krakower cruised around in the early dusk of the evening until he found a black Mercury sedan. He jumped the ignition wires, drove it to Carbo's apartment house, and stripped off the two license plates.

Shortly after ten o'clock, Siegel gave Tannenbaum the stolen car.

"I'm going to get in my car with Frankie," he said. "It's a 1939 Buick convert, parked right in front of the Merc. You follow us, and when we get near Greenie's place, I'll stop and we'll switch cars."

Siegel drove slowly and carefully along Hollywood Boulevard, turned on Highland, and then cruised on Yucca Street until he was two blocks away from Vista Del Mar. He stopped there and climbed into the Mercury with Carbo.

"When we get to Greenie's apartment house, Allie," he said, "we'll turn both cars around and head out. That's a dead-end street right there, and I'm not about to get bottled up. You take the Buick, and you'll be the crash car. If anybody comes after us when we hit Greenie, you know what to do."

"Yeah, Ben, I know."

Moments later, in the chill and darkness of the November evening, Siegel and Carbo were parked on the south side of Vista Del Mar with the car lights out. Allie Tannenbaum was just ahead of them, with the engine of the new Buick barely murmuring. Presently there appeared an old Ford convertible coupe with yellow wire wheels. Harry Greenberg was at the wheel, a folded morning paper on the seat beside him. He pulled the car up parallel to the curb.

At that instant, the door of the parked Mercury was flung open, and the night sky was punctured by sound and light. Big Greenie had no time to cry out, nor even raise an arm against death. The slugs hit him almost all at once and he fell over the wheel. Ben Siegel and Frankie Carbo catapulted into the waiting Mercury sedan, the car leaped into the center of the street, and was a block away before the headlights were switched on.

Allie Tannenbaum followed. Several blocks distant, on a quiet residential street, the Mercury stopped beneath the bare branches of a big elm. Tannenbaum parked, too, and in a moment a third car appeared, a Buick sedan driven by Siegel's friend, Champ Segal.

"Allie," Siegel said, "Champ has to go to San Francisco and he'll drive you there."

"San Francisco?" Tannenbaum said with obvious surprise.

"Yeah," Siegel nodded. "Wasn't that where you were gonna catch your plane?"

Tannenbaum got the message. "Oh, that's right, Ben," he said.

Champ Segal, who seems to have been dragged into a conspiracy about which he knew nothing, drove all night along the coast route, and delivered Allie to the Empire Hotel in San Francisco at seven A.M. Champ went back to Los Angeles, and Tannenbaum, after a four-hour rest, boarded a United Air Lines plane for Philadelphia. The Big Greenie book had been closed.

It has never been explained to anyone's satisfaction why Ben Siegel took a personal role in the sidewalk execution. He had asked for an eastern gunman, and Tannenbaum had been handpicked for the job. Big Greenie was a small-time sinner who didn't merit that kind of attention from the head man. Perhaps Siegel, who had not been involved in a syndicate disciplinary action for several years, felt that he needed a personal killing to emphasize his continuing authority. If so, this was a grave mistake. For there was nothing but trouble ahead.

CHAPTER NINE

Onie Virginia Hill was seventeen when she showed up in Chicago in the summer of 1933. She was five foot four, one hundred and ten pounds. Gray eyes. Well, not really gray. Green-gray eyes. Hair not quite auburn; there was much more red than brown. She was beautiful.

It was a beauty tempered by a barely concealed wariness, like some wild creature willing to be tamed only on its own terms. It was the kind of undeveloped beauty not yet clotted by urban standards. She was then the sort of girl who could use four-letter words and make you believe she didn't really know what they meant.

Considering the coarse crucible from which she came, it is remarkable that she had any poise at all. She was born on August 26, 1916, in the village of Lipscomb, Alabama. Her father, Mack Willis Hill, was a thin and wiry marble cutter and horse trader who lolled around town soaking up grog. The family left Lipscomb not long after Virginia was born and moved to a squalid house in Bessemer, only a few miles away.

There, between tippling and trading, Mack Hill accumulated ten children: Billy, Robert, James, John, Karl, and Chick; Virginia, Ruth, Beatrice, and Toots. "The old man was a terrific trader," Chick Hill recalls. "He could leave home in the morning with nothing but a pocketknife, and come back at night with a horse." Mack Hill also had a violent temper, it seems, and when he showed up one noon and found that his lunch wasn't ready, he told his wife what he thought. Margaret Hill walked out and never came back.

In grade school, Virginia had not yet developed any of the mysterious emanations that would later raise the blood pressure of young and old men alike. She was scrawny, flat-chested, and slightly unkempt. She looked somewhat like a mussed-up kitten, and the feline scratchiness was so patent that she was nicknamed Tabby Cat. Her brothers and sisters and intimate friends called her "Tab." And because she also had a catlike protective instinct, Virginia soon became the undisputed mother of the Hill brood.

When Virginia's first flutters were making her an item for the Broadway columnists, she enjoyed weaving little fantasies about the source of her seemingly bottomless purse. She had eloped at the age of fourteen, she said, with a man named George Rogers who conveniently died and left her $50,000. George Rogers never existed, nor was there any legacy.

Actually, she hung around Bessemer and took care of the other kids, most of whom were kept out of school because they had to work. She did not leave home until just before her seventeenth birthday, and her destination was Chicago.

Mae West was then undulating outside her invisible bedroom in a movie called *She Done Him Wrong*. The anthropoid Italian, Primo Carnera, had just won the heavyweight boxing crown, and prohibition was on the way out. There was also a World's Fair in Chicago, and Virginia got a job as a waitress in a restaurant on the grounds.

There have since been certain elaborations on Virginia's debut in Chicago, including one report that among other moonlighting jobs, she worked as a stripteaser. Chick Hill, who was her favorite brother, and who would soon be living with her full-time, has no recollections about that occupation.

Her moonlighting may have started with a homely, myopic accountant named Joe Epstein who was associated with a commission betting house in Chicago.

The premiere took place in a modest Chicago lakefront apartment where Virginia fussed around in the kitchen and acquired a culinary skill that would one day astound such gourmets as Joe Adonis, Ben Siegel, George Raft, Mark Hellinger, movie producer Howard Hawks, author Irwin Shaw, and other guests at her table.

In Alabama, Virginia's father had difficulty believing that she was wanted for her cooking talents. When he heard about the Chicago love nest, he sent police looking for her because Alabama girls weren't supposed to be on the loose before the age of eighteen. Virginia later talked about her father's futile search when she made her national television debut for Senator Estes Kefauver and his committee to investigate organized crime and admitted she did not go back to Bessemer until she was of legal age.

In the history of the rise of Virginia Hill, there are, as in any Cinderella tale, some persistent legends that defy extinction. One such episode has Virginia appearing at a party wearing a silver-fox cape and a diamond pendant, and an admirer looks at the cape.

"Epstein?" he asks.

"No, Riddle," she replies.

The man then examines the pendant and says: "Riddle?"

"No," she answers. "Epstein."

The point of the dialogue, if it ever took place, was that Virginia had two suitors simultaneously, each of whom was showering her with expensive gifts. Joe Epstein was one. The other was Major Arterburn Riddle (Major was a name, not a rank) an Indianapolis man who started out life banking a high school crap game, made a million dollars, lost it before he was twenty-six years old, and made it again. He owned trucking companies, race horses (The Green Grass Stables), was president of the Riddle Oil Company, and had an interest in the Plantation Club, a gambling joint in Moline, Illinois.

Actually Riddle entered Virginia's orbit some time after Epstein began supporting her in 1934, and the impact was memorable. Three days after the initial meeting, Virginia and Riddle met in Miami Beach by common consent and stayed there together for six weeks. Virginia subsequently declared that Riddle gave her the first nine skins of her sable coat, but Riddle later said she had been fibbing. He didn't give her anything, he said, but he did pick up the rather large bill for the Miami idyll, and he replenished a wardrobe that evidently took a beating on the trip.

Riddle saw Virginia off and on for about eighteen months, and during that turbulent period had one traumatic experience that may have contributed to his final farewell. He and Virginia were in a Chicago penthouse one evening, a whole floor to themselves, when a couple of gunmen came up the elevator unannounced and put a gun in his ribs.

Returning to her modest lodgings at the Medinah Club toward dawn, Virginia was fuming.

"What's the matter, Tab?" her brother Chick asked.

"Two sons of bitches busted into the penthouse tonight and took Maje for everything he had," she snapped.

"No kidding! How much?"

"A hundred thousand."

"Good God!"

"Yes," Virginia nodded. "But I recognized one of the jerks. He's a Capone. And you can bet we'll get it back."

But she didn't. This sort of intramural theft is never reported, and the principals can either negotiate for a deal or hire a hood to get revenge. Since neither Virginia nor Riddle ever operated on this primitive level, they had to take it and forget it. Virginia was later convinced that some jealous Romeo instigated the holdup, and told the invading gunmen where she was—Riddle, cash, and all.

There are few citizens of Bessemer still alive today who can remember when Virginia Hill, who had departed with rustic edges still showing, came home in triumph. Mark Twain once said that virtue has never been as respectable as money, and even crusty Mack Hill had to admit that his daughter, buffed and polished, showed none of the bruises brought on by sin.

She appeared at the family warren in a factory-fresh LaSalle convertible, with her beautiful legs in shimmering silk, a fur neckpiece touching the new sheen of her hair, and more gems than a Reno pawnshop. Lee Mortimer, the late Broadway columnist who feuded with Virginia for years and was in turn labeled by her as "a no-good bastard," once wrote a little essay in which he said she went around Bessemer barefooted, and didn't own a pair of shoes until she went to Chicago.

He meant that literally, and Virginia resented it because, of course, all the Hill children had shoes. In fact, when she came home resplendent—like Cleopatra on a barge—she brought more shoes, stockings, and jewelry for her sisters, and not one of them ever questioned her virtue. She also took presents to her long-suffering mother, who had fled to Marietta, Georgia, rather than take any more from the sire of the brood.

The visit to Bessemer, from Virginia's viewpoint, was mercifully brief. She stayed just long enough to check on the welfare of the family, and to help Chick get packed. The red-haired, laughing young boy was more like son than brother; she had scolded, praised, and guided him through the early school years, and she had determined he would not become a village idler like Mack Hill. "You're going with me, Chick," she said. "Where I go, you go. And you're going to school and learn something if it kills you. Okay?"

"Okay, Tab," he said.

These days, when there is nothing left but a fading image of the incredible years with Virginia, Chick sometimes wonders whether he should have stayed behind in the smoky little steel town where he was born. "You're going to school and learn something if it kills you," she had said. He did go to school. In Florida, Illinois, New York, Mexico, Europe, California. He learned the blistering argot of the gutter, the corrosion of the bribe, the bloody power of gun and knife, the shabby tissue of felonious money, the treachery of the fast-buck crowd. It could have killed him, and almost did.

Back in Chicago, and the pattern did not change.

Stay awake until dawn. Listen to canned music and mob talk. Drink the stingers until they sting no more. Fall into bed. Get laid. Stumble into daylight and cover your eyes from the cruel sun. Buy a new dress. Bless the shadows of evening and the soft lights of the bar. Green eyes looking at green creme de menthe. Belt them by the dozen. And oh—the money.

Joe gave it to her in damp bunches, like lettuce. The bookie joint grew it in clusters, and there was a new crop every day. And this you must say for Virginia Hill—whatever she did, it was not for cash. She did not love for money or hate for money. She was not for sale. But the money was there, and she used it.

Chicago could not hold her very long. Nor could Joe Epstein.

In July, 1938, Chick and Virginia were in Los Angeles.

They had been across the border to Mexico, and it was a fateful encounter. She embraced the country and its people and its happy ambience, and in turn Mexico gave her a sense of security she would never find in the United States. Indeed, when her hour of peril came, and it was inevitable, it was the Mexicans who provided sanctuary.

But in the beginning, as Chick remembers it, there was only the fascination of an ancient land—the color, the music, the food, the *mañana*. "We ate hot peppers the way other kids eat peanuts," he recalls with simple nostalgia. "We always had them in the glove compartment of the car, and we ate some when we got sleepy. I still do it on the lonely roads at night."

Returning to California after the first exploratory trip, they took an apartment at 4071 Havenhurst Street in Hollywood. And because it seemed the natural thing to do, Virginia was drawn to the quiet little Mexican haunts in the neighborhood. One of them was the Serape Club.

There were no big names in the marquee lights for this humble place, and the tempestuous Miss Virginia Hill had not yet met any of the Hollywood stars, so she sat there alone.

The star of the Serape show—if it merited that classification —was a sinuous black-eyed rhumba dancer named Carlos Gonzales Valdez. Virginia, who could be abruptly bold and impulsive when her blood began to move, watched Valdez finish his dance, and immediately summoned her waiter.

"Tell Mr. Valdez," she said, "that I want him to come to my table."

The message was delivered and moments later, with his dark curly hair still damp, Carlos Valdez sat down beside her. He was in her bedroom that night, and he lived there for two weeks until his nightclub booking ran out, and he went on to the next engagement.

She saw him again in Mexico some months later, and on December 7, 1938, they were on a plane which, speeding from Mexico City to Chicago, made its customary customs and immigration stop at Brownsville, far down on the Gulf of Mexico in Texas.

There, Virginia was asked by government agents—and not very delicately—whether she had been copulating with the young Mexican. She denied it, with as much blush as she could manage, and a remarkably restrained anger.

In another room of inquisition, now that Virginia had gone on record, Carlos Valdez was asked the same question.

"Yes," he said happily, with neither blush nor anger. "Yes. The first time was in her apartment in Hollywood."

"Is she a prostitute, *señor*?" an agent asked.

Valdez seemed stunned for a moment. "A prostitute?" he answered after some deliberation. "Of course she is not a prostitute. She is a good woman. Yes—I had intercourse with her, and I am sure I was not the first one. But that does not make her—"

The ruling on Valdez was swift and final. "Entry denied on grounds of moral turpitude."

It was probably the only time in her life that Virginia Hill was hit with this particular kind of penalty for unsanctioned lovemaking. She burned. And long afterward, when the government was no longer so strict about this clause, she made the observation that hardly anybody would get into the United States if they had to prove virginity.

In any case, she had to continue on to Chicago alone, and Valdez was left behind. Just before her plane was airborne, she was overheard telling the dejected rhumba dancer that she would wire him some money, and send her address as soon as she reached Chicago.

She probably did neither. On January 13, 1939, one month after the awkward unmasking at Brownsville, Virginia returned to Bessemer. And she must have been in a defiant frame of mind, for she promptly married one of the town boys named Leon Osgood "Ozzie" Griffin.

When it suited her purposes on subsequent occasions, Virginia falsely identified Ozzie as an All-American halfback from the University of Alabama. Virginia also liked to say that Ozzie gave her a substantial settlement—fifty thousand or so—when they discovered their souls were not in tune and got an annulment a week or so after the wedding.

This was another of her gossamer spinnings that remained unchallenged until the early 'fifties when the government began trying to separate truth from fiction. By that time, Ozzie was unavailable, but his father, Osgood A. Griffin, who owned the Griffin Lumber Company in Bessemer, said his son never had any money of his own and had given her nothing. The senior Griffin said he had to pay the $100 attorney's fee for obtaining the annulment.

Chick Hill described the elopement as "one of those Sunday picnic romances, laced with sandwiches and a little ninety-proof moonbeam." He has never quite understood what got into Virginia unless it was sheer cussedness over the fracas at Brownsville. The temporary backsliding apparently had no effect on faithful Joe Epstein, though, because he continued to send thick bundles of currency along with "wish you were here" cards. The money came by telegraph, cashier's checks, or cash in airmail letters. Eventually, when Epstein began shipping her wads of crisp hundred dollar bills —there would sometimes be as much as $10,000—he put the currency in an ordinary shoe box with a label reading: RX—LOTION.

Virginia and Chick spent most of 1939 commuting between California and Mexico. Virginia was an exuberant and beguiling girl, and was quickly accepted in a social order normally cool and aloof to American visitors. An attractive Mexican society girl named Maria Rosa Lopez Negretti, whose family was wealthy and influential, soon became Virginia's most intimate friend.

Through Maria Negretti, Virginia eventually met powerful Mexican politicians, army officers, diplomats, and police officials. At least two of these men—Chato Juarez, son of the Mexican Minister of Finance, and Major Luis Amezcua, who became Military Aide to President Miguel Aleman—became her lovers. And in time, when Virginia began her last desperate flight to avoid prison, they took extraordinary risks to help her beat the law.

On her frequent trips across the border, Virginia also continued her love affair with Carlos Valdez. Valdez was then living in Nuevo Laredo, just across the Rio Grande from Laredo, Texas, and he and his brother, Adolfo Valdez, were running a nightclub called Las Palmas. There was constant friction between the brothers, and Carlos was determined to get out of Mexico. On January 12, 1940, he tried to get into the United States at the border station in Laredo, but when the officials checked the files and found the Brownsville testimony, he was barred for the second time.

Virginia was so infuriated by the ruling that she went back

to Nuevo Laredo nine days later and married Carlos. As Virginia's husband, Carlos Valdez could now challenge the stubborn immigration men, and he and Virginia entered the United States. Long afterward, when Valdez was only a page in her scrapbook of discarded lovers, Virginia confessed that this marriage was not what Ben Jonson had in mind when he wrote about "a spiritual coupling of two souls." "I just married him," she said, "to help a nice guy get into the United States." The explanation is credible; when a similar crisis confronted her years later, she used the same stratagem in reverse.

Carlos Valdez and his bride traveled around the United States together only when Virginia was in the mood. Usually, when he was booked into a nightclub—as his manager she arranged most of those dates herself—Virginia simply packed her bags and disappeared.

Inevitably, Valdez made fatal errors. Like most Mexican husbands, he believed that he was the ruling member of the family, and that his wife, as Mexican wives do, should stay home and out of sight until the master called. He never quite understood Virginia's mercurial mind, and he never saw the steel lining beneath the soft, perfumed skin. And when his demands became imperious, Virginia knew what had to be done.

Valdez was dancing in a New York nightclub when Virginia came to his dressing room one evening between shows.

"I have another booking for you, Carlos," she said in Spanish. "It is a good one. Sign here."

She gave him a pen and indicated a dotted line. Valdez could not read English and, in any case, he trusted her. He scribbled his signature, and Virginia walked out with what Valdez later learned was not a dancing contract at all, but an agreement for an uncontested divorce. She was on her way back to Hollywood, and the heavens were too big for unimportant stars. He never saw her again.

CHAPTER TEN

Anyone less stupid than Whitey Krakower would have run to Mexico or France or Siberia. Or to any faraway place where the mob couldn't set up the death watch and keep him in sight every day around the clock.

The signs were all there.

The strained greetings from men who used to drink or play cards with him. The fear in the eyes of relatives. The pity on the faces of the fringe people who had heard about the sentence—the bartenders, the cabbies, the newsboys, even the cops on the beat. The whispers were strong, and they were not whispers that could be muted by loud talk. Whitey Krakower had been tabbed for the rub-out.

It is strange that Krakower, who had served on firing squads himself, saw nothing ominous in Ben Siegel's coolness to him or his frequent mysterious trips out of California. Siegel had been in St. Paul, Chicago, Minneapolis, New York, and Newark again. He used the same aliases, stayed at the same hotels, and held conferences with Zwillman, Anastasia, Joey A., and others in the gang. Krakower, it seems, had been gabbing in New York and Hollywood about Big Greenie's death. He wasn't being a stoolie, or making threats, or deliberately getting Siegel involved. He simply had a loose tongue, and loose tongues were dangerous, especially since Whitey had found Greenberg's Hollywood hiding place and set up the kill.

There were some other factors, too. Early in January 1940, about two months after Big Greenie's murder, the syndicate was shaken with the arrest of Abe Reles. He was picked up on a routine vagrancy charge, and he quickly bailed himself out with $1000 in currency, peeled from a thick roll in his pocket.

But some nine days later, when the word got out that he would be drawn into the killing of Red Alpert, a minor burglar who had offended leaders in the gang, Reles inexplicably broke all the rules of gangdom. He surrendered himself to the police, and was lodged in The Tombs, the musty, turreted old Manhattan jail so steeped in legends of despair and death.

Toward the end of March the diminutive professional killer, perhaps prodded by his wife, Rose, chose to sing. No underworld canary in history ever warbled louder or longer, and Reles's arias turned into burial chants for a dozen killers whose names and deeds might otherwise have remained unknown. It was too bad for Whitey Krakower that Reles's confessions did not make the newspapers before Siegel put an X next to Whitey's name. The mob might have given him another chance.

In July 1940, George Raft came to New York and took his customary suite at the Sherry-Netherlands Hotel. He was making personal appearances at the Strand Theater on Broadway, and late at night, after the last show, he cruised the almost deserted streets with two old friends who were detectives on the New York police force.

"Hey, Georgie," one of them said one evening, "I saw Whitey Krakower down in the Village the other night. He was asking about you."

"He was?" Raft said with some surprise. "He's been avoiding me out on the coast."

"How come?"

"Well, he came to the studio a couple of times and said he had to have some scratch. Ben Siegel was out of town and he didn't know where else to go for money."

"So you let him have some?"

The actor grimaced. "Sure, I did. He was one of Ben's boys, and Ben is my friend. I loaned him nineteen hundred bucks altogether, and later when I told Ben about it he bawled me out. 'Don't give Whitey a nickel,' Ben said. I asked him 'Why not?' And Ben said: 'Because he'll never be able to pay you back.' " Grim, prophetic words.

Two nights later, on July 31, Raft was in his dressing room at the theater when his two plainclothes friends dropped in. "There's been a killing on the East Side," one said. "Wanna take a run down? You might get a kick out of it."

Raft agreed to go, climbed into the squad car parked in front of the theater, and moments later, with siren screaming, they were turning a corner into Delancey Street. There was a man's body sprawled on the sidewalk, and a uniformed cop stood there scribbling in a notebook.

"Hello, Mr. Raft," he said, recognizing the sleek-haired star. "This is a dirty business."

"Who is he?"

"Somebody named Ben White," the cop said. "It looks like he was sitting on a sidewalk chair here, and they shot him from a car."

Raft took a closer look at the crumbled body, and instantly recognized the dead man as Whitey Krakower. He was on the verge of telling the cop what he knew when he suddenly had a disturbing thought. Suppose he admitted his friendship with Krakower, and was questioned by the Homicide Squad? It might be awkward to explain why he had loaned money to Whitey, and why he happened to be on Delancey Street only minutes after the killing.

So he kept his mouth shut, and his two plainclothes friends protected him. They drove him out of the neighborhood in a hurry, and he was never publicly involved in the investigation. But Raft suspected who had ordered the murder. So did others. Ben Siegel would discover before long that he had not planned the crime with his usual care.

In The Tombs Abe Reles was fashioning his own tomb, so to speak. It was the most appallingly detailed confession in the history of crime. As Burton Turkus later disclosed, Reles's performance filled twenty-five stenographers' notebooks, and either solved outright or gave clues to no less than 1000 murders during a ten year period. Reles himself committed a dozen of these killings, and with total recall he recited names, dates, and places.

Among the crimes confessed—with an assist from a seemingly repentant Allie Tannenbaum also in custody—was the murder of Harry "Big Greenie" Greenberg in Hollywood. Reles and Tannenbaum were flown to Los Angeles during the summer of 1940, and they gave the Grand Jury a step-by-step account of Big Greenie's fate. The Jury indicted Emmanuel "Mendy" Weiss and Louis "Lepke" Buchalter as the Murder Inc. leaders who ordered the killing, and Ben Siegel, Frankie Carbo, and Harry "Champ" Segal as participants in the actual homicide. Allie Tannenbaum, of course, had received immunity in exchange for his testimony. Ben Siegel would soon be calling for his lawyers.

On a summer morning in Hollywood, when the air was sticky and tempers were short, movie director Rowland Brown had a private chat with the pretty star of the picture he was shooting.

"Look, honey," he said brusquely, "you're just asking for trouble."

The girl looked at him with her eyes showing hostility. "I don't know what you're talking about," she said.

"Oh, yes, you do. You're running around with Bugsy Siegel, and you're doing it where every gossip in town can see you. You want to knock off your career right now?"

"Oh, for God's sake," she snapped. "Are you some kind of a Boy Scout or what? Ben Siegel is a wonderful guy, and he can help me."

"Sure he can," Brown said. "He can help you into oblivion. The studio has a lot of money tied up in you, and they're not about to lose it because of a crummy gangster."

"Ben'll be glad to know what you think of him," she said.

"Tell him," Brown said, walking away. "Give him my regards and tell him."

Two days later Brown was sitting in his box at the Santa Anita racetrack, pencil poised over the *Racing Form*, when Ben Siegel walked in and knocked the pencil out of his hands.

"Listen, you sonovabitch!" he said. "What the hell do you mean preaching to my girl? You get out of line again and I'll wrap a baseball bat around your head."

Brown, a lean, wiry man who had once been a police reporter, slowly rose from his seat. "You use a bat on me, Ben," he said, "and I'll shove it up your ass. I'm just as tough as you are. And I also know your pals Frank Costello and Frank Nitti, and I've got a mind to call 'em and report what you said."

Siegel blinked at Brown in disbelief for a moment, then turned and strode away. Two weeks later Brown was at Santa Anita again when Siegel, grinning self-consciously, came to Brown's box and stuck out his hand.

"I'm sorry, Brown," he said. "Things have been tough lately, and I guess I spoke out of turn. No hard feelings, I hope?"

"No hard feelings," Brown replied. "I don't like carrying grudges around, and I know too many of your friends."

"Okay. Now listen. There's a horse in the fourth race—number three on the program. Get on it. I guarantee it."

"I will, Ben. Thanks for the tip."

Knowing something of the underworld and its ways, Brown went to the hundred dollar window and bought two tickets on number three in the fourth race. He watched the horses break from the gate, but his nerves were steady. He knew it was a fix. And it was. The horse breezed in and paid ten to one. He walked slowly to the payoff window, and there he saw Siegel stuffing his pockets with bills.

"Didn't I tell you, Brown?" Siegel said.

"You sure did, Ben. I see you got on it yourself."

"For two grand," Siegel said, unsmiling. "The way things are going I'm going to need every nickel of it. See you around."

On the morning of August 16, 1940 a group of men gathered in the downtown office of Los Angeles District Attorney Buron Fitts. They had been called together by Chief Deputy District Attorney Eugene Williams, and their quarry that morning was Bugsy Siegel. The gangster had just been indicted for the Big Greenie murder, and reports from a stakeout crew indicated that Siegel was at home, or at least that he had been there the preceding night.

The pavement posse included Detective Lloyd Yarrow, a veteran of the gang feuds; Officers Fletcher Tolbert and Ned Keeler of the underworld squad; Detective Lieutenant Miles Ledbetter, and Detective Lloyd Hurst. Williams, who had never met Siegel, was apprehensive that the handsome hoodlum might put up a fight, and so his raiders were handpicked for their gun skill and their experience in handling tough guys.

The party went to Bel-Air in three cars. When they reached

the house on Delfern Avenue they posted men in the garden at the back of the property, where Siegel's expensive pool shimmered in the sun, and Williams went to the front door with Tolbert and Yarrow.

The bell was answered promptly by a Negro butler who was momentarily belligerent when Williams identified himself and displayed a search warrant.

"I want to see Mr. Siegel," Williams said.

"He's not home," the butler said.

"Oh, I think he's around somewhere. We'll just take a look."

"Mr. Siegel ain't going to like that."

"I *know* he won't like it," Williams said with a half smile.

Two women servants stood with the butler at the foot of the stairs as Williams and his men started for the second floor. In the luxurious master suite the sheets and blankets on the huge bed looked as though someone had flung them aside in a hurry, and Yarrow felt the bed with one hand. "Still warm, Gene," he said to Williams. Yarrow strode to a closet door and suddenly pulled it open, half-expecting to see Siegel hiding behind the suits and sport coats in their orderly rows. He was not there, but on a low shelf he saw a footprint on a pile of linen. Above it, within arm's reach, was a trap door leading to the attic.

"Hey, Fletch," Yarrow said, "take a flashlight and see what's up there."

Tolbert stepped on the shelf, and from there pulled himself through the narrow square. He found himself in the attic, turned on the flashlight, and a few feet away he saw a hand clutching one side of the brick chimney.

"C'mon out, Ben," he called. "We want to talk to you."

The hand slid away from the chimney and Siegel appeared, unkempt, unshaved, and wearing a silk robe. Coming down through the trap door, he faced Williams with a foolish grin.

"What are you doing up there, Siegel?" Williams asked.

"I was going to the barber shop."

Williams and the others reacted with laughter. "That's doing it the hard way," Williams said.

"Look," Siegel said. "It isn't funny. I didn't know you were cops. What's the beef now?"

"Big Greenie," Williams said.

"Big Greenie?" Siegel's blue eyes blinked innocently.

"Sure. The Grand Jury says you helped knock him off."

"Who in hell is Big Greenie? I never heard of him."

Williams nodded to himself. "You never heard of him, eh?" he said. "You never heard of the Hotel Franconia in New York, either, did you?"

Siegel's eyes twitched, but he said nothing.

"And naturally you don't remember the day the New York cops rousted you and Lepke and Doc Stacher and the rest of your mob, and took pictures of all you guys. Funny thing, there was Big Greenie with his overcoat unbuttoned, standing alongside Lepke. Come on, let's go downtown."

Siegel shrugged, slowly got dressed, and went downstairs to the front door. He took a seat in the lead car, and the procession rolled down the driveway to the street. It is generally the custom, when the police want no interference from reporters, to hole up in a hotel or apartment for the first interview with an important suspect in a crime. It was not yet the law of the land to advise a prisoner of his right to have counsel and to remain silent, and so Bugsy was alone when the questioning began.

Williams had taken Room 521 in the Kipling Hotel at 4077 West Third Street in Los Angeles, and when Siegel sat down at one P.M., with stenographer Mildred Evans alongside, he faced Williams and his Deputy V. L. Ferguson, Detective Yarrow, and Officer Hurst. Williams recalls that Siegel was thoroughly relaxed and in a pleasant mood, and the twenty-seven page transcript of that first examination shows that he willingly answered every question, even some which would have made some of his dull-witted collaborators start snarling about a frame-up.

He frankly discussed his thoughts about Tony Cornero's gambling ships, his investment in gambling rooms at Redondo Beach, and his association with Longy Zwillman in the Chicago hot dog enterprise. He didn't quibble about his big money gambling, and admitted that most of his income came from bets on horse races, baseball and football games, and an election now and then.

"Do you know why I am asking you these questions?" Williams said.

"Well—I have an idea," Siegel replied.

"What do you think I am asking you about?"

"About some murder you're trying to implicate me in," Siegel said calmly.

Williams leaned forward in his chair. "Nobody has said anything about a murder," he said.

"I heard somebody talking around the house."

"Is that why you hid out this morning?"

Siegel's eyebrows lifted in what seemed painful surprise. "Why, Mr. Williams," he said. "Certainly not. If you had called me and said you wanted me, I would be right down there."

"You knew Whitey Krakower?"

"Yes, sir. All my life."

"You knew he was bumped off in New York?"

"I heard about it."

"You know why he was bumped off?"

"I haven't the slightest idea."

As the questioning continued, Siegel admitted he had loaned Whitey $20,000 to buy a piece of Cornero's offshore gambling operation, but he denied that he had invested any of his own money in the project.

"Why not?" Williams asked.

The shadow of a smile moved across his face again and he said: "I thought it was crazy because it was illegal."

Siegel's answer was so incongruous that none of them could stifle their laughter, and for a moment they forgot the grim business for which they had gathered in the now smoke-clouded room.

"I want to ask you something," Williams said a moment later. "Did you have any idea when Whitey Krakower was taken that you might be next in line?"

"No, sir," Siegel replied. "I don't know why anybody should take me. I haven't done any harm."

"Did he ever tell you any fears he had?"

Siegel scratched his chin. "Well, no," he said. "But a couple of times going downtown he would always watch this and that. He said it happened sometimes he was trailed."

"So you got the idea he was fearful of something?"

"Yes, the way he acted sometimes."

"Where were you the night he was killed?"

Siegel hesitated a moment, wrinkling his forehead. "I was in St. Paul," he said. "At the Lowry Hotel."

"So you wouldn't have any trouble getting a witness to alibi you the night Whitey was bumped?" Williams said with sarcasm.

"I don't know when he was bumped," Siegel answered, showing irritation for the first time. "But I know I wasn't anywhere near it. Like I said, I think I was in St. Paul."

"I have a description of the guy that did the shooting," Williams said with an accusing stare. "It fits you to a T."

Siegel avoided the prosecutor's eyes. "I haven't the slightest idea what you've got," he said.

During the following fifteen minutes the gangster admitted that he kept at least two guns around the house, that he was afraid of being robbed, and that sometimes he carried a gun when he had large amounts of cash in his pocket. He quickly added, knowing Williams would ask, that he had been given a gun permit by friends in a sheriff's substation. When Williams mentioned police reports about mysterious strangers stationed outside the house at night—"They looked like thugs," he said—Siegel said he had never seen the men, and insisted he had no bodyguards.

The question-and-answer statement, which to my knowledge was never made public, suggests a fencing match in which Siegel, an old hand at this kind of game, skillfully avoided cutting thrusts. He admitted intimate friendships with Frankie Carbo, Champ Segal, Longy Zwillman, and others—they often met at the Y.M.C.A. when he went there for workouts—but he suffered from acute amnesia when it came to knowing where they were the night Big Greenie was slain. He was also vague about his own whereabouts that night, but he thought perhaps he had been back east in Brooklyn, visiting his mother.

In retrospect it appears that Williams, even though he was sure Siegel would have hired a killer for the job, was more anxious to link Siegel with the Krakower murder than the gunning of Big Greenie. Williams never got around to asking the direct question: "Did you kill Big Greenie?"

In any case, he had already made up his mind.

And when Mildred Evans closed up her notebook, he pointed at Siegel and said to Detective Yarrow: "Book him."

In the bedroom of her elegant mansion on North Bedford Drive, the Countess Dorothy DiFrasso stared wild-eyed at the front page of the *Los Angeles Examiner*. Then she crumpled the sheet into a ball and flung it across the room. Ben Siegel was in the County Jail. The charge was murder and there was no bail.

Once not long before, the Countess had lost her self-control in the lobby of the Excelsior Hotel in Venice, and jerked Elsa Maxwell's hair until some strong bystander pulled them apart. But now there was no hair to pull, nor any other way to let her anger explode. She grabbed the phone and made one frantic call after another.

She shouted at lawyers, columnists, editors, and influential friends. But there was no one to arrange a fix, or pull a string, or soften up the D.A. This was the toughest rap of all, and they told her so.

She paced back and forth across the room for awhile, and then suddenly she knew where to go. Moving with cold purpose, she carefully arranged her dark hair, put on fresh makeup, and slipped into a dark, tailored suit. Then, from a locked cabinet built into the wall, she took our her treasure. It was a $50,000 necklace of rubies and emeralds (she often told friends it had been given to her in Rome by Barbara Hutton) and she held it for a moment as the morning sun touched each stone and threw back flashes of light. She finally stuffed it into her handbag, threw a mink coat over her shoulders and drove to the airport.

She chartered a small plane, and within an hour she was standing on the runway of William Randolph Hearst's private airport at the castle of San Simeon. None of Hearst's biographers have ever mentioned this surprise visit, nor is there any record that Hearst himself told anyone that she had come there, or why he consented to see her this time. Perhaps the publisher was in a whimsical mood and her daring flight amused him. He liked her, that much was certain, and she was no stranger to San Simeon.

In any case, the Countess was admitted to his office and there, with remarkable patience, he listened to her plead for Bugsy Siegel. She begged him to use his power to squash the murder charge and get the mob man out of jail, and said she would be willing to do anything in return.

"But Dorothy," Hearst said, "the man has been indicted and there is nothing I can do."

The Countess suddenly fell to her knees and began to sob. "W.R.," she said, "I can't raise any cash right now, but I have something else."

She fumbled in her bag, came out with the fabulous necklace, and flung it at the publisher's feet. "I beg you to accept this," she cried. "It's worth a lot of money, and it's all I can give you. Please. . . ."

Hearst must have been touched by this shameless performance, because he gazed at her with his pale eyes, and when he finally spoke to her in his high, thin voice, he was more embarrassed than angry.

"If this man were my own son," he said, "I could not help him."

He stood up, and the Countess knew that the interview was over. She was silent on the way back to her waiting plane, and when she arrived home she made no further attempts to free her imprisoned lover. She never let him know the humiliation she had suffered, and the details of her remarkable visit with Hearst might never have been revealed if, long afterward, she had not confessed to intimate friends what she had done.

Ironically, she was not aware that Ben Siegel did not need any help at the moment from her, or William Randolph Hearst, or any other outsider. He had the juice, even behind bars, and was enjoying his incarceration.

When Ben Siegel reached the turreted old County Jail building in downtown Los Angeles, across the street from the towering City Hall, he saw that news photographers were waiting to take his picture.

"Hey, just a minute," he protested to his police guards, "I'm not gonna pose for these guys."

"Why not? They'll get their shots sooner or later."

"Because I'm Ben Siegel, and I'm not gonna look like a bum."

"What do you want?"

"Give me a comb and a necktie," he said.

One policeman fished a comb from his hip pocket, and Detective Yarrow took off his own tie. Siegel went into a washroom, washed his hands, and combed his hair in front of a mirror as though he was preparing to go on stage. Perhaps he was. He brushed his checked sports coat, dusted off his shoes and knotted the borrowed tie. "Okay," he said. "I'm ready."

The flashbulbs popped, and Ben Siegel smiled. "Thanks, fellows," he said.

Eugene Williams, satisfied that his quarry was secure, left the building and drove back to the Delfern Avenue house where men from the District Attorney's office had remained on guard since the raid. Two professional safe and lock experts, brought to the house by Williams, went to work on the strongbox behind the sliding panel in the gangster's room, and they got it open moments later.

Almost every man has a secret box somewhere in his home wherein he keeps the little treasures of memories—a faded love letter, perhaps; a creased photo or two of almost forgotten happy times; a dented locket, or the torn half of a World's Series ticket. These treasures sometimes mirror the mind and personality of the man; they can show tenderness and love or hate or greed. Thus, in Ben Siegel's treasures, Williams found almost exactly what he expected to find in the box of a hoodlum who wanted to be somebody. There was a closed-face gold wrist watch, solid gold cuff links, a gold pen and pencil set, a gold cigarette lighter, half a dozen different kinds of gold watches, and a gold-trimmed comb and file set. There were also the tools of his trade—a Smith & Wesson .38 revolver and a .38 Colt automatic—neatly wrapped in oilcloth along with his United States passport, No. 15847, and a safe deposit box key from a bank in Scarsdale, New York.

But it was the three small leather account books, one red, one green, and one maroon, that really reflected the cold precision of Ben Siegel's gambling operations, and gave clues to the goals he had set for himself.

Here were the names and phone numbers of the people he was courting. The movie stars with their unlisted phones; the directors and studio executives; the cops and deputies he had in his pocket; certain bankers who could be counted on for emergency loans; and many a man who was neither saint nor sinner, but who operated in the twilight zone of the law.

The meticulous record of his daily bets suggested fixed races, games or fights, because he almost never seemed to lose except, as

Williams soon discovered, in the crap games which were a late hour pleasure every time he went to New York. In one four-day series, for instance, Siegel won $5750, but lost $5900. He was at Santa Anita every day of the track season, and the account book showed a net profit of $10,000 for the meet.

The books also showed that he borrowed thousands of dollars from racket friends, repaying them promptly. There was only one default on a loan of $7550 from a Hollywood gambler. In connection with it Siegel wrote a cryptic comment in the margin saying: "It will never be paid because of some difference between us." Williams checked on the borrower, and was relieved to discover that he was still alive.

Here and there, as an indication that the king of the underworld was no less vulnerable to family economic pressures, Williams found homey little entries like this: "Gave wife in New York $1000 cash of which she deposited some for me. Balance she used for house and servants for the month." In another entry mentioning his wife, Siegel wrote that he had given her a $50 dividend from the Equitable Life Insurance Company on the same day he won $2670 playing poker.

There was in the safe a little red box, lined with the kind of satin cushion used by jewelers and undertakers, in which Williams found a gold watch engraved: "Ben to Esta—1931." Perhaps he had given her a newer and more expensive watch. Perhaps the old one was beyond repair. Williams didn't know. Later, when Ben Siegel became enmeshed with Virginia Hill, Esta Siegel would be tucked away, too, out of his life, forgotten.

CHAPTER ELEVEN

When Virginia Hill learned that culture—or at least a reasonable facsimile of it—was supposed to include a knowledge of classic literature, she began reading the essays of William Makepiece Thackeray. It was bumpy going at first because she had had limited schooling, was educated only in the bedroom arts, and her late-hour reading was confined to the movie magazines and the Broadway columns.

But eventually, after struggling with the Waverly novels, Henry James, Jane Austen, and Alexander Dumas, she decided Thackeray made sense, and thereafter he was her favorite author. She had a complete set of his works, and she marked with pencil certain passages which, it can be assumed, coincided with her own interpretation of the good life.

In *Vanity Fair*, for instance, she underscored the following:

> "This I set down as positive truth. A woman with fair opportunities, and without a positive hump, may marry whom she likes.
> "I think I could be a good woman if I had five thousand a year."

No one knows whether Virginia understood what Thackeray meant by "a positive hump," but she could examine herself nude in a mirror, as she often did, and be certain that any humps or bumps she had were a positive asset. She never wanted to be what society considers a "good woman," and she would soon discover that five thousand a year would just about pay for one good party.

In the beginning Virginia was not sure what she wanted. Some of the parasites who clung to her as she flitted from Mexico to Hollywood, Chicago, and New York, and back again, had flattered her with the cliché: "You should be in the movies." She toyed with the idea, and when she met the late columnist Lee Mortimer in New York, he told her that she could make the screen if she was seen in the right places and had a publicity buildup. Years afterward, in a reminiscence he wrote for the *American Mercury*, Mortimer said: "She blazed into New York like a prairie fire. She was a wonderful actress even then, and had all of Broadway bamboozled."

She also bamboozled Lee Mortimer and the day would come when, in her quaint gangster moll idiom, she was to say: "Goddammit, the next time I see that sonovabitch Mortimer I'll kill him."

Much later, when Virginia did encounter Mortimer in an alley outside a Chicago nightclub, she leaped on him with long nails clawing. The fight was witnessed by the late Chicago mobster, Jake "Greasy Thumb" Guzik, and he almost fell over laughing. Even though her bare hands were not lethal, Mortimer naturally defended himself, and before the brawl ended he had put long rips in her expensive gown.

She was still muttering about the fight in 1951 when government agents were investigating her finances. She had kept the dress, now repaired, and it brought a remarkably good price during an auction of her personal things.

There were weeks during the early Broadway period when Virginia, with her usual entourage, was in one nightclub or another almost every night. One of her regular joints was a third-grade club called the Waikiki on 52nd Street, operated by a certain Paul Berney. Virginia not only did the rhumba with Berney, who had considerable skill in Latin-American dances, but she always picked up the tab—anywhere from $200 to $1000—for the evening's fun.

She had another favorite club called The Hurricane, at 1619 Broadway, and at the time the place was suffering substantial losses. Mortimer claimed that Paul Berney said one night: "Virginia, you're blowing a lot of money around town on the clubs. Why don't you buy into one of these joints and get your fun for nothing?"

"Which one?" she asked.

"The Hurricane needs dough," he said.

The Broadway chroniclers soon reported that Virginia Hill,

the "Alabama heiress," had bought a one-third interest in The Hurricane for $40,000 and presently she made her first official visit there as part-owner hostess. On one of those evenings Virginia flung aside her shoes and was photographed dancing the rhumba with the Cuban band leader Miguelito Valdez. The picture showed her almost bare-bellied, her red hair whirling across her face, and her breasts welling out of her brassiere. She had her mouth open, as though crying out in some sort of tribal frenzy, and she wore no shoes or stockings. Whenever Virginia made news thereafter, which was often, the photo appeared in newspapers and magazines as though to confirm her wild and wanton nature. She hated it.

Less than two weeks after Virginia bought into The Hurricane, Mortimer reported in his column that she had become bored with her new plaything, and sold out to her attorney David J. Wolper, who had offices in New York and St. Petersburg, Florida.

The truth—Mortimer rarely bothered to check out facts—was that Virginia, rather than having put $40,000 into The Hurricane actually put up $4000, and that money went to Wolper for legal fees. When her partners asked her for more cash she didn't have it. She got the original $4000 by going to a pawnshop in Chicago called Levinson's Loans, and hocking a diamond bracelet she had insured for $15,000. She got two loans from Levinson for this bauble for a total of $6100, and in July 1942, when she failed to repay the money, Levinson's Loans told her she had forfeited the gems. No one seems to know why she abandoned the bracelet. Perhaps it wasn't worth $15,000 to her, and she considered herself lucky to get $6100 for it.

During her breaking-in period in Manhattan, one of Virginia's escorts was the powerful mob leader Joey Adonis. Virginia moved around from one hotel to another—for awhile she was at the Madison, then took a suite at the Savoy-Plaza—but she stayed many nights with Joey A. at the Waldorf.

She was having a couple of warm-up drinks with Joey in the Madison bar one evening when Ben Siegel came in alone. There is no evidence that this first meeting set off any arterial pulsations in either of them; indeed, Virginia later recalled that Joey A. suddenly became edgy, and that Siegel was curiously disinterested for a man who was supposed to have an instant rapport with women.

Perhaps that meeting never even took place. Virginia said it did. Joey Adonis never said anything. Mortimer's essay on Virginia asserts that "rumors began to circulate that the Bug had stolen Adonis' girl . . . a transcontinental gang war was in the making." Chick Hill, who knew his sister better than anyone in the world, says Joey A. was only a stopover on a long bedroom safari, and that Virginia quickly forgot him when Siegel later made her his mistress. In any case, Virginia said so long to Broadway about that time, and moved back to Hollywood for her try at the cinema world.

In keeping with her theory that big spenders and big parties make news, Virginia appeared at Ciro's nightclub one evening and asked for an audience with owner Billy Wilkerson, who was also publisher of the movie trade paper, *The Hollywood Reporter.*

Wilkerson gave Virginia's face and figure a professional appraisal; he liked what he saw and asked what she wanted.

"You're closed on Monday nights," she said. "I want to rent the whole club for a private party."

"I don't know who you are," he said, "and so you would have to make a deposit."

Virginia opened her oversize alligator handbag, and extracted a roll of currency. She slipped five $1000 bills off the top and pushed them across his desk.

"Will that do for a start?" she asked sweetly.

"I'm sure it will," he said, smiling for the first time. "Now, what Monday night would you like?"

Wilkerson later recalled that the cost of the party came to exactly $4800 and that he gave her a $200 refund. Word soon spread in cafe society about the beautiful stranger who was a walking branch bank. The Hollywood columnists mentioned her as possible screen material, and hinted that she was being courted by some of the handsome stars around town. Actually Virginia had not yet met Victor Mature, John Carroll, Gene Krupa, Bruce Cabot, or any of the other suitors whom she would be dating later on. The party she gave had no celebrity guests and Wilkerson did not know where or how she gathered the unknown men and women who did come.

Among them was a sleek young Spaniard named Juan Romero, a dancer like so many of Virginia's early admirers, and presently he emerged from the pack as her picture agent, promising glory and fame. Virginia sat for what the press agents call "leg art," glossy still pictures in which the subject is photographed in provocative poses, exposing as much as the censors would allow. In these shots Virginia looked as sexy as she really was, and Romero got her a seven-year contract at the old Universal studio. It was a standard arrangement offered to pretty young maidens who were photogenic and stood some chance of being touched by the magic wand. But the weekly salary wouldn't have paid for Virginia's suite in the Beverly Hills Hotel.

Virginia was also enrolled in the Columbia Pictures drama school and there she took diction lessons and was instructed on the basic techniques of screen acting. She had an intimate actress friend there named Mara Delgado (her professional name was Adele Mara) and at her suggestion Virginia also enrolled her brother Chick.

Chick vaguely recalls that after weeks of reading lines and acting out bit parts in class, Virginia used a picturesque four-letter word to describe the whole business and walked out. She bought up her contract, and never made another attempt to be an actress. "Tab just chickened out," Chick says. "She knew neither one of us had any real talent, and it was just too much trouble." Juan Romero, who had visions of pocketing 10 percent of Virginia's movie earnings, was stunned by her defection, and was tempted to pull out. But he cooled off, and stayed on the scene as her nightclub escort, a decision he would later regret.

During this flamboyant seasoning period in Hollywood, Virginia entertained constantly. She was virtually a fixture at Charles Morrison's Mocambo Club, also on Sunset Boulevard; Morrison later said she spent so much money there that he couldn't begin to add it up. She always signed the tab—the bill was almost never less than $1000—and Chick would appear the next morning with a wad of $100 bills to settle the account.

Occasionally, to relax, Virginia and Chick went to Mexico City. It was never a true rest for either one, for Virginia could soak up staggering quantities of liquor, and she was seen in the gambling joints so often, her red hair framing a flushed face, that the Mexican casino men gave her a nickname. They called her "The Flamingo" and it was a name that would stick.

In Mexico, where she carefully avoided publicity, and where she moved on a higher social plane because no one knew her humble background, Virginia soon found powerful government friends who could be useful in a country where any trouble is quickly and quietly disposed of through the right connections. One was the young Army officer, Amezcua. The other three were Chato Juarez, Valentio Quintara, an undercover agent for the Federal police, and Rafael Ola, a secretary in the Presidential palace.

A newspaper friend of mine in Mexico City who had heard of Virginia's adventures below the border, but who had never seen her there, once asked me: "What did she do there? What was she really like?"

And I remembered an incident and said: "Well . . . she was many things. She whored around a lot . . . not for money, mind you. She drank a lot and she threw money away. But she had one experience, and perhaps it will tell you something about her."

There was a postman. His name was José Ramirez Segoviano, and he delivered the mail on the Mexico City route where Virginia lived for awhile. One day there came a very fat envelope from Joe Epstein in Chicago, and José remembered having seen another envelope just like it. He watched her tear it open quickly, and take the green money out of it, and when she saw that he was still standing there she threw him a couple of pesos. He thanked her and went on.

One day there was another envelope. José stopped before he got to her place, carefully opened the envelope, and took out the money. There was $5000. He counted it three times, and though the day was cool the perspiration ran down his face. He stuffed the money into his pocket, and took off a thin little scarf he had around his neck. He folded it and put it inside the envelope addressed to Miss Virginia Hill. And his tongue was so dry with fear that he could barely get enough saliva to wet the envelope flap so it would stick and stay closed.

When Virginia came home an hour later and discovered the theft, she knew it was the postman. She had seen that scarf before.

"Chick!" she called to her brother. "Get hold of Bernie Jurado. Tell him we need the cops."

The police came, and with them an official who was one of Virginia's lovers. He told her not to lose any sleep over the mailman because they would get him before the night was out. They found him asleep in his home, and half the money was under his pillow. The police brought José Ramirez Segoviano into the city, to a building which was a sort of precinct headquarters. They called Virginia, told her about the money and said they would have the rest of it before dawn. They roused José's mother from her small adobe house, brought her to headquarters, and left her in a car parked just a few feet from an open window.

"Where did José hide the money?" one of the policeman asked.

"I don't know," she said.

And into the black night, from the open window, came a frightening scream. "That was your son," the policeman said. "They are using the club on him, and the blood runs out of his ears and his nose. Soon it will run out of his eyes."

Virginia and Chick sat in a waiting room nearby, and they heard the terrible cries too. There came wave upon wave of screams, and it was José's mother who broke first. "Stop! Stop!" she wailed. "Let him alone. I have the money. It is in my house. I will take you there."

José Ramirez Segoviano went to jail. Virginia felt a little guilty and she sent money to the jail for him, but money could not repair the cracked skull and the damaged places inside his head. Virginia wished it had not happened, and she said that if another thief stole money from her envelopes again she might let him keep it. She said she hated to see people hurt for a few lousy bucks.

In the fall of 1940 Ben Siegel, locked up in a County Jail cell, was a patient man. He was really not in painful exile. He had the run of the jail floor and was allowed to use the telephone when he pleased. He was hero-worshipped by most of the inmates. One of them served as his personal valet, shining The Bug's shoes and pressing his jail uniform which, unlike the baggy clothing worn by the other inmates, had special notched labels and was made of a better grade of denim. Siegel was also permitted to order meals from outside restaurants, including such delicacies as roast pheasant. In this election year, Siegel was the only prisoner allowed to wear a Roosevelt button on his lapel, a disclosure that subsequently disturbed Los Angeles Democrats because they did not believe Siegel was the kind of campaigner who could help F.D.R.

The fact that Bugsy Siegel, accused of murder, was a pampered prisoner should not have surprised anyone. Graft is as old as the world itself, and there will always be con bosses in penitentiaries and jails when the price is right. And Siegel had the cash. Though he was technically unemployed and had no visible source of money, Siegel reported an income of $57,000 that year—about half what he actually took in. He spread a lot of it around the County Jail.

One afternoon Jim Richardson answered the phone at the *Examiner*, and a man's voice said: "You the editor? There's something phony going on."

"There always is," Richardson said. "Where now?"

"Look, mister, I ain't kidding. I seen Bugsy Siegel on the Strip last night."

"You're seeing things, pal," Richardson said. "The Bug is in the can, and I hope they throw the key away."

"I'm just tellin' you," the man insisted. "I know Siegel like I know my own face. Just ask around."

"I might do that, pal," Richardson said. "Thanks."

Richardson called in Howard Hertel, his top reporter, and told him about the phone call. "The guy might be one of those nuts," he said. "But it's worth a look. Drop anything else you've got, and stick around the jail. Sleep there if you have to. If Siegel is running around loose I want to know about it."

Hertel planted himself at the County Jail and asked questions of people he trusted. Presently he reported to his astounded city editor that the rumors were true. Ben Siegel had been out of jail no less than eighteen times since October 7.

"In God's name, why?" Richardson exploded.

"Well, Jim," Hertel said, "he's been going out on court orders to get his teeth fixed, talk with his attorney or do any damn thing he wants, I guess."

Richardson smouldered. He had never forgotten Mark Hellinger's embarrassing visit on Siegel's behalf, nor the threats The Bug had made. He knew there was a big story in the making, and for Richardson the story came first. He asked reporter Sid Hughes to join Hertel, assigned a photographer to them, and told them to tail Siegel every time he left the jail.

"If you see him on the street anywhere," Richardson said, "I want a picture. And I want one that shows his face."

In the white brick house in Coldwater Canyon George Raft was in a sour mood. The asthma that squeezed his lungs and awakened him in the night with the fear of impending death was worse than ever. He was short of cash, as usual, and the overhead at the house was running him into debt. He was squabbling almost daily with Jack Warner at the studio, and he knew that sooner or later there would be a violent climax which would force him off the lot.

He was staring moodily at the large portrait of lovely Norma Shearer on his desk—and that romance was fluttering away like some of the dead leaves in the garden outside—when Mack Gray walked in.

"Georgie," he said, "you got a visitor."

"I have no appointments today," the actor said irritably, "and I don't want to see anybody."

"That's what I told her."

"*Her*?"

"Yeah. It's the Countess Dorothy DiFrasso, and she's in a snit, I can tell you."

"Take her in the rumpus room," Raft said wearily. "I'll be right there."

The Countess was indeed in a "snit." She had been crying, but now she was white-faced with anger, and the words tumbled out of her mouth.

"George—you know I'm crazy about Ben Siegel—and you're his best friend—and why in hell don't you tell me what's going on!"

"I don't know what you're talking about, Dottie," he said.

"Yes, you do!" she challenged. "He's fooling around with another girl."

Raft spread his hands in resignation. "I'm telling you the truth, Dottie. If Ben has another girl he hasn't said a damn thing to me."

"Don't give me that soothing syrup," she snapped. "I'm no schoolgirl, God knows, but I'm not so stupid that I can't see what's going on."

"So help me," Raft sighed, "if he's playing around I'm not in on the news. I'm at the studio from nine in the morning until seven at night, and I can't watch him every minute. And anyway he's in jail, and I haven't heard that they're sneaking in girls by the back door."

"All right, Georgie," the Countess said. "But do me a favor, please. If you find out anything let me know. Believe me, if I see him with another girl I'll kill her!"

"Take it easy, Dottie. You wouldn't kill anybody."

"Wouldn't I? Try me."

She picked up her mink and swept out, slamming the door. "Women!" Raft said to himself. "Oh brother!"

Raft was mulling over the Countess's visit, wondering whether he should tell Ben Siegel about it, when he got a phone call from Wendy Barrie, the pretty English actress who was having considerable success in Hollywood.

"What's on your mind, Wendy?" Raft asked.

"Oh, nothing really important," she answered. "I know you go downtown once in awhile to see Ben Siegel, and I'd like to go along on your next visit."

"I didn't know you knew Ben."

"I don't really—I met him once or twice."

"I'd be glad to take you, Wendy," Raft said, "but I don't think they'll let you in."

"Oh, yes, they will," she said quickly.

"Okay then. I'll pick you up after lunch."

They made the long drive from Beverly Hills, down Wilshire Boulevard to the Los Angeles Civic Center and, as Wendy had predicted, they had no trouble getting into the jail. Raft recalls that he went into the visitors' room first, shook hands with Siegel and said: "Wendy Barrie's outside. She said she wanted to see you or something, so I brought her along."

"Yeh?"

"Ben—how well do you know this girl?"

"Hardly at all, Georgie," he said, blue eyes looking out the window toward the distant hills. "She seems like a nice kid."

The two men chatted awhile, with Siegel expressing confidence that he would soon be free, and then, as Raft waited in an ante-room, Wendy walked in and talked with the gangster. She was only there a few minutes, and then she and Raft got into his Cadillac, and started homeward.

Sitting at the wheel in the slow-moving traffic, Raft suddenly took his eyes off the road and looked at Wendy. "Listen, Wendy," he said, "when it comes to dealing with Ben Siegel I'm a man and you're a woman, and there's a hell of a difference. I've been publicized with him, and everybody knows we're friends."

"So what does that mean?"

"It means that if you go around with Ben Siegel you'll get hurt. And I mean hurt. Suddenly nobody will want you in pictures."

"I'll take that chance."

"Okay, Wendy. Don't say I didn't warn you."

Neither spoke the rest of the way to her house in Westwood, and a friendship came to an end. Raft says he saw Wendy often after that, both in New York and Hollywood, but she never spoke to him again. Later he was to learn that Wendy mentioned the incident to Siegel, and that Siegel was livid with anger.

CHAPTER TWELVE

Sid Hughes and Howard Hertel, keeping their patient vigil at the County Jail, were suddenly prodded into action one morning when Ben Siegel and Deputy Sheriff Jimmy Pascoe emerged from a side door and got into an official car. The mobster was wearing one of his expensive suits, a gleaming white shirt and a silk necktie, and he was obviously in a jaunty mood. The two newspapermen started their own car, and began to follow their quarry.

Siegel's first stop was on North Camden Drive in Beverly Hills, where he went to the office of his dentist, Dr. Allen Black. He was there for some time, and when he finally reappeared Pascoe drove around the block to Wilshire Boulevard. It was almost noon, and to Hertel's surprise the Sheriff's car turned into a parking lot alongside a popular restaurant called Lindy's. Siegel and Pascoe sauntered in—Hertel noticed that the gangster was not handcuffed, as most prisoners are outside the jail—and sat down at a table like any other customers.

Pascoe let his eyes wander around the room, and he nudged Siegel. "Hey, look, there's Wendy Barrie alone at the bar."

Siegel must have known she would be waiting, and he had obviously tricked Pascoe into having lunch there. In any case, he showed no surprise, and said: "Ask her to join us."

Pascoe subsequently told his superiors that he could not understand why anyone should object to his actions that day. "Siegel said he was hungry as we passed Lindy's," he reported, "and I didn't see anything wrong with letting him go in there for a bite. I saw Wendy Barrie sitting there, and he asked me to bring her over. I did, and they had quite a chat."

This cozy little tête-à-tête between an accused killer and the attractive movie actress might have remained a secret if the *Examiner* men had not been tailing Siegel that day. They were posted on the sidewalk when the trio emerged, and Siegel blanched and cursed as the camera clicked. He ran to the car ahead of Pascoe, trying to shield his face, but the photographer had his shot.

Jim Richardson gave the story splash treatment on the *Examiner's* front page the next day, and as Florabel Muir of the New York *Daily News* later said in her book *Headline Happy*: "All hell broke loose around the County Jail."

A County Grand Jury immediately began an investigation, and Dr. Benjamin Blank, denying any culpability, was temporarily suspended from his post by the County Civil Service Commission. The physician might have come out of it with only a slightly dented reputation if Captain William Bright of the Sheriff's staff had not turned up additional damaging evidence. Captain Bright found out that Dr. Blank had not only permitted Siegel to use his own personal bed in his private quarters at the jail, but that the physician had also brought in the civilian clothes that the mobster wore each time he was taken out on the town.

Worst of all, when Chief Deputy District Attorney Gene Williams took a close look at a box full of canceled checks he had found in Siegel's hidden safe, he saw a batch made out to and endorsed by Dr. Blank. The checks totaled $32,000, and later, at a formal Civil Service hearing, the doctor testified that these payments represented money Siegel once owed him. When his case came up for final hearing, Dr. Blank angrily charged that he was not getting "a square deal," but his protest was ignored. He was fired.

When the scandal broke, the red carpet was pulled out from under Siegel's feet, and he became an ordinary inmate. Unfortunately, as the police saw it, he wasn't behind bars long enough.

On December 11, 1940, Assistant District Attorney Vernon Ferguson went into the court of Superior Judge Crum and moved for the dismissal of the murder indictment against Siegel. It seems that the newly elected District Attorney of Los Angeles, John Dockweiler, decided he did not have a solid case and saved the taxpayers the cost of an expensive trial.

The villain in this shameful miscarriage of justice was William

O'Dwyer, who had given up a $25,000 a year job on the bench to become District Attorney of Kings County, New York. Bill O'Dwyer, as he preferred to be called, informed the Los Angeles authorities that he was not willing to have Abe Reles and Allie Tannenbaum, the key witnesses in the Big Greenie case, travel to California again. They had been there once before, telling their story to the Grand Jury, and he refused to expose them again to what he called the natural hazards of such a trip.

The truth was that O'Dwyer, who wanted a reputation as a crusading, crime busting prosecutor, had his eye on the Mayor's mansion in Manhattan. Though Burton Turkus was doing the dangerous work in tracking down the killers of Murder Inc., O'Dwyer was taking the credit. He had no real concern for the worthless skins of Reles and Tannenbaum, but it was vital to his personal ambitions to keep them alive. He needed them on the witness stand. It was more important to have Turkus put Lepke and his New York mob into the death house than to avenge the murder of Big Greenie. Dockweiler had no choice. And on that December afternoon Bugsy Siegel, accompanied by his lawyer, Jerry Giesler, walked out of jail.

There was one other provocative aspect of that Siegel whitewash that gave Los Angeles newspapermen pause. In her memoirs, Florabel Muir revealed that Siegel had contributed $30,000 to the successful Dockweiler campaign against the incumbent District Attorney Buron Fitts, whom he had never liked. And when Dockweiler took office nine days before Siegel was taken to court, the gangster heard that the new D.A. intended to push the murder charge. Siegel immediately wrote a hostile letter in which he demanded a refund.

Miss Muir and John Roeburt, author of a biography of Jerry Giesler, both wrote that Dockweiler was appalled by Siegel's letter and insisted that he did not know there had been underworld money in his campaign chest. He immediately hustled up $30,000 in cash, and returned it to the angry prisoner in the County Jail. Political campaign experts might find it difficult to believe that a candidate would not know the source of such a large contribution. But that was Dockweiler's explanation, and apparently it was acceptable to the people.

One Sunday morning, a day or two after he was released, Ben

Siegel stuck a loaded .45 Colt automatic into a holster beneath his coat, got into his new Buick and sped to the Raft house in Coldwater Canyon. He didn't pause to ring the bell when he found the front door unlocked, and he strode into the hall. Mack Gray was entering the house from the poolside at that moment, and he greeted Siegel with a smile.

"Hi, Ben," he said.

"Where is he?" Siegel snarled.

"Georgie? He had a big night and he's still pounding the pillow."

Siegel said nothing and started for the actor's bedroom.

"Let 'im sleep, Ben," Gray said. "He can call you later."

"Get out of my way," Siegel said.

He pushed Gray aside, pulled the gun from his pocket and strode to Raft's room. Raft had been awakened by the voices in the hall, and he was sitting up, eyes wide, when his gangster pal came in.

"You snitching son of a bitch," Siegel said. "I'm gonna kill you."

Raft saw something in Siegel's face he had never seen before and, as he said long afterward, "my heart damn near stopped."

"What's eating you?" he said.

"You told Wendy to stay away from me!"

"Yeah—I told her that."

"It's none of your goddamned business!" Siegel was almost yelling now. "In my book that's a doublecross and there's a lot of guys pushing up daisies for that kind of crap."

He fingered the gun, and lowered it almost imperceptibly.

Raft saw Siegel's sudden hesitation, and he calmly returned his friend's accusing stare. "Okay, Ben. You can shoot me if you want, but it'll be the finish for both of us. Now look, Baby Blue Eyes, why don't you put the rod away, and talk to me like a pal."

The sound of his favorite nickname reached Siegel's quixotic temperament; in an instant—as Raft had hoped—he changed from killer to cherub. The self-conscious smile was there, dimples showing, and he slid the gun back into its leather sheath.

"Georgie," he said, "I'm still saying you shouldn't of told Wendy anything."

"You know I was right, Ben."

"Yeah, yeah, I know."

After that day, whenever Ben Siegel was in a rage and a violent quarrel seemed imminent, Raft called him "Baby Blue Eyes." It was like a master key to the gangster's mind, and it always locked off his anger. It was the only nickname Ben Siegel ever had, except the hated word "Bugsy," and only George Raft used the phrase, and knew what it could do.

The searing publicity given to Siegel's jail episode inflicted no permanent damage and, as one could expect, it gave him an even more glamorous cloak in the movie colony. He was a prized social catch and, as Police Chief Clinton Anderson later observed: "He was always most charming around the ladies." The stars invited him to their homes as sort of an exciting Exhibit A, and he was seen with them at the races, at the glittering premieres and in the exclusive restaurants of Hollywood and Beverly Hills. Friends in the police department even drove him home from the racetrack, often with the siren wide open. No gangster in criminal history ever had such open association with the big names of the town, and Siegel was determined to keep it that way.

Exit Bugsy Siegel, hoodlum. Enter Benjamin Siegel, Esq., *bon vivant*, sportsman, raconteur. Also, by the grace of George Raft and a little coaching now and then, perhaps even a movie star.

He kept this gnawing ambition to himself for awhile, but one day, when Raft was making a picture with Marlene Dietrich, he showed up on the set. He watched Raft go through a couple of takes and presently, when the star took a break in his dressing room, Siegel said: "I was watching you out there, Georgie, and I could do that scene better."

"Okay, do it."

Siegel grinned, opened a large briefcase, and took out a 16mm. movie camera. He handed it to Mack Gray and said: "Okay, Killer, I'm going to do this bit and you shoot it for me."

"Roll 'em," Raft laughed.

Gray aimed the little camera, and to Raft's astonishment Siegel reenacted the scene he had just witnessed on the big sound stage. He had not only memorized the lines, but he used Raft's gestures as well, and for a moment the actor was speechless.

"Gee whiz, Ben," Raft said, using one of his favorite expressions. "That's pretty darn good."

"Think I might make an actor?" Siegel asked.

"You might at that."

Thereafter Siegel appeared often at the studio with his camera. When Mack Gray was unavailable, he entrusted the photography to Little Moe Sedway, the ex-burglar who had been promoted to a selling job for Siegel's Trans-America race wire service. Little Moe, who wasn't strong enough to push buttons, and who "sold" his products with ominous threats rather than muscle, was not quite at home in the greasepaint factories. But he did the best he could with the camera, and Raft says that some of the footage, while not quite professional caliber, was remarkably good. Siegel let it be known around the studios that he was available, and that any interested director could look at these personal rushes.

Meanwhile he kept in shape at the Y.M.C.A. gymnasium, spent large sums to keep himself groomed at Drucker's barbershop, made sure his shirts, handkerchiefs, and silk robes were monogrammed in the accepted fashion, and spent many evening hours reading books and magazines to improve his vocabulary. He carefully avoided being seen in public with lowbrow thugs like Mickey Cohen, and though he had a close personal relationship with a Sunset Strip service station operator named Joe Moll, he only saw him at the station, or on the grounds of the Raft home. There, with Leo Durocher usually on hand, Siegel played ball or swam with Moll and Raft, and he was safe from columnists he couldn't elude in public places.

And when he was alone he dreamed of glory.

He waited, and he fretted. The footage of Ben Siegel, actor, dried out and cracked in the round cans, and his camera lens picked up dust and was never used again.

But Siegel was represented in pictures, nevertheless, along with other racket friends, though not the way he wanted. George Raft had long watched Siegel, Joey A., Owney Madden, Al Capone, and Frank Costello—the big names in crime, and they had little gestures and habits that were theirs alone.

As Raft made one gangster picture after another he worked out a "method" system. It was quite simple. He stole the mannerisms of the real mob men, and made them his own on the screen.

Raft always admired Joey Adonis, and made mental notes on how the gang leader used his hands, how he talked, and held his chin at a certain angle. In at least two underworld pictures Raft imagined that he was Joey A. Adonis was so flattered by Raft's interpretation that he asked the actor for coaching help in 1951 when he was called to testify at the televised hearings of the Kefauver Commission crime investigation.

When the hearings were over Adonis asked for Raft's appraisal.

"I thought you were brilliant," Raft said. "You handled yourself very well."

Senator Kefauver was not quite as charmed by Joey A.'s performance, and subsequently wrote in *Crime in America* (Doubleday) a bitter denunciation of Raft's star pupil. "Adonis," he said, "was the evil personification of modern criminality. This man with blood-stained hands for years has set himself up as bigger than the law . . . he was the most determinedly contemptuous . . . and the most sinister of all the racketeers we questioned."

The late Willie Moretti, a high roller who reportedly once picked up $400,000 on a throw for a hard way four, is supposed to have said: "Publicity for gamblers and guys in the racket is nothing but the kiss of debt." If he said it that way—and I doubt that Willie had a gift for the *bon mot*—he was of course referring to the Internal Revenue Service which keeps book—or tries to—on the undeclared cash assets of the underworld boys.

If Siegel had not been so myopic about himself, he might have guessed that his growing pile of clippings would intrigue the government. Inevitably, as special agents began looking into Siegel's bank deposits and withdrawals, he began getting tips about their activities. Knowing that he had reported an income of some $479,000 in an eleven year period up to 1941—though he had unquestionably skimmed that much and more off the top—Siegel went into a characteristic rage.

He rushed downtown to the office of the Internal Revenue Intelligence unit and demanded an interview. He was given the customary courteous greeting, but when it suddenly became clear that he might have to answer embarrassing questions, he refused to say anything under oath. He also declined to submit any canceled checks or bank records for Donald O. Bircher, the special agent assigned to his case.

"It is useless to check my income and expenses," he said. "I don't want trouble with the government, and I report even more than I make, so there can't be any trouble.

"I'll tell you how I operate. I go with friends to a fight or a ball game and we sit down together and we say how much we will bet together—we make no record—and when the affair is over we pay off in cash and maybe I never see the fellows I bet with again.

"I don't remember their names and I keep a note in my diary but there is no way for you to check my wins and losses. I owe maybe $50,000 to friends, but I would not tell you their names as it might embarrass them."

Having thus thumbed his nose at the Government, Ben Siegel stalked out, and he never made another personal call there.

But he would not be forgotten by Donald Bircher, a veteran of the service who, like Javert in relentless pursuit of Jean Valjean, would start assembling a dossier on his man, and wait for him to make a mistake.

In the spring of 1941, when along with other scarce wartime items, there was a shortage of vitamin A, the Countess DiFrasso had another inspiration. She had dinner one evening with Siegel and said: "Ben, I've heard there's a lot of money to be made in shark livers. Why don't we do something about it?" Siegel, whose education had not included a study of ichthyology, was understandably baffled.

"Who in hell wants shark livers?" he asked.

"They're loaded with vitamin A," she said. "And the whole west coast is swarming with sharks. What we need is a boat and a skipper like Bob Hoffman."

"All I know about sharks," Siegel said, "is the loan guys who bleed you to death. But if you want to check on it, count me in."

The Countess called Richard Gully, the young Englishman who had been with them on the *Metha Nelson*, and together they went to Mexico. Their research confirmed the existence of large schools of soupfin and dogfish sharks, long known for the high vitamin A content of their livers, but Gully was skeptical.

Bugsy—at his first arrest.

The nine man lineup after the 1933 raid on a suite at the Hotel Franconia where they had been holding a conference. They are, from left to right, Joseph Rosen (Doc Harris), Benjamin Siegel (Bugsy), Harry Teitlebaum, Louis Buchalter (Lepke the Leopard), Harry Greenberg (Big Greenie), Louis Kravitz, Jacob Shapiro (Gurrah Jake), Philip Kovolick (Little Farvel), and Hyman Holtz (Curley). Two months later Gurrah and Lepke formed Murder Inc. *Los Angeles Herald Examiner*

Countess Dorothy DiFrasso stands with Clark Gable and Richard Barthelmess at one of her famous Hollywood parties. *Los Angeles Herald Examiner*

Marino Bello, promoter of the ill-fated Treasure Hunt to Cocos Island aboard the *Metha Nelson,* 1938. *Los Angeles Herald Examiner*

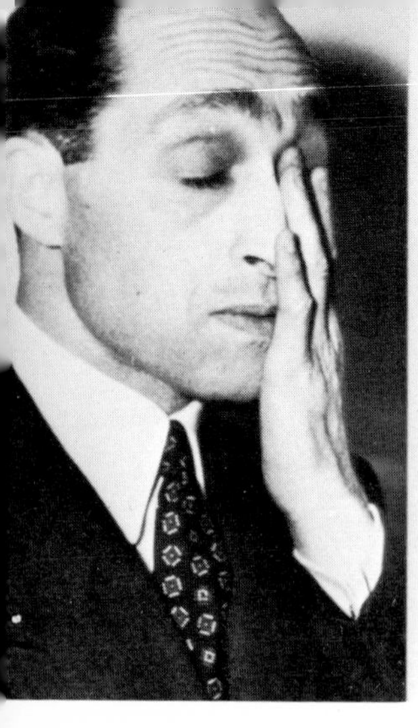

Al Tannenbaum, left, testified that Murder Inc. sent him by airliner from New York to Hollywood with two pistols to kill Harry Greenberg, Lepke gang member. Bugsy Siegel, center, and Frank Carbo, right, were on trial at Los Angeles for Greenberg's slaying. Later Tannenbaum said that Carbo did the shooting while Bugsy drove one car and he drove the second to block possible pursuit. The indictment was dismissed. *Wide World Photos*

Bugsy, after the indictment charging him with the murder of Harry Greenberg was dropped. With him are his attorneys Byron Hanna, left, and Jerry Giesler, November 11, 1940. *Wide World Photos*

George Raft, right, stands with Bugsy, left, at Bugsy's preliminary hearing on charges of bookmaking, July 1944. Raft testified and became so emphatic in his answers that he was warned by District Attorney Harry Hale: "Don't get yourself in contempt." *Wide World Photos*

"Kid Twist" Reles, center, with U. S. Attorneys, 1941. *Los Angeles Herald Examiner*

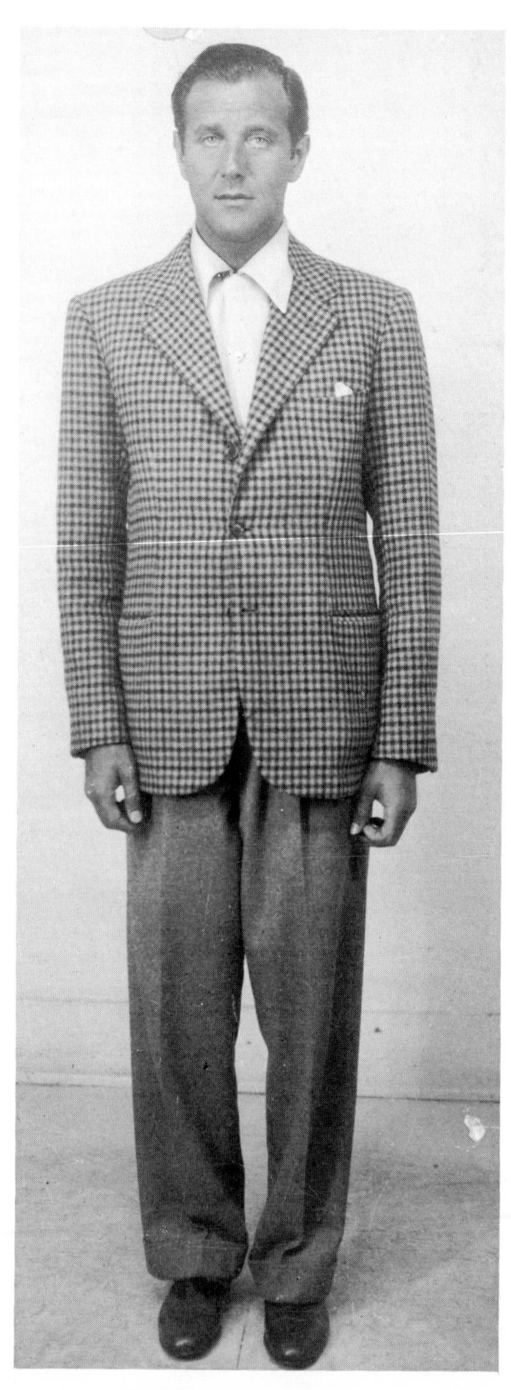

A previously unpublished photograph of Bugsy at the height of his career.

Allen Smiley, who identified Bugsy's body. *Los Angeles Herald Examiner*

Jerri Mason and Chick Hill at Bugsy's inquest, June 25, 1947. *Wide World Photos*

Officer W. L. Ritchey of Beverly Hills stands where Bugsy's killer is believed to have stood. *Wide World Photos*

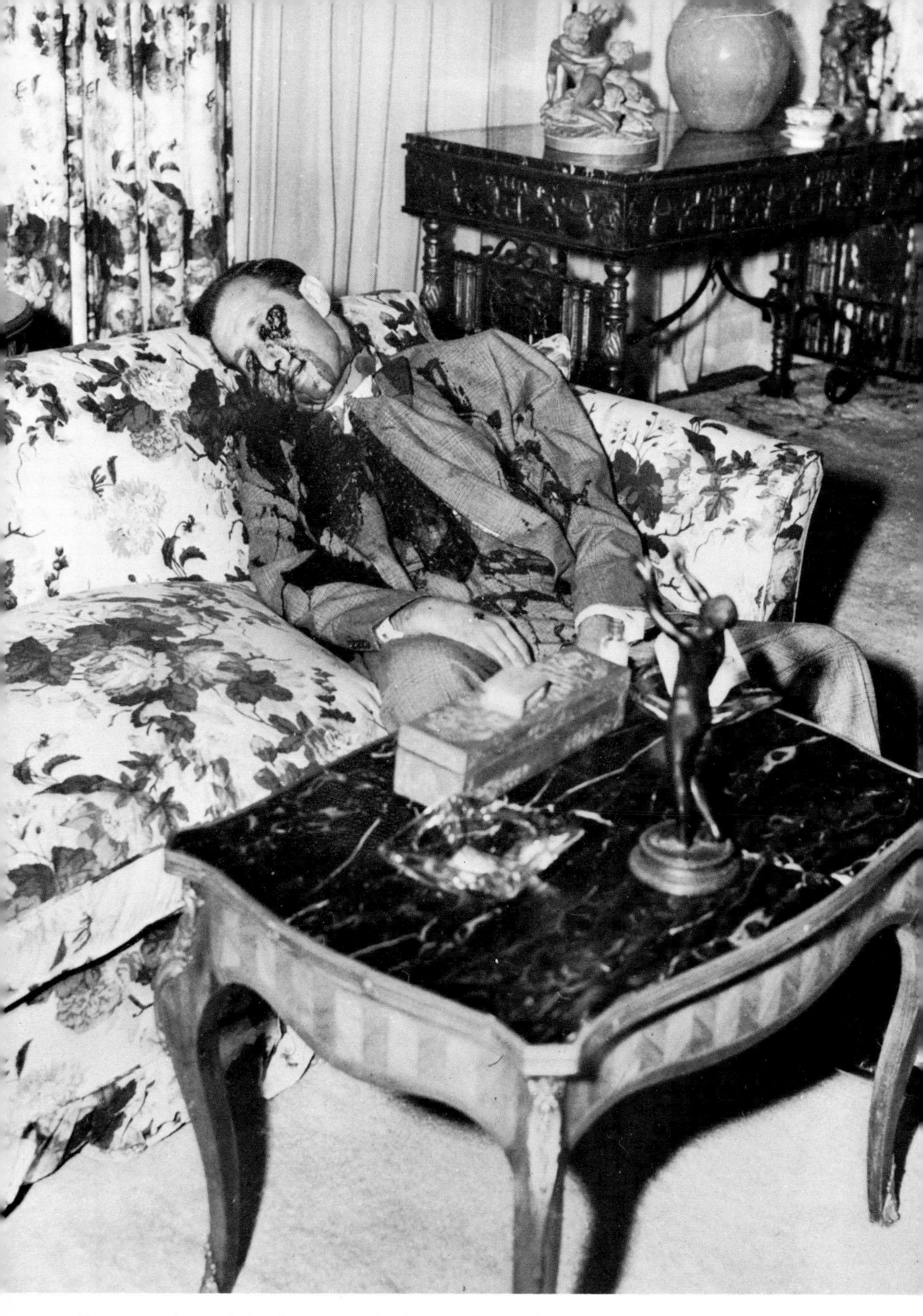

Bugsy, who might have made it on the right side of the law. June 20, 1947.
Wide World Photos

Marie MacDonald in 1947. *Los Angeles Herald Examiner*

Virginia's Beverly Hills home—810 N. Linden Drive. *Los Angeles Herald Examiner*

Virginia Hill in 1947. *Los Angeles Herald Examiner*

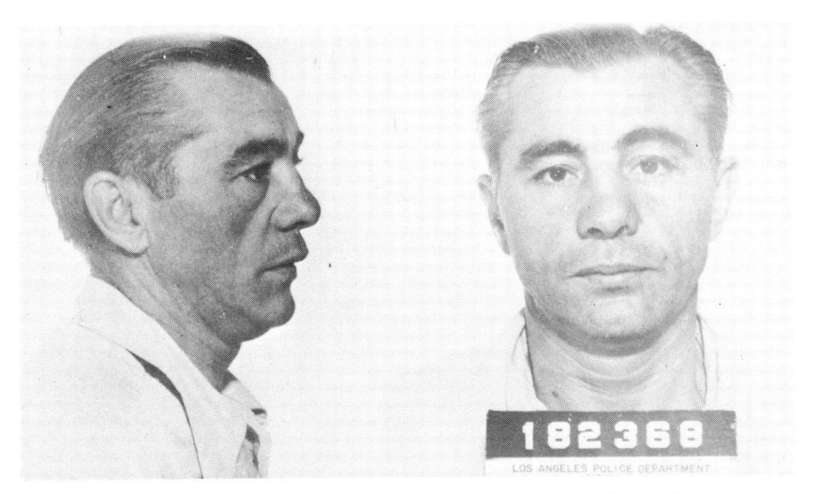

Los Angeles Police Department shot of Joe Sica, 1954.

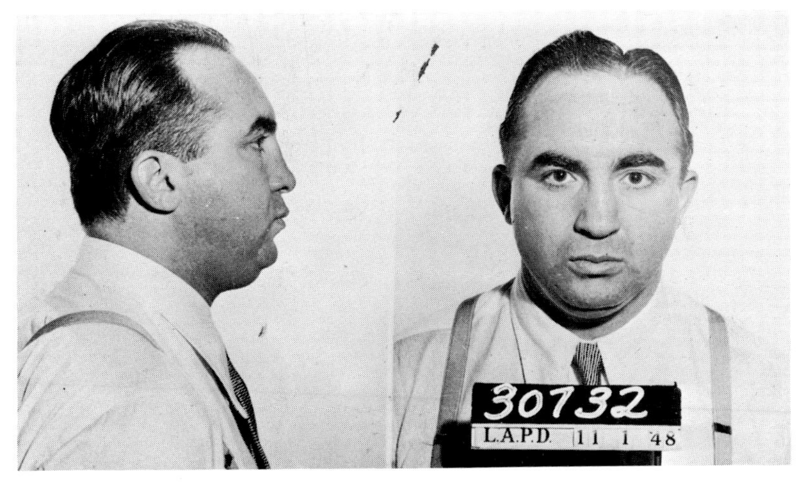

Los Angeles Police Department shot of Mickey Cohen, 1948.

"Swifty Morgan," an associate of Bugsy, is accompanied by Detective Sergeant J. D. Alcorn into Virginia's palatial Beverly Hills home where Bugsy was slain. Police were seeking a clue to the identity of Bugsy's killer, June 1947. *Wide World Photos*

Moe Sedway, who took over some of the Las Vegas holdings of Bugsy Siegel, arrives to testify at a Senate Crime Investigating Committee hearing in Las Vegas, November 1950. *Wide World Photos*

Virginia Hill Hauser expressed pleasantness, talkativeness, and puzzlement over a question put to her at hearings of the Kefauver Senate Crime Investigating Committee, March 1951. *Wide World Photos*

Virginia Hill Hauser with husband, Hans and son, Peter. *Wide World Photos*

"There are boats from all over the world in those waters," he said, "and the competition is very tough. Take my word, Dottie, you'll wind up in the red."

"Oh, for heaven's sake," she said in exasperation. "You're always the pessimist. I'm going ahead anyway."

She went back to Hollywood, and Siegel gave Captain Hoffman a check for $750 for preliminary expenses. Hoffman later chartered a boat, hired a crew of Mexican fishermen, and the venture got underway.

The sharks must have gone south for the winter, and months later, after wasting thousands of dollars, Siegel and his Countess glumly abandoned their futile enterprise.

In September, almost ten months after his cocky exit from the unsocial County Jail, Ben Siegel suddenly had an urgent need for another kind of shark—the keen legal mind of Jerry Giesler. Inexplicably, District Attorney O'Dwyer in New York permitted Allie Tannenbaum to fly west under guard and testify once more about the killing of Big Greenie. This time the Grand Jury indicted only Siegel and Frankie Carbo, leaving out Mendy Weiss and Champ Segal because they felt there was insufficient evidence. Lepke was skipped, too, for by that time he had surrendered to J. Edgar Hoover and Walter Winchell, and was more or less buried in Leavenworth Penitentiary on a narcotics charge.

In his summation to the Grand Jury, Deputy District Attorney Arthur Veitch gave Ben Siegel a new label.

"In gangster parlance," he said "Siegel is what is known as a 'cowboy.' This is the way the boys have of describing a man who is not satisfied to frame a murder, but actually has to be in on the kill in person." Siegel, tight-lipped and almost bursting with fury, surrendered for the second time, and, as some of Giesler's biographers noted, used another chunk of the Dockweiler refund to retain Giesler. Actually, this was the period before Giesler made his reputation defending the virtue of Charlie Chaplin, Errol Flynn, Robert Mitchum, and other actors, and his fees were far less than the $50,000 and $75,000 prices he was to charge later on.

Nevertheless, Giesler was a Blackstone at any price, and he earned every nickel of it with his courtroom sleight of hand. And if the law proved difficult, there was always the element of chance, stronger perhaps because of the persistent legend that Bugsy Siegel was either incredibly lucky or smart—or both.

Back in New York, securely held on the sixth floor of the Half Moon Hotel at Coney Island and watched around the clock by eighteen policemen in shifts, was Abe "Kid Twist" Reles. Boyhood friend of both Siegel and George Raft, Reles was now the traitor ready to pin the Greenie murder on The Bug.

Shortly after seven o'clock on the morning of November 12, 1941, Reles was found dead on a roof extension six floors below his room. The window of the room was open, and from it dangled a makeshift escape line made from knotted sheets and wire which was only long enough to reach the room on the floor below. It looked more like a prop planted there to mislead the guards.

Burton Turkus and his men in the Murder Inc. case were naturally numbed by the untimely plunge of their star witness, and investigations continued sporadically for some ten years afterward. There was talk that Reles's jump was suicide, but his body was found more than twenty feet from the wall. The conclusion was thus almost undeniable that Reles had been heaved out the window for his forty-two-foot plunge by one or more men who had unquestioned entrance to his room. Turkus said as much when he analyzed the case in his book *Murder Inc.* (Farrar-Strauss), but there has never been any solid evidence to prove it.

Joey Adonis or Albert Anastasia could have arranged the fatal fall. So could Bugsy Siegel. All three of them could have been badly hurt on the witness stand by the diminutive killer, and no price was too high to silence him. In any case Reles's death was Siegel's triumph.

The California Penal Code clearly states that corroboration of the testimony of the accomplice in a crime is a prerequisite to conviction. In other words, the story of Allie Tannenbaum, the confessed accomplice in Big Greenie's killing, was not enough to convict Siegel now that Reles was dead. And Jerry Giesler, knowing that, went to trial in February 1942, and asked Superior Judge A. A. Scott to dismiss the indictment against Ben Siegel.

Under the law the court had no alternative, and Siegel was a free man for the second time. Frankie Carbo was eventually tried for his role in the murder, and Allie Tannenbaum was there once more to confess. Other witnesses identified Carbo as one of the men seen running from Big Greenie's corpse, but their stories lacked strength without Reles on hand, and the jury couldn't agree. Carbo was held for retrial, but in New York O'Dwyer (Turkus says: "for some reason I never did learn") would not let Allie out of his sight, and Carbo also got his liberty.

Much later, as a provocative footnote to the death of Reles and the whole sordid affair, Senator Kefauver flatly accused O'Dwyer of backpedaling when it came to exposing bookmaking, narcotics, gambling, murder, and other organized crimes. "The position of Mr. O'Dwyer," Kefauver said of his testimony, "was particularly lamentable—a melancholy essay on political morality."

He also charged that O'Dwyer made no move to go after Adonis and Albert Anastasia, Bugsy Siegel's associates in crime. O'Dwyer remained in Mexico for years, and died without ever washing the stain from his name. Senator Kefauver lived long enough to know that the two gang leaders, along with Lepke, were punished eventually. Lepke died in the electric chair at Sing Sing, Adonis was deported to Italy, and Anastasia was killed by underworld guns in 1957. And Frankie Carbo, who went free twice, was eventually convicted of extortion, and is in prison now.

CHAPTER THIRTEEN

Chick Hill, who was always around as a friendly Peeping Tom during the early war years in Hollywood, does not remember exactly when Ben Siegel first experienced the formidable talents of his sister. Virginia never suffered from false modesty. In her home she was half-naked much of the time, adorning her 120 pounds with the best lingerie money could buy. When Ben Siegel came, she bathed her body with Chanel No. 5. At first she kept the bedroom door locked, and Siegel, to get rid of Chick, would bribe him with a hundred dollar bill.

But as time went on, and Siegel discovered that Chick was neither a blabbermouth nor indignant about his almost daily trips to Virginia's boudoir, he permitted the boy to stick around. Eventually Chick was recruited for morning room service, bringing coffee or cigarettes or anything else the lovers wanted. Chick's pockets were soon swollen with currency, and when he became old enough to drive, The Bug gave him a new Cadillac convertible.

Because Siegel was still pretending to be a family man, devoted to home, wife, and daughters, he and Virginia had to be nocturnal creatures, staying where they thought they were not likely to be caught.

At one time or another, before they were able to drop the masquerade once and for all, they spent time at the following widely known Hollywood and Beverly Hills addresses:

The venerable Chateau Marmont (apartment-hotel) on Sunset Boulevard, where they had apartment 6-D and were known as Mr. and Mrs. James Hill and paid $24 a day.

The Town House on Wilshire Boulevard, where Virginia gave whisky to the employees and tipped them $20 at a time.

The Ambassador Hotel, where Virginia had a suite that cost her $1200 for a few days.

Falcon's Lair, the former home of movie idol Rudolph Valentino, where she "boarded" for awhile as a guest of owner Juan Romero.

A penthouse in the Sunset Plaza Apartments.

A penthouse at 10814 Wilshire Boulevard.

A large house at 1720 Coldwater Canyon Drive, not far from the Raft home, which she rented for $385 a month, plus utilities.

A mansion at 810 N. Linden Drive, which Virginia rented from Juan Romero.

The George Raft home on Coldwater Canyon Drive in Beverly Hills.

In most of the establishments where Virginia bedded down with Ben Siegel, some, of course, where they only stayed a day or two, she used her first name when registering, but had a variety of last name aliases. The WANTED poster eventually issued by the Federal Government listed twenty-one different identities by which she was known. Her favorites were Virginia Norma Hall, Virginia Herman, Virginia Onie D'Algy (Onie was her real first name), Virginia Gonzales, and Onie Virginia Hall.

But under any name, Virginia was the best known of the nonprofessional Hollywood big spenders. The late Hedda Hopper, who had regular reports from her espionage network on Virginia and other people, once told me: "What I remember about this girl is that she had the swingingest parties in town, and had a purse so full of new hundred dollar bills that at least one Wilshire Boulevard store thought they were counterfeit. Imagine their embarrassment when they kept Virginia waiting while they had one of these bills checked, and it turned out to be good. Virginia walked out and never went back there again."

With the exception of the nightclub parties, none of Virginia's spending was tasteless. She bought jewelry from Lackritz and from Reingold, including at least one $15,000 diamond ring. Her wardrobe, including $3500 evening gowns, was created for her by Howard Greer, a movie fashion favorite. Greer once acknowledged that Virginia paid him $43,000 in a little more than two years, but Chick says this was less than ten percent of her actual cash expenditures for clothing.

She always had more than a hundred pairs of shoes; and her furs included no less than four mink coats, half a dozen mink stoles, one ermine, one sable valued at $5000, and two Persian lamb coats. She had her own English bone china, crystal glassware, and a sterling silver service for twelve, carefully carted from one apartment to another. Her supply of sweaters, suits, and sports clothes, most of them imported from London, was big enough to stock a small store.

She drove a Cadillac convertible, buying a new model every year, and would not willingly drive any other make. Once, when her own car was being serviced, she suddenly remembered a dinner date at the Beverly Hills Hotel, and she asked Siegel to get her another Cadillac for the evening.

Having none himself, Siegel called Mickey Cohen, whose car was as well known as the LaBrea tar pits, and asked him to let Virginia borrow it.

"What for?" Mickey demanded.

"She needs it, and that's reason enough."

Mickey reluctantly delivered the gleaming car to Siegel, Virginia drove it to the party and, at 2 A.M., had to go home in a taxi. Someone had stolen Mickey's car from the hotel garage, and it took two days for the police to find it.

Senator Kefauver could be forgiven for being a little snappish with Virginia when she testified under oath that her annual income averaged $16,000 a year—from horse race bets—and that her material possessions, including the items just listed, were gifts from admirers.

"When I was with Ben," she said on the stand, "he bought me everything."

Chick Hill, who traveled with her for years, reluctantly says that whatever she got from her gangster lover was pin money compared to the fabulous flow of cash from Joe Epstein. Chick does remember that when Virginia wanted a little winter place in Florida, Siegel generously offered to put up the down payment.

Virginia picked out a furnished house on Sunset Island No. 1 at Miami Beach. The place was owned by Randolph and Catherine Hearst (he later became President of Hearst Consolidated Publications) and was priced at $49,500. "Catherine and I thought Miss Hill was a nice old lady from Pasadena," Hearst told me. "Instead, much to the embarrassment of the realty company, she turned out to be the notorious Virginia Hill, girl friend of Bugsy Siegel."

Siegel supplied $30,000 in cash, and Virginia made up the difference with a first mortgage on which the payments were $180 a month. It was an expensive toy because Virginia rarely used the place, and did not move her possessions into the house until the dread day when she fled there believing the mob gunmen planned to kill her.

Convinced that the gunmen would show up any minute, Virginia called in electricians who installed a battery of floodlights around the house and grounds, with inside control buttons. Photoelectric cells were placed at strategic points so that any stranger walking through the grounds would automatically set off a noisy alarm and bathe the area with 500 watt lamps. Not trusting the police, Virginia also hired Ed Bishop, head of a private detective organization called Florida Investigation Associates, to post a twenty-four hour guard.

Miami Beach Police Chief Phil Short, who soon learned what Virginia was doing in her fortress, was naturally uneasy about it. He finally made a formal call at the house, and told her he didn't like the setup, and wanted no guns popping in the neighborhood.

"We keep things under control here," he said, "and this is bad for the town."

"I suggest you mind your own business," Virginia replied. "I can take care of myself."

Chief Short lost his temper at that point. "Okay, Miss Hill," he said. "But I have one thing to say. If you're going to get killed —get killed in California, not here."

Actually, aside from the contribution toward the Miami house, Siegel was done an injustice when Virginia told Kefauver that he gave her "everything." For many years Virginia frittered away annually perhaps five times as much money as Siegel could gather in a year. She was overly generous with friends, and impulsively gave them cars, mink coats, jewelry, cash, and other presents.

She once heard from Siegel that one of his charities was the Jewish Home for the Aged in Los Angeles, and when the sponsors hosted a fund-raising luncheon there one winter day Virginia was among the guests. When the chairman called for contributions to the Mary Pickford Bungalow, to be built on the institution's grounds on South Boyle Avenue, Virginia dipped into her mobile safe deposit box, and came up with $1000 in currency. The newspaper reports the next day said that Virginia's almost melodramatic gesture was "one of the striking moments" of the program. She was only identified as a Miss Virginia Hill, naturally, because her underworld background was not known to the good ladies of the Jewish Home.

There can never be any full accounting of the cash Virginia received and spent during those spectacular years. Chick Hill estimates that she must have taken in as much as $5,000,000, but she never bothered to invest any of it in stocks, real estate, or anything except fun.

She did maintain bank accounts in New York, Chicago, Los Angeles, and elsewhere so she could write checks for services rendered. In one twelve-month period her checks on just one Beverly Hills account totaled $10,000, most of them endorsed or cashed by Juan Romero, Miguelito Valdez, and assorted stores and hotels.

During that same period she or Joe Epstein sent forty-seven Western Union money orders to her mother in Marietta, Georgia, the amounts ranging from $20 to $2200. But beyond these bank accounts and their relatively trivial deposits and withdrawals and other records, there was no official trace of the big money she got or where it went. She was not being mendacious with Senator Kefauver about her horse race bets. She was merely understating the size of her wagers.

Chick recalls one afternoon when he was asleep in the Seneca Hotel in Chicago, where he and Virginia were on a temporary visit. She rushed into his room, jarred him awake and stuffed $12,000 into his hand.

"Ben just called me about a horse at Santa Anita!" she said excitedly. "Take this money and bet it. And hurry—it's only fifteen minutes to post time."

"Where'll I bet it? With Joe?"

"Don't be stupid, Chick. Book it at Charlie's. You've been there before. Get going!"

Chick scrambled into his clothes, drove to the bookie's so fast that he dented another car's fender as he turned a corner, and got the bet down. The horse won and Chick was back in the apartment thirty minutes later with $30,000 almost spilling out of his pockets.

Like so many other races on which Virginia and Chick made large wagers when Siegel gave them the tip, this Santa Anita event was fixed. It may be disillusioning to the honest better, but Mickey Cohen once said that the mob needs only one or two fixed races or fights a year to make a major financial killing. Although Siegel's diaries showed losing bets on various events now and then, the amounts involved were relatively insignificant. He never lost the big ones.

Any cash Virginia picked up on these occasional bets was just so much gravy. She did not need horse races or anything else as long as the money flowed in from Chicago—a green river never out of touch.

At first the money came by registered or special delivery letter. Some times it was a Western Union money order or an air express package. After the Segoviano theft in Mexico, Epstein no longer trusted the mails, and the cash was sent to Virginia through Chick, or some personal friend. In the United States at a later stage, when Virginia discovered that she was being investigated by the Internal Revenue Service, she had the money delivered to her personal maid, Delle Gordon, or had it shipped to her in shoe boxes labeled RX–LOTION. At times Epstein brought it to her himself, flying thousands of miles to stay an hour or two.

Only one outsider, reporter Florabel Muir, ever actually saw a money package delivered. Miss Muir says she was in Westmore's beauty salon one afternoon before Virginia came in, and saw a package addressed to her from a J. Epstein in Chicago. "I hung around to learn what the package contained," Miss Muir wrote in her book.* "When she opened it I heard her telling the manicurist

******Headline Happy*** (Holt, Rinehart and Winston, Inc.)**

that someone had sent her ten one-thousand dollar bills. She asked Perc Westmore to change one of the bills . . . and handed fifty dollar tips all around."

As time went on, though, Virginia made arrangements to have the big sums—$10,000 or more—personally delivered to Chick.

When word came from Chicago, Chick would go to the airport in Los Angeles, meet Epstein as he debarked from his plane, and receive an envelope with the cash. In almost every case Epstein immediately took the next flight back to Chicago, and Chick gave the envelope to his sister. Once in Mexico he counted $50,000 in an envelope handed to him at the airport by Epstein.

"I spent half my life going to airports in Las Vegas, Los Angeles, New Orleans and other cities as a money messenger," Chick said. Occasionally, because he was not above a little larceny, Chick extracted $500 or $1000 for himself, and gave Virginia the rest. "She never knew exactly how much there would be," he has said, "and she never missed it." Eventually Virginia was airily contemptuous of her golden goose, and was not above cheating Epstein or lying to him just for the hell of it.

On one occasion, when she unexpectedly ran out of cash, she phoned Epstein with a sob in her voice and said that Chick had been seriously injured in an auto accident. He would be crippled for life, she said, unless he could have an immediate operation by a noted and expensive Los Angeles surgeon. Epstein promptly sent her $10,000, and she and Chick laughed themselves silly.

The question inevitably came up: "Why did Epstein send Virginia these enormous sums all those years? Senator Kefauver and his investigators looked for the answer and got nowhere. Government agents spent endless hours trying to track down the source of the money and a reasonable explanation for its one-way route into Virginia's hands. It was suggested that Virginia had a piece of Epstein's bookie operation. Columnists Jack Lait and Lee Mortimer both said that Virginia was a female gangster, in effect, getting her share of the national rackets. Others guessed that she was a blackmail artist who demanded payoffs in exchange for her silence.

Virgil Peterson, director of the Chicago Crime Commission, has considered the possibility that Virginia was a front for the big gambling interests. Noting that Epstein sent money to Virginia even while she was living with Ben Siegel and other men, he said: "One's credulity is somewhat taxed when he is asked to believe that Epstein continued to furnish Virginia large sums of money solely out of his love for her." One Federal agent believes that originally Virginia made a fortune gambling on fixed events, and stashed it away. Later, he is convinced, she invested in international black market and hijack operations, and kept an apartment in Zurich, Switzerland, to direct these interests.

Only two people—Epstein and Virginia—knew the truth. Epstein, who has been questioned so many times that he begins to twitch at the mere sight of a briefcase, hasn't contributed anything very conclusive. He was conspicuously missing when Senator Kefauver's agents tried to hand him a subpoena, and the Committee counsel, Rudolph Halley, testily said to Virginia: "He [Epstein] appears to be a little elusive. Where would you suggest I find him?"

"Well," Virginia said coyly, "I would call the Clover Bar and ask if he was around."

"That is not a very good way for a Senate Committee to reach a witness . . . to call the Clover Bar . . . is it?"

"Well . . . that's the way I found him."

"Doesn't Joe Epstein have a phone or a place of business?"

"If he has a place of business," Virginia replied, "I never heard of it."

"He must have a home," Halley said, showing some anger.

Virginia shifted slightly in her chair, and tilted her face toward the television cameras. "Oh, he says he has some books," she said. "I used to see him working on books."

Virginia must have stirred up guffaws around the room because her answer was as near as she came to the truth. Joe Epstein had books all right—and a couple of hundred telephones, too. He had then what is reputed to be the largest bookie layoff operation in the world.

Epstein has consistently claimed that all the money Virginia got was her own. He had to say that—or explain where he got it. He once gave a statement under oath to Ray McCarthy, special agent for the California State Bureau of Criminal Investigation, in which he said he was merely a caretaker for Virginia's funds, and maintained a safe deposit box for her in a bank at 33 North La-

Salle Street in Chicago. When Virginia wanted cash, he said, he'd get it out of the box.

And what did Virginia say? In 1965, after years of stubborn silence, an angered and embittered Virginia at last got it off her mind. I found her in Salzburg, Austria, and this is what she said on the overseas telephone: "Epstein gave me all the money I ever had. I hated him. He never gave me any peace. I know hundreds of women in America who were kept by men. Why don't they pay taxes? If they're going to put me in jail for that why don't they put the rest of them? Epstein told me how much tax to pay. He is the one. I took money from no one else. He shoved it down my throat. He always told me if anything happened he could explain it. He's the one. He annoyed me all my life, since I was seventeen years old. Two years ago I told him to go to hell when he tried to get me back. Why doesn't he start talking? I think he could do a little explaining. He's the one."

Chick was standing beside me as Virginia and I talked, and after we hung up I told him what she had said.

"How about that, Chick?" I asked. "Why did he keep on sending her money if she hated him?"

"I don't think he really knows," Chick replied. "My brother Billy and I had dinner with him in Las Vegas one night, and I asked him. He said he had been helping her for so long that he just got into the habit. He didn't know why, or why not. He just said he had her when she was seventeen and he felt sorry for her and he was going to keep on sending it. Maybe he felt guilty about her."

Perhaps she did hate him. Perhaps he did love her—until Bugsy Siegel came on the scene. But hate or love made no difference. The money kept coming from Chicago, and she got it and spent it wherever she was. She thought it would last forever.

CHAPTER FOURTEEN

When World War II started, and American men were fighting to protect the liberties that made it possible for Bugsy Siegel to stay out of prison, the gang chief was busy searching for new rackets that would give him more money and power. He was not interested in flag waving, nor even a fake patriotic attempt to get into uniform. He not only thought he was too old for active duty—he was thirty-five when the United States entered the war—but he knew the Armed Services would have no part of a man with his record.

Ironically, the war years, when money was loose, made it possible for Ben Siegel to spread his criminal empire far beyond his dreams. In Los Angeles, in a warehouse on Antonio Avenue, there was $6,000,000 worth of surplus and salvage material owned by a firm called California Metals Company. Ostensibly it was a reputable firm, like so many groups which handled salvage material during the war, and the stock had been bought from the Lockheed Company at eleven cents on the dollar. A police checkup disclosed that California Metals was organized and financed by Ben Siegel and the eastern mob. The Bug's operating partner was a handsome silver-haired Russian named Aaron Smehoff who called himself Allen Smiley.

Smiley, whose FBI record No. 1-306-286 fills three pages, starting with a robbery in 1926 which sent him to the Preston, California Reformatory, was and still is a suave, smooth-talking adventurer whose destiny was to become irrevocably linked with Ben Siegel's.

While Smiley's salesmen were busy unloading the stored materials, Siegel and Little Moe Sedway were signing up hundreds of new customers for the gang's Trans-America race wire service. There was nothing delicate about these signups at $150 a week for each wire service phone used by the bookie. Many of the joints were already taking the Continental wire, operated out of Chicago by James Ragen, and they could barely afford to duplicate the service. But Siegel, with the muscle furnished by the ominous Jack Dragna and Mickey Cohen combine (Mickey has since admitted they were Siegel's chief lieutenants) was ruthless with the customers. They would buy his wire—or else.

In Arizona the bookies were getting a similar pushing around from a gangling, thick-skinned hoodlum named Gus Greenbaum, who took orders from Siegel. Greenbaum used both muscle and graft.

When Mickey Cohen made the mistake of boasting about his crimes with a microphone in front of his scowling face, he said:

"Listen, Ben Siegel and I sat in an office in Phoenix and I heard a man deal with a Congressman in Washington and some Senators. He had maybe ten guys working for him in his office in downtown Phoenix, and it had kitchens and everything else.

"It was air-conditioned, and here was the tops in our government doing business with the underworld. Placing bets and talking, and actually they were dealing and Siegel had a piece of this. Like this guy would say: 'Senator, take this advice and make this move.' He was a part of the underworld and advising a Senator."

I asked Mickey if the man was an Arizona or California Senator. And he replied:

"There were so many of them. I sat there amazed. I was still a punk, you know. There was some high muckety-mucks that came into the office at different times and had lunch—it was air-conditioned, the most beautiful thing you ever seen. He had three guys working in the kitchen alone. I was down there about eight months, on the lam after the Brophy beating. What the hell, how are you going to clean up a thing like this when the tops in the lawmakers are in on it?"

A fair question.

Mickey's mysterious operator in Phoenix, of course, was Gus Greenbaum, Ben Siegel's protégé. And later, when there was an urgent need for his hard-knuckled services in Las Vegas, Greenbaum pulled up roots in Phoenix and moved to Nevada. But he kept the Phoenix connections going, and that was to be a fatal mistake.

Phoenix was only a detour for Siegel. He had Greenbaum under control there, and anyway the prospects in Nevada were brighter. With Sedway as a combined scout and messenger boy, Siegel went into downtown Las Vegas. It looked like the Promised Land. For many years Las Vegas was a grubby desert orphan alongside Reno in the northern end of the state, but when the mob's money men considered the proximity of millions of potential Los Angeles patrons they began to expand their network.

The California state line was only forty-two miles away, a fast, easy drive to Los Angeles. Union Pacific trains came through the town every day, and even before the jet age, any airliner could make the trip from Los Angeles in an hour and a half.

One of Siegel's first investments was in the Northern Club, and in exchange for a piece of the action he made Sedway his front man on the premises to check the income. As time went on, and the take increased, Siegel summoned Sollie Solloway, a Los Angeles man who had married his sister, Bessie, Gus Greenbaum and Dave Berman, a gunman out of Sing Sing. All were given a percentage of Siegel's Las Vegas investments which, at one time or another, included the Frontier Turf Club, the Las Vegas Club, the El Cortez Hotel, the El Dorado Club and the Golden Nugget, with Siegel's share running from 25 percent to full ownership.

While these assorted enterprises were pouring money into Siegel's pockets (his income from the race wire service alone was estimated at $25,000 a month) he also had some minor receipts in Los Angeles. He owned 5 percent of the Tijuana racetrack; a piece of the Clover Club, an illegal gaming room in Hollywood where the movie people were regularly trimmed for huge sums; and he was playing the stock market through the brokerage firm of A. W. Norris & Co.

There was never any certain method of tracing Siegel's passage through this bewildering complex of money juggling, and after the disastrous troubles when his daily diaries were found during the Big Greenie arrest he simply stopped keeping books of any kind.

Chick Hill says Siegel must have been taking in a minimum of $500,000 a year, but he never gave the true totals to his various accountants. His expenses were enormous and because he was a compulsive gambler who never let a day pass without a bet of some kind, he was always running short of cash. He borrowed money, paid it back, borrowed it again.

Some of his more outspoken friends referred to his personal bets as penny-ante caliber, and suggested they were not in keeping with his status as a big operator. "Oh hell," Siegel laughed, "They're fun and they help the days go faster."

But there was one day, in May 1944, when Siegel's fun bets made the day go too fast. Siegel, George Raft, and Joe Moll were in Allen Smiley's apartment in the Sunset Towers that morning. Raft had just returned from a USO tour, entertaining American troops overseas, and it was the first time he had seen his pal in months. They had the *Racing Form* and other racing sheets, and were sitting around the living room making substantial bets on horses at Churchill Downs in Kentucky.

Siegel was on the phone when the apartment door burst open; the unwelcome caller turned out to be Captain William Deal of the Sheriff's vice squad. Because the apartment house was in unincorporated territory on the Sunset Strip, Captain Deal had proper jurisdiction and he promptly advised Siegel and Smiley that they were under arrest.

"What for?" Siegel growled.

"Bookmaking," Captain Deal said.

He jerked the phone from Siegel's hand, and ripped it loose from the wall connection box.

"You got a hell of a nerve," Siegel said. "We're not booking bets. We're *making* bets of our own."

"C'mon." The Captain was plainly impatient. "We'll take a ride."

Raft says he thought Deal's surprise visit was a deliberate roust, and he was angry. "Take me down, too," he said.

"You stay out of this, Raft," the officer said.

"But I was betting, too."

"Sure you were. With Smiley and Siegel booking 'em for you."

This ignominious arrest was considered a loss of face for Ben

Siegel by his fellow racketeers in Los Angeles, primarily because he didn't seem to have enough money to fix it. He was not only charged with bookmaking, but there was an added conspiracy charge, which was a felony, and thus a threat of a trip to San Quentin.

When the two defendants went to court before Justice Cecil Holland not long afterward, they were represented by the distinguished Isaac Pacht, a former Superior Court judge and member of the State Parole Board. There were stormy scenes in the courtroom that morning, with George Raft deliberately baiting Captain Deal from the witness stand. Raft had been warned by his movie employers to stay away from the trial on the grounds that an admitted friendship with The Bug could damage his screen career.

But he went anyway, posed for pictures with his arm around the gangster, and testified that neither Siegel nor Smiley were booking bets. Producer Mark Hellinger was there, too, in his "uniform" of dark blue shirt and white necktie, and he said under oath that Bugsy was "a man of good moral character." Before the session ended, the prosecutor agreed to drop the felony charge if Siegel and Smiley would plead guilty on the bookmaking count. They agreed, and were fined $250.

Hollywood executives conceded that Raft made a strong gesture when he stood up for Ben Siegel, thus risking his professional future. But Raft's box office appeal actually improved because the public was convinced he was really a gangster himself. He had played so many underworld roles that some people were afraid of him on his personal appearance tours, and there were usually detectives on hand to make notes on any hoodlum friends he might have around.

While the bookmaking affair left Raft unharmed, it upset Ben Siegel. He began to wonder if Los Angeles was getting too hot for him. He knew he couldn't buy a hamburger in Beverly Hills without having some stoolie report it to Police Chief Anderson. He was *persona non grata* to the Sheriff's office, and he was convinced that Internal Revenue agents were watching his bank accounts.

He began to think about selling the Delfern Avenue house. He mulled over the idea of getting a divorce from Esta, and taking Virginia Hill to Nevada. In Las Vegas he could handle the cops.

He could be somebody. Virginia would like that. She was hungry with ambition, too.

Virginia Hill always needed men. Years ago, when she was trying to explain her fun-loving philosophy to the Kefauver Committee, she said: "The fellows I went with . . . if you wanted to have a good time, had a party." Not being totally conversant with her argot, the Committee members may have thought she was referring to the kind of party which is a social gathering, or entertainment for a group. But a party in her lexicon was simply going to bed with a man. She also needed men to take her to dinner, to nightclubs, on shopping excursions, or trips here and there. Even while she was Ben Siegel's mistress, she was almost never without a date.

In her schizophrenic kind of morality she saw no wrong in practicing the art of love—and she was proud of her skill—nor in having men around to be her escorts when Siegel was out of town. But she was rigid in her basic code of behavior, believing, for instance, that a friend should never betray you, that it was good manners to thank people for their courtesies or kindnesses, and that loyalty was a prime virtue. She also believed—as would be demonstrated in violent fashion—that if an enemy worked you over with knuckles or a knife or a gun, that you hit back with the same weapons or anything else that was handy.

The young unattached men of Hollywood found Virginia an exciting, provocative girl who was almost always an item for the columns, and they pursued her wherever she was. During the summer of 1944, on one of her frequent excursions to New York, Virginia met Carl Laemmle, Jr., and for awhile she forgot all the other young men around. Laemmle, who had inherited a multimillion dollar fortune from his father, one of the original movie pioneers, was a bachelor of whom Lee Mortimer once wrote: "The most attractive women in Hollywood, which means at least some of the most beautiful ladies in the world, had been hunting him like a fox for years and getting nowhere." Mortimer claimed he introduced Virginia to Laemmle at the Aqueduct racetrack, although neither of the principals could recall exactly where and how they met.

When Laemmle returned to Hollywood in July—he was then living in Beverly Hills and Virginia was in a rented house on Coldwater Canyon Road—he began a determined courtship. Between June and December his gifts to Virginia included the following:

A War Bond	$750
A diamond bracelet	$750
An antique chest	$300
Silver figurines	$ 50
One rug	$400
One set of dishes	$400

He also escorted her to theaters, restaurants, and nightclubs, more or less regularly, and he later estimated that this nocturnal entertainment cost him about $3000 for a five-month-period.

Actually, Virginia was amused and often irritated by Laemmle's ardent chase, and there were times when she could be incredibly cruel. She conspired with Chick, when Laemmle came to her house, to make him think the place was suddenly surrounded by gang killers. Chick would switch off all the lights in the house and scuttle from room to room making ominous sounds while Virginia cowered in pretended fear.

At one point Laemmle gave her a bracelet engraved: "I Love You"—a tender gesture which she treated with contempt, saying: "Why, the corny jerk." And with that she took the bauble and flushed it down the toilet. Another time, while Chick was driving the couple home, Virginia and Laemmle suddenly began quarreling over some trifle. In a characteristic detonation Virginia pulled off a pair of earrings he had given her, bruising her skin with the violent jerk, and heaved them out the car window.

An hour or so later George Raft, coming home late, saw a man on his hands and knees in the gutter. In the beam of his headlights, Raft recognized him as Laemmle, and called out: "Hey, Junior, what the hell are you doing there?"

"Looking for some earrings," Laemmle replied glumly. "I had a fight with Virginia and she threw them out of the car."

Raft does not recall whether or not Laemmle found the lost gems, but Chick says that turbulent evening marked the death of their romance, and Laemmle never saw her again.

Life brought good news to many people in 1944. Kathleen

Windsor sold a million copies of *Forever Amber*. Bing Crosby won an Oscar for his role in *Going My Way*, Franklin Delano Roosevelt won an unprecedented fourth term in the White House, and Paris was liberated. The U.S. Navy destroyed the Japanese fleet, a costly railroad strike was ended, and the Green Bay Packers won the professional football crown for the third time.

None of these things mattered very much to Ben Siegel, because he and the people in his world had problems of their own. Virginia Hill, for instance, seemed extremely restless, and was not available when he needed her. He missed her by one day in Mexico City. She next turned up in New York where she saw Frank Costello and Joey Adonis, and prepared, with her own hands, a gourmet breakfast for them. Siegel naturally got the word that she had seen Joey A. again, and he seethed with jealousy. Shortly afterward, when Virginia chose to be incognito for a week, and was George Raft's secret guest at his home, Siegel was on the phone night and day demanding to know whether she had been entertaining any men.

Occasionally, just to make sure Raft was telling the truth, Siegel would show up unannounced late at night, and would make love to Virginia on her satin sheets, and talk about his big dream for her.

He had already decided to sell the Delfern Avenue mansion, and when it was placed on the market at a price half its real value, the first potential buyer on the scene was movie star Loretta Young. She and her husband, Tom Lewis, then a Colonel in command of the Armed Forces Radio Service, were delighted with the luxurious house and grounds and made a cash deposit of $8500 on the agreed price of $85,000.

They had the usual termite inspection, and the examiners found that Bugsy's house had more than one bug in it. They estimated that it would cost $350 to exterminate the termites in the cellar, and Loretta and her husband asked Siegel to pay for it.

"Like hell I will," Siegel said.

"Termites are like waving a red flag at me," Miss Young later said. "Termites are dangerous for my money."

But Siegel was adamant, and when the actress canceled her offer, as she had a legal right to do, the gangster was black with frustration, and filed an $85,000 damage suit. Superior Judge Carl Stutsman heard the case and agreed with Loretta that bugs in the basement would make anyone uneasy, and Siegel lost out. With any client other than the beautiful movie star, Siegel might have called in his musclemen and dented her makeup here and there. Instead he took the suit to a higher level, and after two years of litigation the District Court of Appeals turned him down.

Meanwhile, still trying to unload the house, Siegel found another buyer. Just before he vacated the house, Siegel phoned Raft.

"Georgie," he said, "I'm pulling out of here, and I've got some beautiful garden stuff you ought to see."

When Raft got there, Siegel had collected some redwood barbecue benches, a lawnmower, a couple of shovels and other outdoor items, all well worn.

"You can use these things, Georgie," he said.

"What for?" Raft asked. "I've got all those tools already, and I got a gardener who comes around twice a week with his own equipment."

"You're going to buy 'em anyway," Siegel said. "I'll sell 'em cheap. Five bills."

"Five hundred bucks for this junk?" Raft protested. "It isn't worth twenty."

"Don't argue. Give me the cash and I'll get somebody to deliver the stuff to your house."

Raft reluctantly reached for his wallet and gave the money to Siegel. "Well," he said long afterward, "I know he swindled me. But he was my pal, and I guess he needed it."

CHAPTER FIFTEEN

On a summer day in 1945, Ben Siegel and Little Moe Sedway got into Siegel's powerful new DeSoto station wagon, and headed out of Las Vegas on U.S. Highway 91. The temperature was touching 115 degrees, and to the south the 5000-foot peak of Black Mountain seemed to be moving against the shimmering haze of the sky. The creosote bushes, a sea of yellow foam during blossom time in the spring, now stood motionless and bare on the hot sand. The salt bushes and the samphire were naked on the alkali flats, and the Panamint rattlers lay sluggishly against the rocks. The venomous tarantulas were hiding in their holes, and occasionally a brown road runner darted across the sand, head down, searching for lizard prey.

Ben Siegel saw none of these living symbols of the desert land, for his mind was surging with a daring idea.

"Where in hell are we going, Ben?" Little Moe asked.

"I got something to show you," Siegel said.

He swerved the car now and then to avoid a tumbleweed, and he said nothing as they passed the Frontier and El Rancho Vegas motels, then the last outposts at the city's edge. Both these wayside inns were small and unpretentious, built like oversize western ranch houses and decorated with old wagon wheels, steer horns, cattle brands burned into wood, and other conventional emblems of the pioneer days. But at the time they were the best the Strip could offer bored and weary travelers pushing across the forsaken land into Las Vegas, the new boom town of the West, or away from its devouring tables and clanking rows of slots on the road back to California.

At best, Las Vegas was then a sort of cowpoke town where gambling was just another Saturday night diversion for ranchers, toothless and bearded prospectors, workers from nearby Boulder Dam, or tourists who wanted to pick up a tan in the desert sun.

The population was not much more than 10,000 and new homes were just beginning to take shape in the suburb of North Las Vegas. Paiute Indians occasionally wandered through the dusty downtown streets, and it was not uncommon to see a wrinkled squaw with a baby in a basket on her back.

The incoming tide of strangers, which would soon swell to a torrent, had just begun to lap at the edges of the town. Prostitution was a legal attraction in what was then known as "Block 16," and most of the gambling halls—including the Golden Nugget and the Frontier Club—were clustered within a two block area near Fremont and Second streets.

There was gambling money, but at the time it was a mere trickle.

The high-rollers got their action in Reno at the other end of the state, and the stream of planes and trains and cars from Los Angeles had not yet begun to move across the vast stretches of sand.

But Ben Siegel knew the suckers were there, with their itching hands and their pockets full of money. And he would lead them to Las Vegas. Soon.

Siegel had driven about seven miles from Fremont Street in Las Vegas when he came to a stop on the sandy shoulder of the road and said: "Well, here it is, Moe."

Sedway saw a couple of dilapidated buildings, grayed and pocked by the desert winds and sand, and on one of them was a forlorn and faded sign which said: MOTEL. Sedway, who had long suffered from a weakened heart, was panting in the dry and fiery air as he glanced out the window.

"For God's sake, Ben," he puffed, "What is it?"

Siegel's tanned face was alight, and he was obviously bursting with excitement. "Thirty acres, Moe," he exclaimed. "Thirty acres for a few nickels and dimes."

"Thirty acres of nothing," Sedway grunted.

"Moe . . . ," Siegel said, "we're going to buy this hunk of

land. And we're going to build the goddamndest biggest hotel and casino you ever saw."

"You must be nuts."

Siegel ignored the remark. "I can see it now," he said dreamily. "Ben Siegel's Flamingo—that's what I'm going to call it. I'm gonna have a garden and a big pool and a first-class hotel. We're going to make Reno look like a whistle stop."

"But for Christ's sake, Ben!" Sedway said, suddenly realizing Siegel was serious. "Seven miles out of town. Not a tree in sight, and nothing but bugs and coyotes and heat."

"It might even cost two million bucks," Siegel said. "The suckers will drive hundreds of miles just to see it. That's it, Moe." He started the engine, stirring up a halo of dust as he swung across the road, and headed back to town.

The juggling and the scheming began on September 13, 1945, when Margaret A. Folsom, a Las Vegas widow whose rickety and dusty little motel had failed miserably, quitclaimed her thirty acres of land to Little Moe Sedway, fronting for Siegel. Two months later Sedway quitclaimed the same property to Attorney Greg Bautzer, a young Los Angeles attorney who represented many movie stars. Bautzer, then acting on behalf of Billy Wilkerson of the Hollywood *Reporter*, who had been drawn into the project by Siegel, deeded the land to the Nevada Projects Corporation.

No one except the principals ever knew what the land cost, but it can be assumed that Siegel got it for the "few nickels and dimes" he had mentioned. When Siegel consulted Architects Richard Stadelman and George Russell of Los Angeles about his plan, he found out what it would cost and he knew he couldn't swing it alone.

He chose to sell stock to a group of handpicked investors. The Corporation printed certificates for both preferred and common stock, but the sale was limited to the common stock, with a par value of $250 a share, though the true value was nearer $1000. The original investors and their shares included:

Ben Siegel	195
Meyer Lansky, Siegel's partner in the old Bug-Meyer mob	100

Morris Rosen, a reformed burglar from New York, convicted bookmaker and Costello representative	22.5
Louis Pokross, a member of the Bug-Meyer mob	175
Allen Smiley	15
Samuel Rothberg of American Distillers	150
C. Harry Rothberg of New York, a brother of Samuel Rothberg	95
Joe Ross, Siegel's Beverly Hills attorney	45
Hyman Abrahams	22.5
Sollie Soloway, Siegel's brother-in-law	20
Billy Wilkerson	125
Allen A. Block	10
Charles L. Straus, Phoenix banker	100

There was one additional certificate issued, but the holder was never identified. The 1075 shares announced represented a total investment of about $1,000,000, and Siegel wasted no time getting started. In the history of building, the construction of the Flamingo probably is unique for the frenzy, the grand larceny and graft, and the accumulated errors that went into its construction.

Ben Siegel was in a constant ferment from the moment ground was broken in December 1945, and in Los Angeles Esta Siegel finally wrote him off as a lost cause. She went to Reno, filed suit for divorce, and left for New York with a decree that included one of the most generous settlements ever made in the divorce capital of the world. Siegel agreed to pay her $600 a week for life, and since the actuarial tables at the time gave her a life expectancy of some 40 years, he was committed to pay out almost $1,500,000. Ironically, only months before the divorce, Esta had loaned her wandering husband $45,000 because he needed every cent he could raise. It never occurred to her, of course, that she would end up holding the bag.

Siegel probably would have signed anything during that delirious period. He engaged the popular Del Webb to build the hotel, though Webb was dubious about obtaining material in the postwar market when priorities still existed. But Siegel, a man obsessed by the dream that would soon be a nightmare, would stop at nothing. Through Wilkerson, who could and did apply strangleholds on movie executives, he got lumber, cement, piping, and other material that came right off the studio lots. He imported wood and marble and similar items from Mexico and other countries, and he went into the black market for huge quantities of scarce items.

His good friend, the late U.S. Senator Pat McCarran, shuffled the priority lists so the Flamingo could get copper, steel, fixtures, tile, and other things not easily available to the average builder. Indeed, the Veterans of Foreign Wars organization in Boulder City, simmering because their members could not get material for new homes, held protest meetings at which they said there was a very strange odor about the Flamingo project.

Siegel ignored the complaints, and showed up early every morning to make sure there was no slowdown. The big trucks thundered down the road to the building site, delivering black market goods. Sometimes they returned late at night, stole the material and resold it to Siegel a day or two later. He paid as much as $50 a day to carpenters, plasterers, and other artisans, flying them in from other cities. He ordered walls and foundations of double thickness, saying: "No goddam wind or earthquake is going to blow this place away. It'll last forever." (There were so many yards of concrete in the building—it was much like a wartime pillbox—that it took an enormous iron ball wrecker three days to knock over one wall during a recent remodeling at the hotel. It required two full days of jackhammer pounding just to tear down one bannister in the old casino room.)

Siegel designed the penthouse suite in the main hotel building for his own use, but unfortunately there was a beam across the ceiling only 5′8″ from the floor. When The Bug realized he would have to duck every time he crossed the room he exploded like a gas tank. "Tear that goddam thing out of here!" he cried.

"That's an expensive job, Mr. Siegel," the job foreman said.

"Never mind the cost," Siegel said. "Get it out."

They got it out—for $22,500.

When the kitchen was being built, Siegel walked in one morning, noticed that the big ovens had a narrow passageway and blurted: "What kind of a layout is this? If you turn around in here you'll fry your ass. Fix it." It was fixed—for $30,000. Siegel decided the boiler room was too small, and it was enlarged at an extra cost of $115,000. Each of the ninety-two hotel rooms had its own private sewer system, and the total plumbing bill—Siegel yelled about that for weeks afterward—exceeded $1,000,000.

Someone made a mistake on the heavy curtains for the main lounge and casino because they turned out to be highly inflammable, and had to be sent back to Los Angeles for chemical fireproofing.

There was only one happy event for Siegel that first summer. The rivalry between the Continental race wire directed by James Ragen in Chicago, and the syndicate's Trans-America service, Siegel's baby in the West, had never been settled. In Chicago, Jake "Greasy Thumb" Guzik and other Capone mob musclemen finally went to Ragen with an offer to "buy in" for $100,000 cash, and retain him as a profit-sharing partner. Ragen was convinced that even if he accepted the offer he would be killed soon afterward, but he told the Capone boys no. He predicted to friends and officials alike that he had the big X on his name. On June 24, while Ben Siegel was relentlessly driving his workers in Las Vegas, Ragen was shredded with shotgun blasts on a Chicago street. He clung to life in the hospital for some six weeks and then, when it appeared that he might survive the shooting, he became violently ill. He died in writhing agony, and an autopsy later showed his body was loaded with mercury. Some unknown Borgia with access to Ragen's room had been regularly dropping poison into his drinks. Ben Siegel and his mob had won another deadly round.

Shakespeare once wrote: "Base men being in love have then a nobility in their natures more than is native in them."

There are men and women living today who never quite understood the deep emotional relationship between Ben Siegel and Virginia Hill. Sometimes they hated, sometimes they loved. But it was not true hate, nor true love as these words are generally understood. These were the surface ripples that others saw, but the real bond between them was nameless, invisible, and, in its own fashion, stronger than any words that came from their tongues.

Once, in a happy schoolboy mood, Siegel wrote a love poem for Virginia, scrawling it down laboriously with a pen, and gave it to her on her birthday. He put it into an envelope on which he had written "To My Sweetheart," and she later told Chick it made her cry. Long afterward, when she was talking to reporters in Florida about Ben Siegel, she said: "You know—he was never as tough as you guys made him—look at this lovely poem he wrote for me." She opened her purse and took it out, the paper now wrinkled and torn, and she started to read it aloud. Then, as though an unseen hand had touched her shoulder, she slowly folded it and put it away, and her eyes froze.

"Oh, the hell with it," she said. "You bums wouldn't get it anyway."

Ben Siegel would never have admitted to any tenderness at all. But he knew—as did Virginia—that their relationship was far more interlocking than mere physical union. He had known a hundred women, and Virginia had long since lost count of the men who had her, but she also knew that she and Ben had something denied to those nameless others. She found a classic little book called *Forever* (Alfred A. Knopf, Inc.), by Mildred Cram, which was to become her private bible, and his, too.

It is a short and charming fantasy, written in 1938, about a man and a woman who, unable to be together in life, believe that they will die, and then be reborn. And in the rebirth they will be lovers for eternity. Virginia carried the little volume everywhere, and she had marked the lines that would be her creed until the end:

> JULIE: If you should go first. . . . And then what if I could never find you again? Or you me?
>
> COLIN: We'll find each other. Somewhere. Somehow. You'll be born knowing about me. Wanting me. And some day we'll come back here.

And on the last page she had underscored the line that meant so much, that she would always believe: "Julie lifted her head. 'This is forever,' she said."

In the fall of 1946 Ben and Virginia flew to Mexico for one day, and were married there. Siegel had bought a ruby and diamond ring, and he slipped it on her finger, and when the Spanish ceremony was over they left there as man and wife. Siegel never mentioned this brief and hasty wedding, and five years passed before Virginia even identified the ring she had. Then she showed it to newspapermen, saying only: "Ben gave me this. It was to be our wedding ring."

The ceremony might have remained a secret if Virginia had not mentioned it in a garrulous mood one day to a friend named Betty Cromwell in Mexico City. Mrs. Cromwell, a Connecticut divorcee who lived in Mexico for many years, was Virginia's most valiant and unswerving defender, refusing to believe that Siegel was a gangster or that Virginia was anything but a misunderstood girl who was crucified by the American press. In 1951, when Mrs. Cromwell was interviewed by American Government agents, she confided the facts about the Siegel-Hill wedding. But the news went no further, and has never before been printed.

Virginia was proud of her ring, though—it cost Ben Siegel $500—and it was her most treasured possession. "I'll never take it off," she said once. "Never." But once she forgot that vow.

The long hot summer was over, and the night winds of fall cooled the vast desert. Far out in the dusty wasteland where once had been only jackrabbits and coyotes, Ben Siegel fumed and cursed with impatience as the Flamingo Hotel took shape against the sky. He had determined to stage the opening on December 26, when Las Vegas would be crowded with Christmas vacationers, but there had been frustrating delays, and it seemed certain that he would not get a piece of the holiday purse until the following year.

During the day, eyes bloodshot from lack of sleep, Siegel prodded and goaded the workmen. He prowled the gaming rooms, picking up cigarette butts and muttering: "I'd like to catch the dirty pig who dropped these." He emptied ashtrays and gathered up stray bits of paper or lint. Once he found a sooty handprint on a wall and yelled for the foreman. "What the hell is this?" he said angrily. "You think you're working in a cheap bar somewhere? This is the Flamingo—and don't forget it!"

Once more he was the dreaded Bugsy and the men on the building crew avoided arguments that might trigger one of his notorious tantrums. It was not that they feared bullets from Siegel himself, because they all knew he carried a gun only when there was a specific need for it. But he was always with such sinister confederates as Hymie Segal, a scowling thug who had done ten years in Sing Sing on a robbery rap; the evil Little Moe Sedway; Dave Berman, and a tough handyman whose real name was John Greenberg, but who was better known to the mob as Fat Irish Green.

Any one of these, who were known collectively as Siegel's "muscle," could be very unpleasant indeed, for this was the period when opposition was crushed with a pistol butt on the skull or a slug between the eyes. There were few men in Siegel's orbit who were not aware of the frayed nerve ends at the time, and Little Moe Sedway found that even he was not immune.

Moe was playing a friendly game of gin with Charlie Resnick at the Health Club, in rooms above the Las Vegas Club, when Hymie Segal stalked in one afternoon. "Moe," he said, "Ben wants to see you."

Little Moe nodded, dealt out another hand, and began sorting the cards. Hymie's lips tightened as though they had been squeezed. His right hand swept down and sent cards and score sheets fluttering halfway across the room.

"Now!" he snarled.

Little Moe stood up, pale and shaking, put on his sports jacket, and silently followed Hymie down the stairs.

The great casino was completed before the end of November, and in Los Angeles Billy Wilkerson hired a talented young press agent named Paul Price to start beating the drums. The cheesecake went into the ovens, and an assembly line of glossy prints poured out for newspaper and magazine editors in every city and town within a five hundred mile range. The half-naked bosomy young maidens not only said "cheese" as shutters were snapped to show a seductive smile, but the inference in their poses was plain to male readers. The ladies were at the Flamingo, and available for lonely high rollers.

There were still no press agents on the payroll in Las Vegas, and Ben Siegel, who knew that publicity was the oxygen of show business, realized that time was running out. One morning he was at the office of the *Review-Journal*, then the only newspaper in Las

Vegas, discussing the problem with Editor Al Cahlan. In the composing room that morning was Henry "Hank" Greenspun, a young Brooklyn-born lawyer who had left New York after he was discharged from the Army and come to Las Vegas to build a future.

As a starter, while he studied for the bar examination to enable him to practice in Nevada, Greenspun had conceived a miniature monthly magazine called *Las Vegas Life*. It was frankly no more than a puff sheet to advertise the night life in town, and it was loaded with girlie pictures. Greenspun's fledgling enterprise was having a bumpy ride, for the golden age of the big budget and big money was still four years away, and during the off-season the downtown casinos were content to catch the relative few who paused there on the grim and lonely ride across the sands. Al Cahlan was showing Siegel around the plant when he saw Greenspun reading proof sheets for *Las Vegas Life*.

"Hank," he said, "do you know Benny Siegel?"

"Glad to meet you, Ben," Greenspun said.

Siegel gave him a beguiling smile, and Greenspun conceded later that the ambitious young gangster had more charms than a witch doctor. "Say," Siegel said, "aren't you the fellow with the little magazine?"

"That's me."

"How much for the back page?"

Greenspun studied Siegel for a moment, knowing that his publication was only two months old and might founder at any moment, and decided to gamble. "Two hundred and fifty," he said.

"In color?"

"Three-fifty," Greenspun said.

"Okay," Siegel said. "I'll take it every month."

That same day Siegel also gave Al Cahlan the Flamingo advertising account and shortly afterward this typed notice appeared on the editorial room bulletin board:

FROM THIS DAY FORWARD MR. SIEGEL OF THE FLAMINGO WILL NEVER BE REFERRED TO AS "BUGSY." MAKE IT BEN OR BENJAMIN.

In December, with the opening less than a month away, Siegel's friend Swifty Morgan suggested, in one of his few serious moments, that Siegel import an assistant manager to help Chuck

Gaskell. Swifty just happened to know about a young man named Dick Chappell, then working at the palatial Fairmont Hotel in San Francisco, and Siegel persuaded him to come to Las Vegas at once. The pressure was on.

News Item—1946

Los Angeles (AP) Benjamin O. Siegel, 30 year old recording company executive, is very tired of explaining that he is not Benjamin "Bugsy" Siegel.

So yesterday, in a petition filed in Superior Court, Benjamin O. Siegel offered to surrender his surname if the court allows him to adopt a new one. He proposes to be known as Benjamin O. Siegert. He says the name similarity has caused him considerable embarrassment.

Chick and Virginia Hill came to Las Vegas in December and, without telling anyone that it was legal, Virginia moved her nightgowns and toothbrush into Siegel's private penthouse. The apartment, known as Suite 401, was on the fourth and top floor of the still unfinished guest rooms building across the garden terrace, and from a balcony she could look down on the blue water of the pool. Virginia was so glad to be living with Siegel that she ordered a Scott radio phonograph from the Penny-Owsley Music Company in Los Angeles, and had it delivered to him, gift wrapped, in Las Vegas. It cost $1129.80, and she paid for it from her inexhaustible cache of $100 bills.

Chick took a room in the El Rancho Motel, and was promised a job as a "robber"—a gaming term for the trusted hands who make regular rounds of the coin-swollen slot machines and take the money to the counting room. Neither Siegel nor Virginia kept track of the cash gifts they gave him, but Chick, who had just turned eighteen, never had less than $1000 cash in his pants pocket. And he would need every nickel of it for the expensive girl hunts that were his favorite sport.

Like so many hoodlums who served their apprenticeship in New York, and were misled by the false halos that went with the Walter Winchell school of name-dropping, Siegel was convinced that one way of achieving respectability was to associate with the men of the press. He tried to buy their favors with costly gifts or outright bribery. There was many a handshake which transferred a crisp new hundred dollar bill, or, for the more sensitive, the currency would be delivered in plain envelope. Cases of whisky were sent to the homes of important newspapermen along with courtesy cards that guaranteed a free ride on everything except the gaming tables and the night shift girls who prospected for business in the casino. Although, when the need was acute, Siegel let it be known he would even pick up the tab for girls.

Believing that names make news and profit, if they are around to be conned, Siegel compiled a handpicked list of movie stars he wanted for the Flamingo's formal opening. Billy Wilkerson, who knew them personally, was persuaded to front for the unveiling and issue the invitations.

Just before Christmas, when Wilkerson dolefully reported that most of the stars had turned him down, Siegel phoned George Raft in a panic.

"Hey, Georgie," he said, "what's the matter with these jerks that they don't want to come for the big party?"

"Well, Ben—"

"Yeah, yeah, I know," Siegel interrupted. "They don't think I'm good enough for 'em. But I'm on a spot, pal. We gotta get somebody. What about all your buddies at MGM? Joan Crawford, Greer Garson, Spencer Tracy, Ronald Colman?"

"I don't like to tell you this, Ben," Raft said. "But old man Hearst has passed the word around the studios that he's against the whole idea, and everybody's been told to stay away."

"The crummy son of a bitch!" Siegel exploded. "What's he got against me?"

"I don't know, Ben."

"What about you?"

"I'll be there. Georgie Jessel's coming up and so is Charlie Coburn."

Siegel terminated the conversation in a fury, and for nearly an hour he seriously considered canceling the affair. But Virginia Hill, who had just received a flaming orange-red $3500 gown created for the occasion by Howard Greer (he called it "The Flamingo" not only for the hotel, but because it was also her nickname) was not to be cheated out of her entrance. "Forget those dumb bastards from Hollywood!" she said angrily. "They'll come around when they hear about the place."

Siegel backed down, and in a mellow mood he summoned Chick and gave him a thousand dollars in cash. "Here, Chick," he said, "take this dough and do some shopping for me in L.A. Get some nice presents for the columnists and people like that. Neckties, shirts. Oh, hell, you know."

Chick flew to Los Angeles, and quickly blew the thousand. He came back to Las Vegas loaded down with packages, but Siegel showed no interest in the gifts and said: "You take care of 'em, Chick." Chick did; he kept most of the stuff for himself.

Just before the opening, the December issue of *Las Vegas Life* came out with Hank Greenspun's first article about Ben Siegel and the Flamingo. It said:

> Youngish, baby-blue eyed Benjamin "Ben" Siegel has spent a great deal of his forty years running around the periphery of big time respectability. The few direct encounters he had with it were either head on or passing through.
> It was obvious after a few years that you don't get in the blue book by making book, so Ben decided to go into the hotel business. Result of this Siegelian course of action is the Flamingo—the world's most lavish conception of hotel resort, casino, cafe and playground all rolled into one.

Siegel, who was unable to read between the lines and didn't know or didn't care that the plug had cost him $350, was so delighted with the story that he summoned Greenspun for lunch and offered him a job as permanent resident press agent for the hotel.

"Thanks for the compliment, Ben," Greenspun said. "But I can't handle two jobs at once—at least not now—and I want to stick with the little magazine."

"That's okay, Hank," Siegel said. "Maybe later. I'm going down to test the big fountain and waterfall at the front entrance."

The waterfall, made of rock, plaster, and lumber, was an ingenious and imposing structure with a circulating pump that would keep the water tumbling around the clock. At night, spotlights would throw color on the spray, and Siegel had boasted that motorists would be able to see it a mile away. When Siegel reached the base he found a grounds keeper waiting.

"All set?" Siegel asked.

"Yes, sir. Except—"

"Except what?" Siegel said impatiently.

"Well, sir," the man replied, "we're gonna have to flush out the damn cat first."

"Cat? Where?"

"In the sump. The cat crawled in there last night and had six kittens, and we'll just have to flood 'em all out of there."

"Listen," Siegel snapped. "You bother those kittens and you just lost a job."

The grounds keeper shrugged and said: "You're the boss, Mr. Siegel. But you won't have a fountain for the opening."

"The hell with the fountain. It can wait."

"I didn't know you were a cat lover, Mr. Siegel."

"I'm not," Siegel said. "I hate 'em. But it's bad luck for a gambler to touch a cat."

And so the fountain valve was kept shut for opening night. Later, remembering that disastrous evening, Hank Greenspun thought Siegel might just as well have bucked the curse. The luck couldn't have been worse.

On the evening of December 26, Ben Siegel appeared in the lobby wearing a sports shirt, with no tie or jacket. Virginia took one withering look at her lover. "You crummy peasant!" she said." Go back and get into a dinner jacket. This is your big night, remember?"

Siegel looked at the shocked faces of guests milling around the lobby, but he turned without a word and went back to the penthouse. When he returned, wearing a dinner jacket and a flower in his lapel, and began the ceremony of opening the casino doors for the first time, there were more employees than customers. It was all too obvious to the staff that they were participating in a monumental flop.

The Constellations Siegel had chartered were empty on the runways in Los Angeles, held there by winter storms. The movie stars Siegel hoped to see were at home, and the half dozen at ringside were not the names that would draw crowds. George Raft had made the 350 mile trip from Los Angeles in his new Cadillac. Monocled Charles Coburn, who was almost seventy then, had traveled by train. Sonny Tufts and George Sanders were there with Georgie Jessel and Jimmy Durante, the Flamingo's first headline act.

In the protocol of Las Vegas, it is almost mandatory for the owners or operators of the major casinos to attend the opening of a new gambling hall. But there is nothing in the rules which says a visiting gambler can't get lucky and take his new rival for every dime in the house bank. It was almost certain that Siegel's competitors in downtown Las Vegas not only conspired to sabotage the Flamingo with whispering campaigns and other subtle weapons, but also hoped to break him with big winnings during those critical first forty-eight hours.

In defense of their operation, the Vegas mob has often sanctified the fiction that the games are honest and that cheaters can't get away with it. Nevertheless, Siegel's casino losses during the opening week were staggering and it does not seem to have been a matter of pure chance. Guy McAfee and Gus Greenbaum, neither of whom had any loving feelings for Siegel, each took him for thousands of dollars. Even McAfee's girl, presumably brought along just to brighten the scenery, could not lose. George Raft emerged as the only pigeon among the high rollers, losing $65,000 in a *chemin de fer* game, but his contribution wasn't enough to balance the disastrous loss.

Ben Siegel was frantic. He switched dice, changed the cards, and moved dealers from table to table like a losing coach desperately switching lineups. The percentages were not only running against him in an unprecedented lopsided fashion, but he was also being clipped by his own dealers and stickmen. Siegel and Chick Hill were standing behind a roulette croupier at one point, perhaps five feet from the table, when Chick saw the man pushing chips to a player although he was not hitting winning numbers. He nudged Siegel, and together they watched the croupier and his confederate perpetrating their obvious swindle.

"You get the pit boss to take him off the table," Chick whispered, "and I'll handle the phony player."

Siegel nodded, as though in agreement, but his mounting anger suddenly took control. "I'll kill the son of a bitch!" he said. He moved quickly behind the croupier and kicked him so hard with his right shoe that the man was catapulted out of his chair. He landed nose first on the felt tabletop, scattering chips like bird seed, and he didn't wait for the next blow. He scrambled across the table, ran out to the road, and was never seen in Las Vegas again.

On the evening of December 27, when the disorganized casino crew showed up for the night shift, George Raft came into the big room and sat down at the *chemin de fer* table.

Siegel saw him sliding into a chair, and greeted him with a scowl. "What are you doing here?" he said curtly.

"Trying to get my money back," Raft said.

"Beat it, Georgie. You're not playing here tonight."

"What's eating you, Ben?"

"I said you're not playing."

"Look, Ben, I stuck my neck out and drove up here from LA because you begged me to," Raft said. "I dropped sixty-five gees last night, and I'm entitled to another shot."

Siegel ignored his friend and glared at the players. "If anybody deals a hand to Raft," he said, "this game's closed for the night." He strode away and Raft, hurt and angry, left his Cadillac at the hotel, took a cab to the airport and caught the first plane back to Los Angeles. That evening one *chemin de fer* player made nine passes with the shoe—a streak that Raft later said could have made him even with the game, and it was weeks before he spoke to Siegel again.

Chick Hill was the next victim of Siegel's petulance. He was in the dollar slot machine section of the casino, stripping the coin boxes, when Siegel walked in. His delicate mouth was twisted, as a choleric baby sulks, and he looked at the cloth bag in Chick's hand.

"What are you doing with those cartwheels?" he said perversely. "Stickin' 'em in your pocket?"

Chick's jaw dropped. "W-h-a-a-t?" he sputtered.

"You heard me," Siegel said. "I ought to take a poke at you."

"What the hell's the matter with you, Ben?" Chick asked. "Just because the joint's a flop you're taking it out on everybody else."

Siegel's right hand shot out suddenly, but Chick ducked and instinctively swung the heavy coin bag. The improvised blackjack hit Siegel's right shoulder, and because he was off balance he toppled over. He sprawled there for a moment, then rose to one knee. The scowl vanished from his dark face, and he began to laugh.

"Forget it, Chick," he said.

"No hard feelings, Ben," Chick said. "I wasn't really sore. I guess it was the old Army training."

Siegel stood up, carefully dusting his expensive suit. "I think both of us better get some sleep," he said. "Nothing like a little sleep to fix things."

And he walked out, slowly, and crossed the garden where some of the casino girls sprawled in the low winter sun on their beach towels. Their swimsuit halters were down below their breasts, and they turned slightly as Siegel walked by, deliberately baring white flesh, and smiling at him. But he did not know they were there, and he took the elevator to his bedroom, and he slept. It did not fix anything.

CHAPTER SIXTEEN

Las Vegas gambling establishments are not charitable institutions. They are in business to separate the customers from their money. They operate on long established odds in their favor, and if the books show a loss, the two most reasonable answers are (1) they're not getting a play or (2) they are being clipped by crooked employees or phony dice or cards used by sharpies.

Siegel, examining the red ink for the first two weeks of operation, was smouldering with the knowledge that the Flamingo's net gaming loss was already touching $300,000. The outstanding bills from contractors and suppliers were formidable, and the building costs were spiraling toward $4,000,000. The hotel rooms were still not ready for overnight guests, and the cost of furnishing each room was estimated at $3500. The casino alone needed fifteen special cops around the clock to keep an eye on the money, the dealers and known cheats, and there were scores of other employees to be paid.

These problems would have been minor if the casino had been crowded with players every night because the law of averages and of gambling odds would work toward a profit. But the pigeons were roosting somewhere else.

It was soon apparent to Siegel that the money hustlers in downtown Las Vegas wanted no part of him and his Flamingo Hotel. They couldn't go in and knock him off with guns, but they could be just as murderous with gossip. They planted whispers that the Flamingo was a hangout for eastern gangsters—which it was—and that honest citizens should double their life insurance if they hung around the hotel too long. Siegel himself was pictured as a violent man who might rap you with a pistol butt just for the fun of it, and when he lost his temper, which was often, the whole town soon heard about it.

One such incident involved Cliff Leonard, a Las Vegas laundry operator who was walking through the lobby with his family one evening after seeing the show. Leonard, a plump and jolly man who was proud of his community, spotted Siegel and impulsively reached out to shake hands.

"Great place, Bugsy!" he said. "You've done a wonderful thing here."

Siegel glared at him and said: "Were you and I ever introduced?"

"No," Leonard replied, still smiling.

"Do you know anybody I know?"

"No, sir," Leonard said, suddenly aware of Siegel's hostility.

"Then who told you to call me Bugsy?"

Leonard fumbled for an answer. "Well—I thought—that is—well—everybody says that's your name."

"You thought wrong!" Siegel snarled. "I never want to see you here again. Get out! Get out!"

Leonard backed away, and Ben Siegel never saw him there again. In time, these episodes, or versions of them, multiplied, and Siegel soon realized that he was being portrayed as an evil man to both townspeople and visitors. He knew that new images are not easily spun, and when Hank Greenspun once asked for approval on a piece he had written called "What makes Benny Siegel Tick?" accompanied by photographs, he refused to let it go out.

"Look, Hank," he said, "I don't want this. You mean well and it's well written. I love it and you're very flattering."

"So what's wrong with it, Ben?"

"You know what will happen. It will come out hoodlum, or noted mobster, and all the good stuff will be gone. Talk about the Flamingo—yes—but forget about Benny Siegel. Every time an article appears it hurts my kids, and it kills me."

Greenspun never wrote another piece in praise of the gangster, nor did any other press agent. Ben Siegel remained an enigma to the Las Vegas public, but his anonymity was still not enough to make the Flamingo popular. There were other factors, too. He had insisted on an all-male staff in the dining room, and people who were used to favorite waitresses in other places had no friendly rapport with the Flamingo's waiters and captains. Bud Bodell, chief of the security force in the hotel at the time, also recalled that the dealers were in white tie and tails—Siegel's conception of elegance—and that no visitors were allowed to wear hats in the casino. "The local people were just plain insulted when we made them take off their hats," he said.

In January 1947, when Siegel saw that he was up against the wall, hundreds of thousands of dollars in the hole, he closed the Flamingo and said he would not reopen until the whole establishment was finished—hotel rooms, pool, gardens, and all.

Virginia Hill, who gradually developed an acute allergy to the desert area, especially a kind of hay fever she got from cactus plants, impulsively packed her bags when Siegel closed the hotel, and went back to Beverly Hills. She said she was sick of taking Benadryl, and promised to come back when the Flamingo was completed. She rented a mansion at 810 North Linden Drive from her friend Juan Romero, and settled down there with her jewels and her incredible wardrobe.

She once said her rent was $500 a month, but Chick Hill, who commuted to the house from Las Vegas, said she actually paid nothing at all. Moreover, she celebrated her liberation from the cactus by buying a $10,000 diamond bracelet from Lackritz in Beverly Hills, and acquired a new Cadillac convertible.

She engaged an interior decorator named Alice Allen to brighten up the Linden Drive house—her bill for advice alone totaled $2638—and spent many more thousands on new furniture, rugs, draperies, a $1200 radio phonograph identical with the one she had sent to Siegel in Las Vegas, and had a wall safe built to hold $100,000 worth of her jewelry.

It was like old times. Beautiful gowns, parties, late hour trips to various nightclubs. And lovers. Outwardly, during this intermittent stay at the Romero house, she was as vivacious and carefree as ever, but Chick and others close to her sensed an acute agitation which was manifested by frequent outbursts.

Barney Ruditsky, a former New York policeman who had

started a private detective agency in Los Angeles, and had been hired by Siegel to run down Los Angeles losers who had left rubber checks at the Flamingo, got an excited phone call from Virginia one evening.

"You better get over here right away!" she yelled. "I have trouble at the house."

Ruditsky, who knew that anything was likely to happen in her dangerous little world, grabbed his shoulder holster and hurried to Linden Drive. There were four or five people at the dinner table —he recognized only Allen Smiley and Siegel's favorite clown, Swifty Morgan—but Virginia was in the living room alone. Despite the late hour, she was wearing a thin, revealing bathing suit, and she was standing there, legs apart like Annie Oakley facing a target, and she had an automatic in her hand.

"I'm going to kill everybody in this house!" she screamed. "The maid, the Chinese butler, and everybody else."

"Now take it easy," Ruditsky said softly.

"I'm going to give it to 'em," she said shrilly. "They've been stealing from me."

Ruditsky recalled that none of the diners dropped a fork or even raised an eyebrow, and concluded they had all seen this routine before. He finally persuaded Virginia to sit down and put the gun on a table, and she seemed reasonably calm when he left. He later told the Kefauver Committee that, in his opinion, she was "an absolute screwball. I think," he added, "that she is psychopathic."

Ruditsky was not qualified to make psychiatric judgments, of course, and he never got very close to Virginia. But Chick knew the answers. Virginia hated the Flamingo and the desert life, but she also knew that Ben Siegel was in the fight of his life to save the hotel for which he had schemed, begged, borrowed, and killed. She knew that Billy Wilkerson, disenchanted with Siegel and the failure of the Flamingo, was in a hurry to pull out. It cost Siegel $120,000 to buy up Wilkerson's shares at a time when he needed all the cash he could assemble. She also knew that Little Moe Sedway was no longer the weak-witted messenger boy he had appeared to be. He had so much money coming in from the bits and pieces thrown to him by Siegel that he could now afford a fine home and an expensive car and could peel off a C-note without having to count what was left.

He became a poseur, who was playing both ends against Siegel. He was chummy with the hoodlums he secretly despised, but he also cultivated the respectable citizens of the city and dropped a grand now and then into the charity and church hoppers. But at the same time, according to Ed Reid and Ovid Demaris, he was a stool pigeon for the Las Vegas office of the FBI, and made regular reports about the activities of the gangsters who were finding Las Vegas a private and secure retirement community.

Eventually Little Moe decided to get into politics as a candidate for the state assembly, perhaps, or a spot in the city government. Little Moe's ambitions were duly reported to Ben Siegel and, according to Reid and Demaris, The Bug grabbed the little man one day and said "We don't run for office. We own the politicians!"

About that same time (Chick Hill was a witness to this) Siegel had an argument with Little Moe. Instead of belting him on the chin, which would have been the normal tactic, Siegel gave him the blow of disgrace. He dropkicked with his right foot, as he had with the cheating croupier, and connected with Moe's rear end. From that moment on the hate was mutual.

Siegel gave orders that Sedway was permanently barred from the Flamingo, and Little Moe prudently obeyed. Worse yet, Siegel contemplated having one of his musclemen take Moe for the one-way ride. "Before I die," he said to Chick Hill one night, "there's two guys I'm gonna kill. Sedway and Wilkerson, the two biggest bastards that ever lived."

In November 1946, a passenger freighter from Italy docked at Havana, and a scowling, swarthy man with one drooping eyelid went ashore. He was met by another man who picked up his bags, and they drove off in a taxicab. The dark-haired stranger, who apparently had no customs or immigration problems (Cuban government leaders subsequently insisted they didn't know he was in Havana or how he got there) was Charles "Lucky" Luciano, master drug salesman, pimp, killer, and the former Mr. Big of the underworld.

Earlier that same year Charlie Lucky, as he was called by the mob, had been deported to Italy after being released from Dannemorra Prison in New York by Governor Thomas E. Dewey. The Manhattan police, who had suffered the indignity of seeing Luciano living like an emperor in the Waldorf Towers, were relieved to get him out of the country. Enforcement officers at every level of city, state, and Federal government, who had seen Luciano's hand in all the branches of organized crime, naturally believed that he was gone forever.

Suddenly there he was—ninety miles from the American mainland—holding court, exacting tribute, plotting new rackets, and ruling the kingdom just as he had years before.

Luciano's presence in Cuba naturally spawned some intriguing stories. It was rumored that he was once more the leader of the syndicate, and would remain in Havana to direct its international operations. There were ominous reports that he had come there to personally knock off some of his old enemies. Eye witnesses said there was a steady procession of mob executives arriving for meetings with Charlie Lucky—Frank Costello, Joey Adonis, Meyer Lansky, Willie Moretti, and others.

The most remarkable tale of all was that Bugsy flew to Havana with six of his gunmen in February 1947, and had a showdown with Luciano about the race wire war, and the disastrous flop of the Flamingo Hotel. When Siegel stalked out of this meeting after telling Luciano to go to hell—according to some versions—the syndicate board of directors voted unanimously to kill him for his defiance and because he had lost $3,000,000 of their money out in Nevada.

This confrontation between Luciano and Siegel never took place.

During the entire period Luciano was in Cuba (he was arrested on February 22 and sent back to Genoa on the Turkish ship *Bakir* on April 12) Siegel was seen almost daily in Las Vegas by Chick Hill and other companions, and he was also under surveillance when he occasionally flew to Los Angeles. In January, in fact, he was politely asked to call on Chief Anderson at Beverly Hills police headquarters.

"I hear there might be some trouble," Anderson said. "I don't want anything unpleasant happening here in Beverly Hills."

"Don't worry, Chief," Siegel said. "I'm spending most of my time in Las Vegas now. I don't live here anymore."

Government agents, who knew from day to day where Siegel

was living and what he was doing, said that Siegel didn't get within a thousand miles of Charlie Lucky. They also said that the so-called vote to execute Siegel, while a romantically chilling idea, was unrealistic. The case against Siegel was far more complex.

Every man in the mob, and dozens of outsiders in Los Angeles and Las Vegas, knew that Siegel's immediate problems at the Flamingo were so acute that he barely had time to sleep, much less take trips. The books of the Nevada Projects Corporation showed that checks payable to Siegel during the first six months of the hotel's operation totaled $75,375.00, and that all these checks were in turn endorsed over to associates from whom he had borrowed money.

At one point, when the financial pressure was extremely heavy, Siegel went to Beverly Hills and put the arm on George Raft for $100,000.

"My God, Ben," Raft said, "I don't have that kind of money lying around."

"But you can get it, Georgie. Right?"

"Yeah, I guess so."

Raft says he raised the cash by borrowing on his substantial annuity fund, and he adds that he had no qualms about lending it to Siegel. There was no collateral put up by the gangster, and Raft got no receipt of any kind. He could not know he had kissed it good bye forever, and in 1965, when he was indicted for income tax evasion (he eventually pleaded guilty to one count) Raft said he guessed he wasn't a very good businessman and was a little careless about money.

Siegel set the second opening of the Flamingo for March 1. No drums beat for this affair, no banners fluttered, no Kleig lights probed the sky. The hotel room section of the Flamingo was still not finished, and as the hour neared, Siegel doubled the number of workmen, and they took one room at a time. The rug layers went in first, and when the last tack was driven a second group carried in the furniture.

Still another squad hung the draperies, and they were followed by maids who made up the beds, hung towels on the bathroom racks, and put small items in their proper places—soap, stationery, phone books. At eight P.M. there were guests in the lobby, waiting to check into rooms that were still without furniture.

As Ben Siegel stood by the reservation desk, appraising the visitors, Manager Chuck Gaskell came into the lobby for a last look around.

"Chuck," Siegel said to Gaskell, "have the beds been turned down as I ordered?"

Paul Price says: "Chuck's face was something to see. He had forgotten all about that."

"Yes, sir," Gaskell lied. "The beds have been turned down."

Moments later Gaskell, Price, and Dick Chappell, the assistant manager, with their wives pitching in, raced from room to room turning down the beds and switching on lights on the bedside tables. Siegel had ordered most of the room lights left on at night to make passing motorists believe the hotel was jumping with business, and for the first few days he spent considerable time in the main lobby, greeting new arrivals and politely asking how they happened to choose the Flamingo.

On the green felt tables the dice bounced and rolled against the backstops, and the riffle of the cards was like soft rain falling. The roulette balls danced in and out of their moving slots, and the one-armed bandits made their metallic sound as the levers were pulled.

Business looked good. People were driving out to see this glittering new temple in the desert, and at night the colored lights touched the bubbling fountain. The veil of light hung in the sky, and the Flamingo, the fabulous Flamingo, could be seen for miles across the sands.

Business looked good. But it was not. The grim truth came out in the counting room, where Ben Siegel and his trusted men looked in vain for their gambling profits. The unbelievable run of bad luck was still blighting the casino, and the net operating loss, which was to total $774,000 for the first six months, was turning Siegel into a raging insomniac.

At the peak of his depression, when Virginia had come up for the weekend, he went to the penthouse and found her reading *Time* magazine.

"What in hell are you doing with that crummy magazine?" he said.

"It's got a story about the race wire business," she said.

"Never mind that baloney," he said with a snarl.

"I'll read what I damn well like," Virginia said stiffly.

Siegel's hand made a looping sweep, knocking the magazine from her grasp, and as she leaned over to retrieve it, he gave her a violent shove with his foot and she sprawled in a heap on the floor. She was on her feet like a cat, clutching her left shoe like an ice pick, and the long sharp spiked heel cut a deep gash in Siegel's head. She hit him again and again, until blood ran down over his eyes, and before he could stop her with his fists she was out of the room and down the stairs out of sight.

Siegel slowly walked into the bathroom, wiped the blood from his head, and touched the slashes with iodine. Then he went looking for Virginia, but she had left the hotel in a hurry, and was already in the air on a flight back to Beverly Hills. She knew him well enough to stay away until his anger cooled, and a full week passed before he saw her again.

During that period columnist Westbrook Pegler, who had regularly been writing nasty words about Siegel, Raft, and Leo Durocher, inexplicably showed up at the Flamingo for a personal look at the operations of the men he had called "Siegel and a group of henchmen carpetbaggers." Pegler had also written that J. Edgar Hoover had personally phoned Billy Wilkerson and warned him that he was mixed up with "the worst bunch of gangsters in the underworld." Hoover says flatly he made no such phone call to Wilkerson, but Siegel chose to believe Pegler.

Now the hated Pegler was in the Flamingo, and the moment Siegel heard about it he ran into the casino. He saw Pegler yanking a slot machine lever, walked up to say something, and almost immediately whirled away and found Chick Hill standing by another bank of machines.

"That son of a bitch called me Bugsy!" he said. "I'm going to kill him, Chick. I'm going to kill him!"

Chick, who has arms like a gorilla, put a half Nelson on the gangster, yelled for two security officers nearby, and the three men wrestled Siegel into his private office.

"For Christ's sake, Ben!" Chick cried out. "You want to ruin everything?"

"This guy's been cutting me up," Siegel said breathlessly. "If he isn't out of my hotel in five minutes I'm going to take him."

"You're not taking anybody, Ben."

Siegel stared out the window for a moment, both fists clenching and unclenching, eyes glazing, and lungs sucking in air. He looked at the half open center drawer of his desk, and he could see the butt of the gun he kept there. Chick and the two guards watched him. The color come back into his face, and at last he said: "Yeah. You're right. Go out there and hang around, Chick. And let me know when he leaves." Chick walked back to the casino, but Pegler had left, and neither Chick nor Ben Siegel ever saw him there again.

It was spring in Las Vegas, and on the desert the wild flowers rippled in the wind. The sun was higher and warmer, and when the last of the dust-blackened snows had melted from the shoulders of the roads the cars once more began to whine along the dark ribbons of highways running east and west out of Las Vegas.

But it was still cold winter in Ben Siegel's mind, for nothing was going right. There was that strange afternoon, for instance, when the shimmering pool was filled with Flamingo guests and suddenly the water vanished as though it had been sucked out by some giant subterranean pump. By the time Siegel got to the pool, there was not one drop left, and the bathers were standing there, mutely staring at an enormous crack across the center of the pool. Some of the more irreverent guests mumbled that the hand of God had drained the pool as a warning against the sinners in the place. Others blamed it on an earthquake far down below the dry land, and the more nervous men and women quickly checked out.

Actually what seemed like a phenomenon of nature was quickly traced to a construction fault, and within hours Siegel had repair crews pouring new concrete, reinforced with heavier steel rods. Water poured into the big bowl, and the swimmers and sun bathers gradually came back.

Virginia Hill came back, too, and Siegel, knowing her inflammable spirit, morosely said to Chick: "I wish to God she'd stay away until we get things going around here."

But Virginia needed to be seen and admired and loved, and she would let nothing interfere with these needs. She was not popular with the workers in the hotel, especially the waiters and doormen, and she let them know, in her own arrogant way, that she was Ben Siegel's girl and could get them fired if they got in her way.

She had a particular dislike for Hank Greenspun, who was temporarily helping out, and the feeling was mutual. Greenspun had learned from experience that often, when Siegel and Virginia were together, it was like a short circuit in a power line. Sparks jumped, and the air crackled with strong language.

"She was worse than most men," Greenspun recalls. "When she let go she had nothing but foul language, just like the hoodlums around her."

From the beginning, if Virginia sat down at a table where he and Siegel were talking business, Greenspun simply stood up and walked away, saying: "See you later, Ben."

Siegel finally called Greenspun to the executive office and said: "Hank, listen, my girl's unhappy."

"What about?"

"Because she says you're snubbing her. Every time she comes near you, you walk away. Why do you treat her like that?"

"She's not my girl, Ben. She's yours. I got a job to do and I'll do it."

"Damn it, Hank, she doesn't like it."

"It isn't my fault, Ben," Greenspun said. "There is nothing in our agreement that says I have to sit and talk to your girl. I just don't want to have anything to do with her."

Greenspun went back to his publicity office, and the subject was permanently dropped. He continued to avoid Virginia, and his obvious dislike only aggravated her tension. She began to suffer from jealousy, an emotion which was new to her, and she had a new quarrel with Siegel when the Countess DiFrasso unexpectedly appeared at the Flamingo one day.

The Countess had heard of Siegel's critical money problems and, despite the certain knowledge that he had discarded her for Virginia Hill, she had come to help.

"Ben," she said, "I know you need cash. I have had some financial difficulties of my own, but I have borrowed money on my jewelry. Fifty thousand, Ben, and you're welcome to it."

This gracious and unselfish gesture must have touched some remnant of conscience, for his response was out of character.

"You're a real sweetheart, Dottie," he said. "But I don't need it now."

"Don't fool me, Ben," she said. "Everybody knows you've been losing your shirt."

"We're coming out of it now," he lied. "We're doing okay."

The Countess returned to Beverly Hills with her fifty thousand intact, and she never saw Ben Siegel again. His refusal of the proffered loan was one of the few decent acts in the remaining weeks of his life, for he actually needed ten times fifty thousand. He persuaded George Raft to buy $65,000 worth of stock in the Flamingo, and he raised huge sums from his mob pals in the East.

But whatever he got wasn't enough. The total cost of the Flamingo had now soared to $6,000,000, and many of his checks were bouncing. Virginia put up cash for some of the smaller ones, but even her treasury wasn't rich enough when Siegel wrote a $50,000 check to Del Webb. The check, No. 1384 on the Nevada Projects Corporation account, came back to Webb stamped "Insufficient Funds," and for once in his merciless life Ben Siegel was forced to make abject apologies. He also assured Webb that the money would soon be available.

Virginia was in the casino or at the bar almost every night through this crisis, watching every move Siegel made, especially when he sat down with or talked to other women. One evening Virginia was in the bar alone when a honeymooning couple from Los Angeles were toasting each other with highballs.

Virginia watched them for a few minutes, then strode to the bar and dropped a $1000 bill on the mahogany top. "I want these young people to have champagne," she said to bartender Steve Stevens, who had been brought to the Flamingo by Billy Wilkerson. "The best you have." She smiled at the honeymooners and walked into the casino. Hours later, when Virginia had not returned to pick up more than $900 in change, which was still lying on the bar top, Stevens called Siegel on the house phone.

Siegel came to the bar immediately, and pocketed the cash.

"How long has this been here, Steve?" he asked.

"At least four hours, Mr. Siegel."

"I tell you," Siegel said with a frown, "this girl must be going nuts. Thanks for watching the dough, Steve." He tipped the bartender $20 and marched out.

Virginia *was* going nuts—as Siegel phrased it.

She was convinced that Betty Dexter, a pretty blonde girl who had the hatcheck concession in the hotel, was making a play for Siegel. The suspicion grew in her mind until it was out of control, and every time she walked past the check booth she made vicious remarks that could be heard ten feet away even with the din from the gambling room. Finally, when her caustic tongue failed to arouse the girl, Virginia suddenly cracked. She grabbed Betty by the hair, hit her a one-two clip with a speed any fighter would have admired, and then raked the staggering girl with her long nails.

Ben Siegel and Chick Hill finally separated the two screaming girls, and Virginia fled from the building and sulked in the penthouse. Betty Dexter was taken to the Clark County General Hospital with a dislocated vertebra, and a dozen scratches and bruises. When she recovered, her attorneys drew up damage suits against Virginia and the Flamingo Hotel, but they were never filed and the details of the battle were withheld from the press until Miss Dexter chose to talk about it several years later.

That week, one evening long after midnight, Dick Chappell was in the terrace garden taking a few minutes off for a cigarette when he heard a strident voice calling his name. He looked up at the penthouse balcony, and Siegel was standing there in shirt sleeves.

"Dick!" he cried. "Get up here! I need your help."

Chappell ground out his cigarette butt and went up the hotel stairs on the run to the penthouse. When he got there he found Siegel, obviously unstrung, slapping Virginia's face with cold wet towels. She was lying on her back on the bed, a faint bluish tinge in her cheeks, and she was barely breathing.

"We had a fight about the Dexter girl," Siegel said. "She's taken a slug of sleeping pills. Gimme a hand and we'll get her to the hospital."

They picked her up, struggled into the elevator, and carried her to Siegel's station wagon. Chappell, who along with Chick had been favored with a set of keys for the car, took the wheel and raced the vehicle in and out of heavy traffic toward the Southern Nevada Hospital, five miles away on Charleston Boulevard. The speedometer was touching ninety when they heard a siren in the distance, and saw a red light winking in the blackness.

"Never mind the goddam cop!" Siegel said, holding Virginia tightly in his arms. "Give him a bill when we get there."

They were at the hospital in minutes, where orderlies lifted Virginia to a stretcher, and wheeled her into the emergency unit. Chappell, who remained outside, gave the pursuing highway cop a hundred dollar bill—he later thought it was a wasted gesture under the circumstances—the officer took it, and went on his way. Hank Greenspun says it was not the first nor last time Siegel had handed out a hundred dollar bill to a policeman, and recalls that only one had ever refused it. On that occasion the man let the bill flutter away in the wind, and when Siegel retrieved it from a nearby sand mound he mumbled: "There's a dumb guy who's going nowhere."

Virginia's life was saved that night by a stomach pump, and, as was her custom after a losing round, she flew back to Beverly Hills to be alone for awhile. Chick Hill, who had seen the near-fatal effects of barbiturates in that first suicide attempt, says that he begged Virginia not to have the pills so easily available. But she filled endless prescriptions for sleeping pills thereafter, and, when he found them, Chick flushed them down the toilet bowl.

At least twice, when Virginia sent him to Schwab's for a bottle of phenobarbital, he emptied the drug out of the capsules and laboriously refiled them with powdered sugar. "I'm no psychologist and you can think what you want," he said not long ago, "but when Tab took the sugar pills she slept just as well. If I had been around her all the time, I might have been able to stop her from that terrible thing she did."

CHAPTER SEVENTEEN

In the frantic scramble for cash customers during the spring of 1947, Paul Price and Hank Greenspun tuned their tom-toms to every legitimate pitch. Girlie photos went to the nation's newspapers by the box load; visiting celebrities were interviewed or photographed in the now lush terrace garden. Jackpots were increased in the slot machines, and almost every week there was something new—door prizes, contests of all kinds, special midweek room rates. The male waiters in the dining rooms were replaced with pretty young girls, and an internationally-renowned Italian chef, who later had the audacity to go on strike in the middle of a major banquet, was brought in to plan gourmet menus.

One of the gimmicks worked out by Greenspun was a lottery which offered a new Plymouth car every week. Greenspun ran a large and expensive ad in the *Review-Journal* announcing that the first drawing would be held at one P.M. the following day, and when the time came the casino and the garden were swarming with people. At 12:45 Greenspun went to a house phone in the lobby, three steps above the level of the casino, to tell the chief operator to announce on the public address system that the drawing would be held in a few minutes.

Greenspun was still chatting with the operator when Ben Siegel, who had been standing in the casino, suddenly made the three steps in one leap. "He had fire in his eyes," Greenspun says, "and he made a lunge at me with his right arm. I thought he had gone crazy and I know he intended to jerk the phone out of my hand."

Instinctively, Greenspun let fly with his right fist and the blow hit Siegel on the shoulder. He dropped to the rug, rolled down the stairs with an incredulous expression on his face, and almost immediately scrambled to his feet. He was ready for battle with both fists knotted, and Greenspun, still clinging to the phone, said: "Benny—don't you ever take a swing at me."

"I wanted you to get off the phone," Siegel panted. "I wasn't going to swing at you."

"I'm sorry. It was a misunderstanding."

"I want you to hold the drawing off for another hour. We got a big crowd out there, and if we make 'em wait another hour that'll be good business."

Siegel again reached for the phone, and Greenspun blocked him. "Ben," he said firmly, "we announced the drawing for one o'clock, and that's when it's going to be. You can't bring people here and then trick them."

The winsome smile that had been seen so rarely those days illuminated Siegel's face, and he self-consciously began brushing lint and dust from his suit. "You're right, Hank," he said. "Absolutely right." He went back into the casino, where the dealers once more went about their work, and the drawing was held on schedule.

Greenspun says that up to that point in their relationship Siegel had been unbearably autocratic about every activity in the hotel. He was so emotionally involved in his beautiful but soulless castle in the desert that he had lost perspective on people—yet believed he was an expert in public relations—and he insisted on making all the decisions. He consistently refused advice from his closest associates, and, like most mediocre executives, he wanted to run the entire operation by himself. He tried to supervise the kitchen crew, hire the big name entertainers, appoint the pit bosses, choose the decor for the hotel rooms, and personally approve every employee.

He simply could not stay in the background, nor was he able to clear his reputation as a gangster with a vile temper. He came there as Bugsy Siegel. He remained Bugsy Siegel.

And as his despair grew and the losses increased, he dropped his veneer so often that he ruined the friendly image Greenspun and Price worked so diligently to create. Some of the Siegel legends, which were the talk of the town, were total fabrications. Some were true. There was one report that still shows up now and then that he forced Abe Schiller to crawl on his hands and knees around the Flamingo pool. Siegel held a gun against the press agent's head —or so the story went—and threatened to spill his brains. The incident never happened. Schiller was working at the El Rancho, not the Flamingo, and was never threatened by Siegel.

There was another rumor that one of Siegel's cars struck and killed a little girl on a Las Vegas street. If the incident actually happened, there seems to be no record of it—though the skeptics claim he paid a huge sum to soothe the bereaved parents.

Many of the people who worked with Siegel during those tense months remember that his disposition steadily became more savage. On one occasion he saw a man in a dinner jacket sitting by the pool and mistook him for an employee. Siegel knocked the chair over, threatened the unfortunate stranger with his fists, and then had to apologize when the man identified himself as a paying guest. Dick Chappell recalls that Siegel saw Mrs. Chappell taking a sun bath near the pool, and snapped at her: "That's no goddamn place for a sun bath." That same week, when a little girl became nauseated in the lobby and lost her breakfast on the rug, Siegel raged like a madman. But the child was the daughter of a guest and he couldn't do anything about it.

That evening at dinner time Paul Price missed his three-year-old daughter, Pam, and blurted to Mrs. Price: "Holy cow, this is no time to have a child wandering around loose with Ben raising hell. That's all he needs."

Price hurriedly searched the grounds and the hotel area, thinking she might be playing with other youngsters. Finally, glancing through the casino entrance, he saw Siegel holding the child in his arms, and helping her pull the lever on a silver dollar slot machine. "I thought my job was gone right then," Price said, "but no one could tell which way Ben was going to flip. He handed Pam over to me, and said he got a kick out of watching her face when he was putting the dollars in the slot."

Among others who came close to being scorched by Siegel's wrath was a nationally-known band leader whose orchestra was then playing at the Flamingo. Siegel summoned Paul Price to his office one morning and said: "I hear that so-and-so is using that name I hate, and I'm going to throw him and his whole goddam band out."

"What name is that, Ben?" Price said innocently.

"Now look here, Paul," Siegel said. "You know damn well what I mean—*that* name."

Price nodded. He knew. "Funny thing, Ben," he said, "I was talking to this guy last night, and he was telling me what a fine fellow you are, and maybe he just doesn't understand."

"Maybe he thinks it's a nickname?"

"I'm sure he does," Price said quickly.

"Okay, Paul. You tell him it isn't a nickname, and to quit using it. Or else."

Price went out, wiping his forehead, and the bandleader's job was saved.

Early in May the people of Las Vegas were busy preparing for their Heldorado Days, an annual event celebrating the founding of the city in the pioneering days. It is the kind of carefree festivity familiar to visitors in many old western towns, when the men grow whiskers, and wear boots and cowboy clothes, and the women pin up their hair and go square dancing in bonnets and hoop skirts. It is a time of unrestrained revelry, when liquor and money flow freely and the cops tend to forgive those who trespass against them if no one gets killed or hurt.

The main event was the Heldorado Parade, with bands, costumed marchers, and flower-decked floats. First place in the commercial division of the parade floats won a coveted prize, and Ben Siegel was determined to have it.

Among the more scenic attractions due in Las Vegas for the Heldorado fun was Mrs. Vic Orsatti, who was better known to the movie columnists as Marie "The Body" McDonald. She had a close friendship with Ben Siegel and Virginia Hill, and Virginia knew she was booked for a six week stay in Las Vegas to get a divorce from her movie agent husband. Virginia asked Marie if she would ride in the parade as Queen of the Flamingo float—Siegel had already allotted a large chunk of cash for it—and the actress said she'd be happy to do it.

Two days before the parade, which was scheduled for May 17, there was no sign of the lovely blonde star, and Price was pacing the floor. The float, featuring a giant-sized flamingo with a platform on which Marie would sit, had been completed, and Siegel had chosen a dozen dazzling show girls who would circle the float at the foot of the big flame-colored bird. It was an expensive entry, but Price had assured Siegel that the parade would be covered by all the wire news services and scores of photographers.

Price was nervously waiting for word about Marie when Virginia heard that she had checked into the El Rancho.

Virginia phoned her in something of a pique, and Marie was sobbing. "Honey," she said, "I can't come to the Flamingo."

"Why not? You belong here if you're going to ride our float."

"Well, I was in here, and when I started to check out, the room clerk said: 'Miss McDonald, you don't want to go to the Flamingo! Don't you know the place is run by gangsters and murderers?' "

"Who said that?" Virginia demanded.

"The clerk here. I'm not sure of his name—a Mr. Karsen or Konsen. Something like that."

Virginia asked Marie to sit tight, and immediately called Siegel on the house phone. He and Paul Price were discussing the parade as he picked up the phone, and Price heard him say: "What? When? Just now? All right." He banged the receiver into its cradle, snatched up the .38 revolver from the top desk drawer, and stuck it into his waistband.

He marched into the lobby, yelling for Hymie Segal and Chick Hill, and the three jumped into Siegel's car as Paul Price stood by, ashen-faced. Chick took the wheel, and shot the big car down the road at full throttle. He pulled up in front of the El Rancho with the tires smoking, and waited there while Siegel and his muscleman went inside. They found the offending clerk, whose name was Ray Kronsen, and they let him have it with their gun butts until he dropped, half alive, with his face and head a bloody bas-relief.

Then they walked out to the car, as casually as though they

had just gone in for a pack of cigarettes, and Siegel nudged Chick. "There's one son of a bitch who won't be talking for awhile," he said. "Okay, Chick, let's go."

Sanford Adler, a gambler who first got his name on a police blotter in 1926, and who had worked his way up to become manager of the El Rancho, was clever enough to keep his mouth shut about this brutal episode, and the identity of the victim was a public mystery until Chick Hill began talking about it almost twenty years later. The cruelty of Siegel's attack so upset Marie that she refused to go through with her promise to ride the float. She not only complained to Virginia about the Kronsen clubbing, but added that she didn't feel like riding in public with a bunch of second-rate chorus girls.

"Well, goddam her!" Siegel swore.

He found her in the garden that evening, pushed her up against a wall and cuffed her once or twice. "You're going on the float, you hear!" he said.

"Yes, Ben," she said meekly.

And she rode the plaster Flamingo and she never looked more beautiful. Ben Siegel won first prize and he gloated about it. But he lost more than he won. Now there was talk all over town, as well as in Los Angeles and New York, that Siegel was going to be taken. Siegel heard the rumbles himself, but laughed about it and said there wasn't anybody around strong enough to take him. The Flamingo was crawling with his gunmen. He had a gun himself, and in the penthouse suite there were rifles and pistols. He could handle the punks himself if he had to. He told Chick and Virginia to quit worrying about anything.

"Ben," Virginia pleaded one evening, "why don't you sell this crummy joint before you fall apart."

"You talk like one of those dumb broads hanging around the bar, Tab," Siegel retorted. "I'm not falling apart. I just need time. And don't call it a crummy joint, see?"

Virginia later tried to explain to the Kefauver Committee that Siegel told her the Flamingo was "upside down," a cryptic remark that was never made quite clear. What Siegel probably meant was that big gambling casinos are not supposed to run in the red. Business was so bad, for instance, that the great Lena Horne, one of the major attractions in show business, had to go on one night with only fourteen customers in the theater room. Secretly, Siegel regretted that he had put so much time and effort into a business for which he was not professionally trained. He often told Virginia and Chick that he should have stayed in the rackets, where the profits were certain, rather than having the gamblers make him look like a rube.

But he could never bring himself to admit that the Flamingo's failure was his own fault, and so he passed the blame along to Billy Wilkerson, Little Moe Sedway, Gus Greenbaum, and others who had encouraged the project. Toward the end of May that year he was being so inexorably squeezed that the downtown Las Vegas experts were sitting around like vultures, predicting that Siegel would be forced out of the Flamingo in thirty days. He knew they were right.

"If I can raise enough to hang on until the summer tourist season starts," he said to Chick, "we'll come out of it okay."

"And where are you going to get the dough?" Chick asked.

"I got an idea," Siegel said. "There's some guys who won't like it, but the hell with them."

Contemplating those tense days, Chick Hill confesses that he himself had no real concern for Ben Siegel's crisis. First, because he was only nineteen years old at the time and was getting all the money he needed from Virginia, and second, because he was more interested in the female body than he was in the Flamingo's vanishing bank account. There was a new girl in town, and Chick wanted her.

Her name was Jerri Mason, a pert and saucy redhead who was then working for Marie McDonald as a combined maid and secretary. Chick was with her in the terrace garden one evening when Virginia saw them. Later she took Chick aside and said: "You making any time with Jerri?"

"Aw, c'mon, Tab."

"It would be handier if she wasn't tied up with Marie, wouldn't it?"

"Well—"

"Okay, Chick. Starting tomorrow, she'll be working for me."

Jerri was offered $100 a week, more than she was receiving

from Marie McDonald, and she came to work for Virginia. Long afterward, stirring the ashes, Jerri Mason said she would have taken the first plane out to any remote corner of the earth if she could have had just one little glimpse of the terror ahead. A Year of hell, she called it. Perhaps it was.

There was a time when Joe Moll sat disconsolately in the cluttered little office of his service station on the Sunset Strip, and griped to himself because business was so slow. Then one day George Raft wheeled his gleaming Cadillac alongside the gas pump, and Joe hustled out to greet the famous movie star. Raft was used to this obsequious kind of service, but he was also shrewd enough not to give anyone the brush.

"You from New York?" Raft asked. "You got the accent."

"Yes, sir, Mr. Raft," Joe said. "I used to be a driver for some of the Tammany guys."

"Well, what do you know," Raft said. "You look okay to me."

"Thanks, Mr. Raft. Next time you need a polish job lemme show you what I can do."

In time Raft not only gave all his automotive business to Joe —he had two Cadillacs and a Mercury at the time—but he also brought Ben Siegel, Leo Durocher, and other celebrities there. Joe acquired a reputation as a "character," and had to hire extra young men to pump gas for the many cars that rolled into his place.

Joe never concealed his adulation for Raft and Siegel and if they needed anything he was happy to get out of bed in the middle of the night. During the war he had black market fuel for his pals, and he could get tires and parts that weren't available elsewhere at any price.

One day, after Raft had spent half the night doping the races, as was his custom before going to the track with three or four grand in his pocket, he invited Joe to his private box at Santa Anita. Joe bet a few dollars on Raft's tips, won a modest amount, and thereafter became a regular afternoon patron at both Santa Anita and Hollywood Park.

Inevitably, he promoted himself from the two dollar window to the fifty and hundred dollar section. And just as inevitably, losing horses made his checks bounce. First he went to Raft, who admits he was always a pushover for a soft touch, and he borrowed all he could get. It was barely enough to handle the action for one week and then, because now he was irretrievably hooked by the horses, he dreamed up an ingenious idea.

Cadillacs and other fine cars were as scarce as rain in Los Angeles during the postwar years, and some of Joe's customers offered him eye-popping sums of cash if he could find them a Cad. Joe was a con man at heart, and he was going color-blind with all that green stuff being waved in front of his eyes.

"Tell you what I'll do," he said to a customer one day. "See that beautiful Caddie over there?" He pointed a grimy finger at George Raft's convertible, up on the rack getting a grease job. "I can get you that car in two or three months."

"No kidding, Joe."

"Sure I can. But you gotta put up a deposit."

"How much you want, Joe?" the eager buyer asked. "I got it right here."

"Oh, a couple of grand will hold the car for you," Joe said.

The happy chump peeled off twenty hundreds, and that afternoon Joe was back in line with the rest of the betters at the track. "I don't know how many times he sold my two Cads," Raft said, "but he did it over and over, and I didn't know what was going on. He quit coming to the house to play baseball with me and Ben, and I heard he was making trips to Vegas."

Joe also "sold" Ben Siegel's car now and then, or any other hard-to-get car brought into his station for service. Because his business was all under the table Joe didn't have to worry about income tax, and sooner or later the big long shot would thunder down the stretch at the track, and he would be out of the hole.

Three months went by, and the first victim came to the station one afternoon, complaining because his Cadillac wasn't ready. And then came the second and third. And Joe suddenly realized that he was at the end of the line. It was time to blow. But first he went to the Beth Olam Cemetery in Hollywood, and bought himself a crypt in the mausoleum there. It took almost all the cash he had, and he said to the manager: "Write it down. If anything ever happents to Ben Siegel, if he dies before I do, I want to be in a crypt right over his. Got it? Right above him."

With that he walked out into the street, and George Raft and Ben Siegel and all the people he had clipped never saw him again.

Virginia Hill, still brooding about her last quarrel with Ben Siegel, was beginning to tire of the pace.

She had come back to the Linden Drive house with a determination to stay away from the Flamingo until Siegel's fortunes improved, but somehow Beverly Hills no longer seemed quite the same. She was almost thirty-one, and there were long nights when her body and her mind seemed a century old. She was drinking too much, and she was using more and more sleeping pills to soothe her nerves.

Virginia was debating her next move when her landlord Juan Romero came for dinner one evening. She told him her problems, and he said: "Have you ever been to Europe?"

"No," she said. "What the hell would I do in Europe? I don't know anybody there."

"Sure you do. Remember that young Frenchman I brought here once a couple of months ago? Nick Fouillette?"

"Yes, I remember him. But Juan—he's just a kid."

"Kid or not, he's rich and his family is powerful in France. They own Mumm's champagne, and God knows you've bought it by the case. Listen, he told me he'd show you around Paris if you ever got there."

"Paris—," she said dreamily. "I always wanted to go there."

"Summer in Paris," he said. "You'll have a ball."

"By God!" she exclaimed. "I'll do it."

Chick says his sister was "crazy with excitement" after she made the decision to go, and flew to Las Vegas immediately to tell Ben Siegel about it. His reaction was one of jealousy and anger.

"You're not going," he said.

Virginia stiffened, and looked across the room where Chick and another brother, Billy, who had just arrived in Las Vegas, were sitting on a divan. "Who do you think you are?" she said challengingly. "You don't own me, Ben Siegel." She motioned to her brothers. "C'mon," she said. "The hell with him and this whole goddam place."

She handed her weekend case to Chick, threw a mink stole

around her neck, and pushed the button for the penthouse elevator. Ben Siegel made no move to interfere. He stood by the window, staring down at the guests lying in the sun beside the pool. He heard the elevator doors slide open, and then close with a soft thud. He saw her striding across the garden, followed by Billy and Chick, and they disappeared inside the casino. The cab stand was just outside, a door slammed, there was the sound of gears meshing, and they were gone.

The little book by Mildred Cram was in Virginia's bag. It was always there but she was not thinking about Colin and Julie that day. She was aching with anger and defiance, and she did not want to look back at the tinsel built for her and in her name.

But later she would read the story again. "At the end it was Colin who cried: 'Julie, I believe we're dead. Both of us! Of all the astounding luck!' And with his arm across her shoulder Julie lifted her head and said: 'This is forever.' "

Virginia Hill flew to Chicago on June 10. She had bought a new Cadillac convertible for Chick, and had asked him to stay at the Beverly Hills house with Jerri. "Ben will probably show up one of these days to get his clothes and the other stuff out of his room upstairs," she said. "Tell him I don't know when I'll be back."

"Okay, Tab," he said.

"And one more thing, Chick. Keep Jerri around as long as you like, but don't be a sap and marry her."

Chick almost betrayed himself with a self-conscious grin. He was already planning to marry Jerri while Virginia was out of the country.

"Have fun, Tab," he said.

"I will," she said.

Joe Epstein met Virginia at the Chicago airport, stayed with her overnight in his apartment, and the next day they took a flight to LaGuardia Airport in New York. Virginia, Epstein, and a friend from Chicago named Mrs. Jacques Grimaldi occupied a suite at the Hampshire House on Central Park South, and remained there until she boarded the plane for Paris on June 16.

Epstein said later he had given her $2000 in cash which he said he took from her own safe deposit box in Chicago. He may not have known that she already had $5000 in cash and another $5000 worth of travelers' checks in her bag. When applying for her passport, Virginia said her primary purpose in going to Paris was to make arrangements for a deal with the Fouillette family. She said she planned to establish an import agency in California to handle French wines and liqueurs, and she had already written to Nicholas Fouillette, who was then only twenty-one years old, that she wanted his services as a guide around Europe. "Money is no object," she wrote, "and I'll pay all the bills."

Virginia had no intention of importing wine to California, or going into any other business. It is likely that she concocted this fiction to mislead the Fouillette family and other prominent Parisians. Neither Nick Fouillette nor his mother knew that she was the notorious Virginia Hill, consort of killers and gangsters.

CHAPTER EIGHTEEN

The rumbles were heard from coast to coast, and toward the middle of June the unemployed gunmen in Las Vegas became jumpy when Ben Siegel was around, and instinctively fingered their guns.

The rumbles were heard in the New York police department. In Beverly Hills Chief Anderson got a tip. In Chicago the mob men said Virginia Hill had gone to Europe to get a reprieve for her man from Lucky Luciano. Lee Mortimer spotted some notorious eastern gunmen in a Beverly Hills hotel—or so he wrote long afterward. They told him they were there for a little talk with Ben Siegel, and they were going to ask him what happened to their money in his casino. Meyer Lansky arrived at the Flamingo, and Siegel introduced him to Paul Price.

"This is my old friend, Mr. Lansky," Siegel said. "He's staying with us for a couple of days."

Meyer Lansky was not officially registered at the Flamingo, and he was not seen outside his room. But the gangsters in town knew he was there.

Ben Siegel went about his daily business, trailed by Hymie Segal and Dave Berman and Fat Irish Green, and if he was aware of the rumbles he said nothing to anyone. He was more irascible than ever, and sent word to the major bookies in Nevada, California, and Arizona that he wanted them in Las Vegas for an important conference.

They showed up as he had ordered, and during a stormy

meeting in the hotel, he told them he was doubling the price of his wire service. There was open rebellion, and many of the small operators complained that Siegel was forcing them to pay for the big losses at the Flamingo. The mutiny was so flagrant that even Hank Greenspun and Paul Price, who had carefully avoided direct contact with the underworld elements, heard threats against Siegel from half a dozen sources.

On June 13, when the bookies had gone home grumbling, Siegel phoned Price at home and said: "I have to fly to LA, on some money business, Paul, and I want you to come along."

"Sure, Ben. When?"

"Right now. Meet me at the airport."

Price glanced at his watch and saw that it was almost midnight. He threw a razor, clean shirt, and socks into a little suitcase, and went to the field. Siegel was waiting there alone and they soared away with Del Webb's pilot in Webb's private plane.

They landed in Glendale about two A.M. and found the airport deserted. It took some time to get a taxi, and they were taken directly to the Linden Drive house. They sat around for an hour in the living room talking business. Chick and Jerri were not home. Siegel made fresh coffee for Price, and he himself sipped a small glass of RemyMartin cognac.

"I never saw a man more calm in my life," Price recalls. "The curtains were all pulled away from the windows in the house, and he walked right through the front door with no hesitation. If he had any fear do you think he would be out alone at night with just a press agent? I'm sure Ben didn't suspect anybody wanted to hit him. He had as tough a crew as you'll ever see, and they were always around at the Flamingo. But that night he was wide open for it. All alone in that house. I was convinced all the rumors didn't mean a thing."

Siegel and Price returned to Las Vegas the following afternoon, and once more his personal gunmen followed him around. If there were killers nearby, they couldn't have hit him with a cannon.

In Beverly Hills the next evening, Chick and Jerri were asleep on the second floor of the big white house. Just before midnight,

Jerri suddenly shook Chick into wakefulness and whispered: "Chick! I hear someone downstairs!"

Chick leaped out of bed, grabbed his gun and went to the head of the staircase. "Who's down there?" he called. As he had hoped, his voice was heard by the unknown intruder, and the silence was broken by the sound of someone running. He snapped off the safety on the gun, switched on the downstairs lights from a wall button, and went down to the living room. He felt a current of cool air, walked to the kitchen and discovered the back door was wide open. He had locked it every night, and there were scratches indicating the prowler, whoever he was, had forced the latch.

He stood there for a moment, listening for sounds in the darkness outside. Then he closed the door, left the lights on there and in the living room, and went back to bed. It was a warm June night, but Chick suddenly felt a chill. "I don't like it, Jerri," he said. "I don't like it a bit."

Just before noon on June 19, four men who looked like underworld gorillas, marched into the Flamingo Hotel, collared the first available bellhop, and demanded to know where they could find Siegel. He refused to say anything at first, but when one man pulled a gun and threatened to belt him behind the ears, the bell boy said the boss usually came in around two P.M. The men left, and Siegel was notified at once. He sent Hymie and Dave into downtown Las Vegas on a frantic search for the tough guys, but they had disappeared.

All through that day there were long distance calls for Siegel, and when he answered the phone a voice would say: "Bugsy—you've had it," and then hang up. Siegel finally asked Dick Chappell to have the hotel operators trace the calls, and he left word at the switchboard that he would not answer unless the callers were people he knew.

Siegel also had a curious session with Little Moe Sedway that day. He did not discuss it with anyone, and it was not mentioned until 1951, when Sedway was on the stand at the Kefauver hearings. Sedway, who was keenly anxious to be identified with the respectable people in Las Vegas, was chairman of the United Jewish Appeal campaign that year, and claimed he and Siegel were together at the Flamingo to discuss a fund-raising dinner to be held in the hotel.

"Siegel said he thinks he can get Al Jolson down for the dinner," Sedway testified, "and I said that would be a big thing for us."

"Did he say anything that might indicate he was in fear of his life?" Rudolph Halley asked.

"No, he never said anything. He was supposed to call me the next day about Jolson. He never did call me."

One suspects that this conversation between Siegel and Sedway never took place at that time. Sedway was No. 1 on Siegel's black list in Las Vegas, as everyone knew, and he was not permitted inside the Flamingo under any circumstances.

Early in the afternoon on June 19, Siegel put in a call for Chick Hill. "I'm coming down tonight with Swifty Morgan," he said. "I've got a meeting with Paul Price at Joe Ross's law office in the afternoon, and I want to get my clothes, too."

"Anything I can do?"

"No. Don't wait up for me because I'm not leaving here until after midnight."

"Okay, Ben."

About eight P.M. Siegel went into his private office, and sent for Fat Irish Green. The fat man, who was not only one of Siegel's bodyguards but was also employed as a timekeeper, came in presently and sat down.

Siegel opened a briefcase and let Green see that it was jammed with currency. Green later said it was only $60,000, but government investigators now believe there may have been as much as $600,000.

"I'm going to Los Angeles tonight for a couple of days," he said. "I'm going to leave this bundle with you, Irish."

Green squirmed in his chair and fumbled for a cigarette. "Jesus, Ben," he said. "That's an awful lot of jack for anybody to be carryin' around."

"Nobody in Vegas knows you've got it," Siegel said.

"What's going on, Ben?"

"Nothing. I'm leaving it with you—just in case," Siegel said.

"If anything happens to me you just sit tight and there'll be some guys who'll come and take the money off your hands."

"Well, if that's the way you want it."

"That's the way I want it. I'll see you in a couple of days."

At midnight Siegel joined Swifty Morgan, and they were driven to the airport. Swifty looked more and more like a leprechaun, with his long moustache and his little goatee, and he was full of gags as usual as they boarded Western Air Lines flight 23 for Los Angeles. The plane took off at 12:53 A.M. and landed at Mines field in Los Angeles about 2:30. Siegel and Swifty called a cab and went directly to the Linden Drive house.

Chick was awake when they arrived, but Siegel was too tired for conversation. He went upstairs and took Swifty to a guest room. The largest of the four rooms on that floor overlooked the street. It contained Virginia's antique four-poster bed, with a canopy over it, and the safe which was concealed by a swing-out panel. Siegel looked in there out of habit, then went to his own room next door. He went to sleep at once.

In the morning, Siegel, Chick, Jerri, and Swifty were served breakfast by Virginia's Chinese cook, Lee, and shortly afterward the phone began ringing as steadily as the alarm in a fire house. Siegel had long conversations with many people. Chick does not know their names because he was not in the bedroom where Siegel was using the phone. He does recall that Siegel eventually came downstairs and said he was going to Mickey Cohen's house in Brentwood. Siegel took Allen Smiley with him, but when they got there it was obvious that he wanted to see Mickey alone.

"Take a walk, would you, Al?" he said.

Smiley knew what that meant. "I'll wait in the car," he said.

Siegel went into the house after Mickey had looked at him through his front door peephole, and he said: "Mick—I hope this place isn't bugged."

"Not this one," Mickey laughed. "It's been tried."

"I don't want to take any chances,' Siegel said. "Let's go outside."

They went out through the back door, and Siegel said: "Mick, you got any guys with equipment?"

"Well, Hooky Rothman's in town. Woody may be here, too. They can both handle a rod pretty good."

"Ask Hooky to see me tomorrow," Siegel said.

"I'll have Hooky call you," Cohen said. "What's up, Ben?"

"Nothing much," Siegel replied casually. "I'll see you."

Reconstructing this brief exchange later, Mickey said he had never seen Siegel so knotted up. "I should have asked more questions," he said, "but Ben was the kind of guy who told you only what he wanted you to know. If I'd had any idea what was coming up, I'd have hung around closer myself."

Enroute back to Virginia's home, Siegel drove to the George Raft house in Coldwater Canyon, and found the actor just starting breakfast. Raft was shocked by his friend's pallor and his jerky speech and movements, and he said: "Gee, you look terrible. Why don't you get out in the sun more? Take a vacation. Get away from the hotel for awhile."

"I'm tired, Georgie," Siegel said. "And I am going to get away for a few days. My two daughters are coming out from New York by train in a couple of days, and I promised to take them to Lake Louise up in Canada."

"Now you're talking sense," Raft said.

Siegel glanced at his watch. "I got to get going, pal. But how about having dinner with me and Al Smiley tonight? We're going to a new place—Jack's at the Beach."

"I wish I could, Ben," Raft said. "But you know I'm trying to start a picture company of my own, and I have a date with some people."

"Okay. Take a rain check. Maybe you can drop around at the house tomorrow."

"Will do," Raft said.

At two P.M. Siegel walked into Drucker's barbershop to meet Paul Price, and he took what Price calls "the full treatment"—shave, haircut, manicure, neck and shoulder massage, and shoeshine. They left there together, and walked to Joe Ross's law office a few blocks away.

Siegel was alone with Ross for perhaps an hour, going over the account books and discussing legal problems in connection with the hotel. There was probably also some talk about Virginia, because at the time Ross was not only preparing her income tax returns, but was also receiving money on her behalf from Joe Epstein in Chicago. During one four-year period, cashier's checks from Epstein to Ross totaled $10,000. Ross also disclosed later that Ben Siegel had given him approximately $50,000 which he had turned over to Virginia on various occasions. "I don't know where Miss Hill gets all her money," he said once, "and I don't want to know."

That day Ben Siegel probably wished he had the $50,000. He was being crushed in a financial vise, and he was so touchy about it that he quibbled with Paul Price about a small expense account that afternoon in Ross's office.

"Look, Ben," Price said, "I got a lousy little expense statement here that you have to sign, and you've been ducking me on it. How in hell do you expect me to operate if you don't sign it?"

"How much is it?" Siegel asked wearily.

"A measly thirty-five bucks."

Siegel signed the paper and said: "I suppose you're busted?"

"Sure I'm busted when I can't get expenses paid."

Siegel pulled out his wallet, counted out three one hundred dollar bills, and stuffed them into Price's hand. "Now you're not busted," he said. "Forget it."

Siegel and Price agreed to meet at the airport the following day for the return flight to Las Vegas, and each went their separate ways. It was now four P.M.

Siegel drove back to North Linden Drive, and joined Chick in Virginia's bedroom. The warm sun danced through the window and played on the wall. It touched the gun lying on a bedside table, and the barrel of the Colt threw back the light. Siegel turned slightly to keep the reflection out of his eyes, fingered the gun that he had taken from the safe only moments before, and spoke to Chick, who was lolling in a chintz covered chair.

"Chick," he said, "put the rod back in the safe and lock it up, will you?"

Chick uncoiled himself from the chair, smoothed out his brown alpaca sweater, and walked past the big bed with its gold damask spread.

"Don't you want the rod, Ben?" he asked.

"Hell, no," Siegel said. "Who needs it here?"

Chick closed the door of the safe, spun the dial twice, and then swung the concealing panel in front of it.

"You know Tab's jewels are in that safe, too," he said. "They cost her a hundred grand, and it makes me nervous having them in there."

"That's your sister's worry, kid," Siegel said. "I got enough on my mind."

"The stuff's not insured."

"So it's not insured. You think this is some Alabama hillbilly town like Bessemer? You're in Beverly Hills, where the cops come along this block every half hour." Siegel glanced at his watch. "Let's go in my room," he said. "I want to make some calls."

The telephone was ringing just as they stepped into the room, and Siegel answered the call.

"Hello," he said. "Oh it's you."

He listened for a moment as the other party talked, and Chick saw Siegel's face darken, and he was clenching his teeth. "You son of a bitch!" he bristled. "Over my dead body you will! You haven't got the guts!"

He dropped the receiver into its cradle, and stared out the window.

"Trouble, Ben?" Chick asked.

"Just some wise guy who thinks he can take me," Siegel growled.

"Anybody I know?"

"Yeah—you know him. Look, Chick, leave me alone for now. I got urgent business."

Chick went back to his own room, trying to guess the name of the man whom Siegel obviously did not want to identify. He never mentioned the incident to the police or any other official, and he is still guessing.

"If Ben had only confided in me that afternoon," he said recently, "we'd have had somebody to put the finger on."

In New York City, Police Chief Clinton Anderson of Beverly Hills got into a police squad car on the afternoon of June 20 with New York Police Lieutenant Francis Phillips and a uniformed patrolman, and started out on Riverside Drive heading toward the

Bronx. In Beverly Hills some months before, a robber had held up Mrs. Samuel Genis in her apartment and taken $114,000 worth of jewelry. When Chief Anderson let her riffle through a stack of mug shots, the usual procedure in such cases, she quickly picked out one photo. "That's the man who did it," she said.

"Albert Greenberg," Chief Anderson said. "A tough excon. You're sure?"

"I'm positive," Mrs. Genis said. "I'd know that face anywhere."

Greenberg was eventually traced to New York and was found in a Bronx apartment. Tough or not, Greenberg put up no resistance when the three policemen walked in that day, and he quietly admitted his identity. Later, when Chief Anderson questioned him downtown, he said: "I didn't do that caper, Chief. I wasn't even in Beverly Hills."

"Where were you?"

"At the Flamingo in Vegas. I was there two days before the robbery, and two days afterward. Never left the joint."

"Anybody see you there all that time?"

"Sure, Chief. Bugsy Siegel himself saw me there. He'll be my witness."

"He will, eh? All right. I'm taking you back to Beverly Hills, and when we get there I'll ask him."

"That's fine with me, Chief," Greenberg said. "Bugsy will tell you."

At seven P.M. on June 20 Ben Siegel phoned the Hollywood office of *Daily Variety* and asked for Florabel Muir, who was then doing a column for the show business newspaper. "I just want to thank you for your review of the Flamingo floor show," he said. He told her he was planning a major advertising campaign, and had booked the Ritz Brothers for a September opening. "I'm paying them $25,000 a week, but I think they're worth it."

At seven-thirty Allen Smiley pulled up at the curb in front of the house in his new powder blue Cadillac convertible. Siegel said: "Hi!" to Smiley and then turned to Chick. "Chick," he said, "your car's parked in the driveway, so we'll go to Jack's in Al's car. Tell Jerri we're all set."

Siegel sat in front with Smiley driving; Chick and Jerri were in the back seat. The night was warm, with no overcast to blot out the stars, and there was a soft but cooling breeze from the sea when they reached Jack's restaurant in Ocean Park. They had a leisurely seafood dinner, and Siegel seemed cheerful for a change as they watched the slow rollers snaking in from the sea, and breaking up in foam on the sandy beach. Siegel's back was toward the door, though he usually sat against a wall, as all gangsters learn to do, and he went through dinner without once glancing over his shoulder. Chick says there was no one in the restaurant Siegel or Smiley had ever seen before, and neither man made nor received a phone call.

Shortly after nine o'clock Siegel paid the dinner check, tipped the waiter, and walked out to call for the car. While he was standing there, someone handed him a copy of the morning *Los Angeles Times* (Chick does not remember whether it was Sonny Meyers, one of the owners, or the cashier). On the front page was stamped: *Good Night. Sleep well with the compliments of Jack's.*

Siegel tucked the paper under his arm, and as they started for Beverly Hills he said to Smiley: "My nose feels a little stuffy. Stop at the Beverly-Wilshire drugstore and I'll get something." Minutes later Siegel went alone into the pharmacy, and bought a bottle of Campho-phenique. He came out, holding the medicine in a small paper bag, and Smiley drove out Wilshire Boulevard to Whittier Avenue, turned right for a few blocks, and parked in front of the Linden Drive house.

Siegel reached into his pocket for the solid gold key Virginia had given him, unlocked the front door and switched on the hall light.

He stopped suddenly, sniffing the air like a hunting dog. "Chick," he said, "there's a very strong odor of flowers in here. Like carnations."

"I don't smell anything," Chick said. "There isn't a flower in the house."

Siegel ignored Chick's remark, and looked irritably at Jerri Mason. "Can't you smell them, Jerri?"

"No, I can't, Ben," she said. "If your nose is stopped up I don't see how you can smell anything."

Siegel went into the big living room, his nostrils still flaring, and sat down on the chintz covered divan. "I'm going to talk to Al for awhile, Chick," he said. "But take a look around. Somebody must have sent us some flowers. I can still smell 'em."

Chick went from room to room, but there was nothing. And then he remembered the folklore his mother had told him when he was a little boy in Alabama. "When someone smells flowers and there aren't any in the house," she had said, "it means they're going to die. That's what it means, Chick. They're going to die."

Chick walked upstairs with Jerri, and he told her what his mother had said long, long ago.

"Did you ever know anybody who died after smelling flowers, Chick?" she asked.

"Well, no," he said.

"Of course you didn't. So forget it. It's just one of those silly superstitions, like walking under a ladder or breaking a mirror. C'mon, let's go to bed. I'm tired."

Cars sped along Sunset Boulevard in Beverly Hills, tail lights spattering the dark like tracer bullets, glowing pale red as the traffic flowed, changing to flarelike color when the street corner signals showed yellow, and the stream slowed down. Just east of the Benedict Canyon Intersection, where the curved driveway of the Beverly Hills Hotel makes its exit, Arthur Day, Jr., sat at the wheel of his Yellow Cab, listening to music on the radio. Business had been slow on his shift that evening, but later, when dances and parties were over, he would be busy rolling through the tree-lined streets, driving fares to apartments and homes.

He was twisting the tuning knob when he heard a voice outside his window, calling: "Hey, Mac!" The street corner was bright with overhead lights, and alongside the curb he saw an old Pontiac sedan with crumpled fenders and dents in the body—not the kind of car usually seen on the streets in this prosperous neighborhood of shining Cadillacs and Lincoln Continentals. In the front seat, looking at him, was a stout, black-haired man who wore a seedy snap-brim hat pulled down over his eyebrows. The man at the wheel was in the shadows, but there was a third rider in the back seat, whose dark hair was long and unkempt, and whose white shirt was open at the neck. All three, Day decided, were Italian or Mexican.

"Hey, Mac," the man nearest the window said again, speaking

with a Brooklyn accent, "how do we get to North Linden Drive from here?"

"You're almost there," Day replied. "You keep going three blocks to Whittier Avenue. You make a left there, and Linden is the first street coming into Whittier from the left. You can't miss it."

"Thanks, Mac."

The man in the back muttered: "C'mon, let's go," and the battered old car moved on. Day turned up the volume on his radio, but his mind was on the three strangers in the Pontiac, and he said afterward he had never seen three tougher looking characters on that street, and he was glad they were not riding his cab.

Twenty minutes later he heard the sound of sirens, and two police cars shot out of Canon Drive to his left. The sirens screamed, red lights flashed their warning, and in an instant the cars were out of sight. But the sound was still strong, and he listened until it faded away. Now he could hear the music again, and he said to himself: "Some poor slob's in a jam."

At midnight, tuning in the news, Arthur Day heard a bulletin that shocked him, and it brought back the gruff sound of a man's voice. "Hey, Mac!" He shivered a little, because now it was all very clear. He was suddenly afraid, but he knew what he had to do.

Ben Siegel and Al Smiley sat side by side in the living room of Virginia's house, and as they talked the *Los Angeles Times* was spread open, like a napkin, across Siegel's lap.

Despite Virginia's expensive redecorating, it was not an attractive room, and the flowered sofa seemed incongruous in the Moorish-style setting. There was an oil painting of an English dowager on one wall beside the fireplace, and among other rococo touches was a small bronze statue of Cupid beside the fireplace tongs and poker. The coffee table in front of the sofa was French Provincial, but the valances on both windows were flowered print material. The curtains were parted on the windows, and a scant twenty feet away was a plant-covered latticework frame separating the property from the driveway of the house at 808 North Linden, owned by Martin and Anna Belousoff.

There was a car parked at the curb just ahead of Smiley's Cadillac. Ben Siegel did not see it. There was a man outside the window, standing behind the lattice frame. Ben Siegel did not see him.

There was a .30-30 carbine resting in a notch of wood, and the finger on the trigger was trembling. Lined up in the sights was Ben Siegel's handsome face. He did not see death; neither did he hear it, nor feel it. Here in the peace and stillness of the night he was safe. In thirty-five years there had been only two killings in Beverly Hills, killings of noncelebrities, and both were quickly solved. "We have a unique community in this respect," Chief Anderson has said. "The streets are patrolled every half hour, and strangers are quickly detected. It is a safe and pleasant place to live."

The first slug crashed through the window glass into Siegel's skull and drove his right eye fifteen feet away and plastered it to the tile floor of the dining room. Baby Blue Eyes, George Raft had called him. His long eyelashes were sliced from the eyelid, and were later found glued to the door jamb. The second bullet broke up the rest of his face, driving into the neck and out.

There were seven more bullets. One of them ripped through the sleeve of Allen Smiley's coat. Another hit the painting on the wall. There was a little figure of Bacchus, god of wine and pleasure, on the top of Virginia Hill's piano, and the white figure fell apart and bits of marble dropped on the ivory keys. Siegel's head rolled away from his neck and rested against the back of the sofa, and his flowered necktie was sticky and red.

"It was like firecrackers," Chick Hill said later. "We didn't know he was dead. We didn't know a goddam thing. Smiley yelled to douse the lights, and I did. And when I turned them on again there was Smiley inside the fireplace. I don't know how he got in there. Maybe he doesn't know himself. Jesus Christ, we were scared."

Chick ran back toward the stairs, and Jerri Mason was standing there, eyes staring, stricken dumb by blood and death.

"Call the cops!" he yelled at her.

She came out of it with the whip of his voice, and ran to the phone. She riffled through their phone list with fumbling fingers, found the "P" section and dialed the number marked Police. But it was not the police number at all; it was the emergency phone for

Barney Ruditsky's private detective office, and she screamed at the man who answered, and he said: "I'll be right over."

The instant she picked up the phone Chick remembered the safe in Virginia's room. He bounded down the hall, opened the panel, and unlocked the steel box. His hands came out with a handful of fire—Virginia's $100,000 cache of jewels—and he stood transfixed, brain working, hands clutching the gems, wondering where to hide them before the police showed up. He went to the laundry chute and dumped them inside, and they landed on the dirty linen piled up at the bottom of the chute.

And then he began to shake, and fell into the nearest chair and waited. He did not want to go downstairs again.

He was no longer afraid. The gun had come for Ben Siegel, and the gunner was gone, job done, and he would be miles away now, returning to a house and wife and children perhaps. In Chicago or Detroit or Frisco or some other city. Someone would hand him a thousand or two, and he would ask about the next job, and they would promise to let him know.

Chick waited in Virginia's room, bracing himself for the exhausting hours ahead. He would have joined Smiley, who was downstairs staring blankly at the hole in his sleeve while the perspiration of fear welled from his every pore. But he did not want to see Ben Siegel again, ripped apart on the couch, no longer a man, just a thing.

Good night. Sleep well with the compliments of Jack's.

CHAPTER NINETEEN

In Las Vegas the sand struck the city as though it were fired from a spray gun, pitting and peeling the paint from walls, driving under windows and piling up in drifts wherever it struck. The telephone wires sang like harp strings, swaying in the fierce storm, but they clung to the weathered poles, and calls were going through. One of them was from Los Angeles for Little Moe Sedway, another was for Gus Greenbaum. No one knows who made the calls, or exactly how it was said, but the message was clear, and Sedway and Greenbaum moved.

Twenty minutes after the burst of bullets smashed through the window and into Ben Siegel, Little Moe and Gus strode into the lobby of the Flamingo. The police cars were still arriving at 810 North Linden Drive, and the night crew at Beverly Hills police headquarters was still not sure who was lying dead in the house. But Sedway and Greenbaum knew.

Little Moe had not been seen inside the Flamingo for months. He hated Ben Siegel, and feared him. But now there was nothing to fear, and he and Gus, joined by Morris Rosen, the exburglar from New York, sent the word to the staff. They were taking over.

Hank Greenspun, dead tired from bucking the sandstorm on the long round trip from his home in Boulder City, dragged himself into the Flamingo toward dawn. In the casino the roulette wheels spun like tops, and the little white ball bounced in and out of the number slots. The stickmen at the crap tables mumbled their toneless spiel, and the cards floated silently to the felt at the blackjack tables. Ben Siegel was dead, but the games didn't die, and the players had no concern for life or death outside the little islands where they stood.

Hank joined Dick Chappell in the office, and the young manager was hollow-eyed from worry and lack of sleep.

"I got a phone call from a man in New York," Chappell said, "and he wants me to get the strongbox in the penthouse."

"Who made the call?"

"I don't know," Chappell replied. He probably did know, because he would not have obeyed an order from an anonymous gangster in New York, but there was no point in discussing it with Greenspun. "Will you come with me? I don't want to go up there alone."

"Sure," Hank said.

They crossed the garden, took the elevator to Ben Siegel's suite, and found the key to the strongbox where the New York man said it would be. They opened it, but there was only about $800 and a small diamond ring. Chappell dutifully called New York to report what he had found, but he never discussed the eastern gangster's reaction to the small amount of cash they found.

"Years later," Greenspun said recently, "it occurred to us what damn fools we were for going up there. We could have gotten our heads blown off. Suppose they thought there was a million dollars in the box. They might have thought we heisted it. But both of us were so damn naive we never gave it a thought."

Actually, the mob men never doubted what Chappell and Greenspun reported. And the reason they were never bothered or questioned about the strongbox is no mystery at all now. The mob soon discovered that Fat Irish Green had the money, and when the time came he surrendered the cash, as Siegel had told him to do, and he got his reward. For the past nineteen years Green has been living at the El Cortez Hotel in Las Vegas. He has never had a bill for room and board, and he gets small cash handouts now and then to pay for drinks and the other needs of life. The syndicate may cheat and rob and pay graft and kill, but they take care of a loyal man.

Police Chief Anderson was still in New York the night Siegel was slain. And so the first Beverly Hills officers who reached the house were Captain William White and Lieutenant P. R. Smith. But within an hour the house was swarming with newspapermen, special agents and other representatives of the District Attorney's staff, and men from the coroner's office. Photographs were taken of Siegel's grotesque corpse—he looked as though he might have been sitting up reading the *Times,* if he had not been so spattered with blood—and the house was searched as though there were mob men hiding in every room. In the driveway at 808 North Linden were found the nine .30 caliber shells, spewed there by the murder gun, and in a house across the street, at 807, officers talked with a man named Lou Shane, who said he heard the rattle of shots. He ran outside in time to see the vanishing tail lights of a car which he said was "really traveling."

Siegel's body was removed from the house after the photographs were taken, and at the morgue the onetime darling of movie society suffered the last indignity. He was laid out nude on a slab, and the *Los Angeles Herald-Express* published a front page picture of his right foot, with an express-type label dangling from the big toe. On it was written: Homicide, and his name was misspelled Benjamin Seigel. And that same morning, as the hawkers in Hollywood made their pitch for bus customers on the daily tour of movie star homes, they cried out: "Special today. See the house where Bugsy Siegel met his end!"

It seemed ironic at the time that Allen Smiley, who barely missed having a bullet tear through his chest instead of his coat sleeve, was an immediate suspect. Mickey Cohen has since said that the bullet which brushed Smiley was a sheer accident, and that the assassin was there to knock off Siegel and no one else. "These guys don't miss," Mickey said, forgetting that at least six of the nine shots went wild, "and if they had wanted Smiley they would have taken him." But the fact that Smiley did survive gave the investigators pause. Smiley had two new arrests—one for participating in a big crap game, the other for being involved in the near-fatal stabbing of movie actor Jon Hall at an all-night party. Smiley was accused of using a knife on Hall, but was later acquitted.

Smiley, who was already being investigated by the Immigration Department and would eventually spend a year in the penitentiary for falsely claiming American citizenship, had a formidable rap sheet, including two arrests for robbery and two as a murder suspect. Who knew almost every movement Ben Siegel had made that day? Smiley. Who knew when Siegel left Jack's Restaurant? Smiley. Who led the way to the sofa in front of the window where Siegel became a sitting duck? Smiley. It made sense for awhile, and Smiley was taken into "protective custody" and booked at Beverly Hills police headquarters.

Chick Hill was also a suspect, even though it was definitely determined he was on the second floor of the house at the time. As he reviews the horror of that night, Chick still seethes with anger. "The police and the D.A. gave me a bad time," he said. "They treated me like I was some hardened criminal just out of the pen. They promised me no photographers or newspapermen, but when I got to the D.A.'s office they were all there. Not only that, somebody stole all my neckties and one of my suits. The whole house was crawling with people. They even took some of Ben's clothes."

Chick and Jerri were both taken to police headquarters with Smiley, and all three were questioned by relays of officers, and a group from the District Attorney's office which included Leo Stanley, chief of the Bureau of Investigation, and his assistant, Captain Everett Davis. Smiley was put into a jail cell temporarily, but Chick and Jerri were allowed to return to the house.

Martin Belousoff, Virginia's neighbor, remembered that for weeks he had seen a small sedan parked across the street from her house. There was a man at the wheel—the same one each time—who wore workman's clothing and stared at the house. He was there for hours at a time, often far into the evening, but it never occurred to Belousoff to jot down the license number.

Arthritic Swifty Morgan, who was once a professional card player on transatlantic liners and whose source of income in the late years of his life is a mystery, was roused from bed at the Roosevelt Hotel, but he contributed nothing of value. Paul Price, Joe Ross, George Raft, and Mickey Cohen knew only what they read in the papers.

Actually, Mickey Cohen was clean; he had nothing against Ben Siegel. As Mickey once said in his forthright way: "I never killed nobody that didn't deserve killing by my standards." Mickey was never tried for murder anywhere, but he did talk himself into Alcatraz on an income tax conviction. Perhaps he should have remembered the plaque he had seen on a wall behind Chief Anderson's desk which reads: "Oh, Lord, help me to keep my big mouth shut unless I know what I'm talking about."

Even Esta Siegel was not immune to the frantic search for information. The dead gangster's blonde, blue-eyed exwife was taken to the District Attorney's office for questioning, and while she nervously tamped out one lipstick-stained cigarette after another, she defended Siegel as a "fine husband and father," and said they were divorced only because he was never home. She had not the slightest idea why anyone would want to kill him, and after the funeral she and her two daughters returned to New York.

Chief Anderson, meanwhile, had arrived at his own analysis of the case, and he was determined to get the story from the one man whose name had not even been mentioned in the thousands of words filling the newspapers on the case. And the order went out to his men: "When Moe Sedway shows up here from Vegas—and he will—pick him up and bring him in. I've got questions for him."

In a little town in the Sacramento valley, a seedy young man in a cheap hotel picked up the morning paper and saw the black headlines: BUGSY SIEGEL SLAIN. He poured a slug of whisky in a dirty glass, tossed it down his throat, and slowly read the story, over and over. There was a picture of The Bug, and he was smiling, and the long eyelashes made him look almost soft and feminine. The man carefully folded the paper, put it on top of a bureau, and for a long time sat there, looking out the window at the flat brown land, dried and burned by the blazing summer sun.

Then he walked steadily to the bathroom, emptied a bottle of small red capsules into the palm of his hand, and washed them into his stomach, three and four at a time, with whisky and water. When the pills were gone, he stretched himself out on the bed and went to sleep. He was found dead there the next day, and as he had requested, his body was shipped to the Beth Olam Cemetery in Hollywood. They put him in Section M-2 of the mausoleum in the fourth row from the floor, and on the crypt in the third row, directly below him, was the plaque which read: *"In Loving Mem-*

ory from the Family. Benjamin Siegel—February 28, 1906–June 20, 1947." Joe Moll had come at last to be with his friend.

At Beverly Hills police headquarters Chief Anderson found himself enmeshed in the skein of confusion that inevitably turns up in a major homicide. There were the endless false leads, the screwball letters, the anonymous phone calls. In Redwood City, 400 miles north of Los Angeles, an exconvict named Edward Ross confessed that he had shot Siegel. In Waurika, Oklahoma, a Missouri State penitentiary graduate said he drove the getaway car. On the border at Mexicali, narcotic smugglers bumped off Police Chief Juan Menesen, and the crime was blamed on members of the Siegel mob. Frank Orbi, a Mexican drug peddler, was picked up for questioning because he had once complained that Bugsy had cheated him out of $6500 in a smuggling deal.

None of these incidents—and each one had to be investigated—turned up any valid link to the killing.

Little Moe Sedway came to Beverly Hills, as Anderson knew he would, and was immediately brought to headquarters. He was in poor physical condition, trembling and struggling for breath, and he promised that if he could rest overnight he would be happy to see the Chief the next day.

When Anderson kept the appointment, he was told Moe had been rushed to a hospital. He found the little hoodlum in a room marked NO ADMITTANCE. OXYGEN, but he went in anyway.

"I'm a sick man, Chief," Sedway gasped. "I can't talk to you today. Come back tomorrow."

"All right," Anderson said. "I'll be back."

The following morning Anderson was chagrined to discover that slippery Little Moe—perhaps rejuvenated by the oxygen—had taken a night train to Las Vegas, and was thus out of the Chief's jurisdiction. Anderson did not see him again until 1951, when both were called as witnesses during the Kefauver crime investigation.

At the time Sedway had already suffered three heart attacks, and was being treated for stomach ulcers and intestinal abscesses. "I never had a chance to talk to him," Anderson now says, "but I was convinced, and still am, that he had a hand in the Siegel killing. He knew who did it." While Anderson was trying to see

Sedway, taxi driver Arthur Day decided he could no longer keep silent about his secret. He was driving along Santa Monica Boulevard one evening when he saw a parked Beverly Hills police squad car, and pulled in behind. He told the two officers, whose names he could not remember, what he had seen the night Siegel was killed. Then, when he finished his shift and took his cab back to the Yellow Taxi garage, he related his experience to the supervisor there.

Some weeks afterward, when it suddenly occurred to him that he might be the only man alive who had seen the killers on their way to murder Siegel, he grew taut with fear. Each new rider in his cab looked like a gangster, and he stared at them so anxiously in his mirror that sometimes he forgot where he was going. At home he was suspicious of every passing stranger on the sidewalk, and he was sure the mob would blast him some night. When his apprehension almost led to traffic accidents, he quit the cab company, and got a job in an aircraft plant miles away from Beverly Hills. He was found there by State Special Agent Ray McCarthy, who had patiently followed up a tip from the cab company, and once more he told the story in detail.

"I'll never forget that one man's face," Day said to McCarthy. "I'd know him anywhere."

"Give me that description again," McCarthy said. "We might find someone who'll fit it."

"Let me see if I can make a little sketch for you," Day said.

He found a sheet of paper and a soft pencil, and in fifteen minutes he gave McCarthy a drawing of a swarthy, scowling man —the one who sat in the back seat of the Pontiac that night. McCarthy returned to the plane factory several days later with a sheaf of police mug shots, including one which looked almost exactly like Day's crude sketch. He spread the photos out, and he was not surprised when Day excitedly selected the likeness of the man he had drawn.

"That's the guy!" Day exclaimed. "He was in the back of the car." He examined the other photos, and plucked up another one. "Hey—this is the fellow who asked me how to find Linden Drive."

"You're sure?"

"Yes, sir. I'm sure."

The initials of the two excons—and this is the first time their possible role in the murder has been even mentioned outside police circles—were J. T. and T. D. T. Both had long records. Both came from Arizona. And both were known associates of the Gus Greenbaum gang in that state. McCarthy flew to Arizona, though he had no jurisdiction there, and tried to determine whether the two men were out of the state on the night of June 20. Unfortunately, he was in no position to make an official investigation, interview the two hoodlums, or pick them up on suspicion. He is still convinced, as I am, that they were taking orders from Greenbaum, and that they were in Beverly Hills that fatal evening. Perhaps no one will ever know.

Chief Anderson never heard of Arthur Day, Jr.—evidently the two cops in the prowl car failed to report the cab driver's story—and he is inclined to doubt that the two Arizona gangsters knocked off Ben Siegel. "This crime was well planned," he says. "The gunmen knew every move Siegel made from the time he left Las Vegas. They had cased the house, knowing our police cars were patrolling that street every half hour. They wouldn't have to ask how to get to Linden Drive."

But he does believe that Sedway and Greenbaum had a hand in planning the deed, and says they were the kind of men who could easily import gunmen from another town to do the job. "These people outside the law," he said, "have to solve their quarrels differently. They can't go to the courts or to the police, so they handle it themselves. They can hire gunmen for a few bucks, fly them in and keep them in storage until they're ready."

Little Moe Sedway, unfortunately, died of his multiple ailments in 1952 before anyone could extract from him the hidden pieces of the puzzle. Moe lies in the same mausoleum with Ben Siegel—perhaps fifty feet away—and his floor-level horizontal crypt is far more imposing and expensive than the file-like slot that holds the remains of the man he hated.

On North Linden Drive and on Whittier Avenue on June 21 the cars crawled along the pavement, bumper to bumper, and the drivers and their passengers looked for the number 810, and gawked at the house. Traffic cops were posted here and there along the block, trying to break up the jam, and forcing drivers to move on. The sidewalks swarmed with pedestrians, and the nervier ones darted up the driveways to peer in the windows. Some even dared to ring the doorbell. The mailman brought letters from morbid people offering to rent the house, and messengers came with telegrams.

Chick and Jerri stayed out of sight in the house, curtains drawn, and they were together upstairs when the call came from Virginia Hill in Paris.

She told Chick how she heard the news at the houseboat party. Her voice was hoarse, and he said: "Tab—are you all right?"

"I'm all right now," she said. "There is nothing I can do now. It's over. Chick, you're okay, I hope."

"Sure, I'm okay. The cops kept me at headquarters for five hours, but they let me come back here."

"Who did it, Chick?"

"Damned if I know, Tab. The cops don't know anything, and they wouldn't tell me anyway."

"Listen," she said. "What about my stuff in the safe?"

"I got it all, Tab," he said.

"Get out of the house as fast as you can. Take my things and ship them to Florida. I'll meet you there."

"When?"

"God knows," she said. "I'm not going to hang around Paris. Too goddam many nosy reporters. I'll call you at Miami. And Chick—"

"Yes?"

"If you need money to move, call Joe in Chicago. I've already talked to him. So long."

For the next three days Chick and Jerri worked frantically gathering up Virginia's personal possessions and packing them for shipment to Florida by truck. Richard Lee Morley, a young television producer who was among Virginia's suitors, came to the house and helped them pack her silverware, dishes, and linens. Later that same day Chick and Jerri drove to Morley's apartment, the Villa Italia in Crescent Heights, and entrusted him with the dazzling heap of jewelry Chick had retrieved from its hiding place.

Morley kept the gems wrapped up in what he later described as his "dirty socks and laundry."

That evening Morley and Chick had dinner at King's Restaurant, and in a phone booth there Chick called Epstein in Chicago, and told him his urgent need for cash. A packet of money—Chick can remember only that it contained several thousand dollars—soon arrived by air wrapped in plain manila paper, and Chick immediately began paying off Virginia's accumulated bills. He gave Morley $1000 in cash to settle up her Schwab's drugstore account, but he handled the other bills himself.

Chick had just returned from an all-day round of visits to various stores and individuals when Mack Gray, George Raft's factotum, appeared at the front door.

"Georgie's out in the car," he said. "He wants to know if there's anything he can do."

Chick was suddenly bursting with resentment. "Oh, he does, does he?" he said. He ran down the stone steps to the curb, where Raft sat at the wheel of his convertible, and shook his fist at the actor.

"You crummy son of a bitch!" he cried. "Our friend is dead, and you send your boy in instead of coming yourself!"

"Now, Chick—"

"Don't give me your song and dance. You should have been here long ago when we needed help. Now get the hell out of here, and I hope you never come back."

Raft understood Chick's anger, but he could also do some bitter philosophizing himself about their "friend." He still had his little piece of the Flamingo stock, but he knew his $100,000 loan had been burned up in the burst of gunfire. "You know," he said later, "Virginia Hill was at my house one time, and she said: 'If Ben Siegel asked me to push a lump of sugar from here to Chicago with my nose, I'd do it.' Well, that's the kind of guy he was if he was your friend. If he had lived, he would have paid the money back. I know he would."

And George Raft also thought about the night of June 20, and how lucky he was. Suppose he had gone to dinner with Ben Siegel at Jack's? He would have been sitting on the couch with Smiley, and he too might have had his head blown off. He thought about Virginia and he wondered who would have her now.

CHAPTER TWENTY

The new faces at the Flamingo were like the old faces. The eyes and hair and ears were different, like an assortment of Halloween masks, but behind the makeup they were the same. Mob men with mob money. Men with police records from coast to coast. The list of those who were involved in wiping out all remnants of the Bugsy Siegel rule included Little Moe Sedway, Gus Greenbaum, Morris Rosen, Meyer Lansky, Dave Berman, and Israel "Icepick Willie" Alderman.

These All-American ruffians, aware of their underworld reputations, picked urbane Sanford Adler of the El Rancho to front for them. His police record was not generally known, he could get the money to buy approximately 48 percent of the stock, and as a professional gambler he had the experience to protect the other investors. So Adler's name went on the state gambling license, and he moved into the front office. It was a big promotion but it is certain that he can look back on it as a nightmare that almost put him in a crypt, too.

At the time it seemed like a sound move. As Sedway testified later: "The place was in a very bad spot. It was ready to close if we didn't get a buyer. They weren't doing much business on account of all the adverse publicity that Siegel was getting."

On July 2, Virginia Hill checked out of her $35 a day suite at the Westminster Hotel in Paris, and drove a rented car southward toward the Riviera. She stopped at Aix-en-Provence overnight, and the following day checked into the Beach Club at Monaco. She was seen in the world-famed casino one evening alone, moodily watching the players in their evening dresses and dinner jackets—a prince at one table, a countess at another. Alone in a foreign land, surrounded by people babbling a language she could not understand, and with an escort she described as a "bare-faced kid," Virginia was in an agony of loneliness. She went back to her hotel and swallowed all the remaining pills in her ever-present bottle of barbiturates.

She was found unconscious by a maid who came to her room earlier than usual with a breakfast tray. Virginia was taken to the Villa Albert I Clinic in Monaco where emergency treatment saved her life. She moved into a suite at the Hotel La Reserve in nearby Beaulieu-sur-Mer where she spent four days with nurses watching her around the clock.

On July 23 she got a bill from the French physician who treated her at Monaco. His fee was 22,000 francs, but she only gave him 10,000 francs, and promised to send the rest from Paris. Months later the doctor complained to American authorities that he never heard from her again, and said somewhat acidly that perhaps she was penalizing him for helping her stay alive.

In Paris, Virginia took a large and expensive suite at the Ritz, and once more she began making the rounds of the nightclubs and restaurants with Nick Fouillette. She had already spent $4600 on her first Paris stay, plus the considerable expenses on the Riviera, and the S.O.S. went out to Joe Epstein in Chicago. Airmail letters began arriving, and Fouillette, who was standing by when Virginia ripped open and extracted several one-hundred dollar bills, assumed they all contained cash.

Four days after checking into the Ritz, Virginia once more gulped down sleeping pills, and an ambulance took her to the American Hospital in Neuilly. While she was recuperating, Virginia reported to the American Embassy that she had lost her passport, and urgently needed a replacement so she could fly home. As this request was being processed, one of the hospital employees gave a newspaper reporter a tip that Virginia apparently had a secret lover in Paris whose last name was Fluctuat. The tipster said Virginia was wearing a scarf with that name on it when she came to the hospital, and the excited newsman, who hadn't been around the city very long, spent hours searching for the mysterious suitor.

Eventually the reporter discovered to his chagrin that Virginia had purchased the scarf herself, and that on it was printed the official motto of Paris: *Fluctuat Nec Mergitur.*

One day after her departure, the Embassy people discovered that they, like many other trusting officials, had been tricked by her. Room maids at the Ritz, cleaning up her bottle-strewn suite, found the "lost" passport stuffed behind a sofa cushion. In 1947 French government rules specified that Americans had to write down, on pages 9 and 10 of their passports, how many American dollars were brought into France, either in person or by mail, and how many dollars were converted to francs. These two pages had been torn out of Virginia's passport, and once more she had beaten the law.

There was a curious sort of retribution for this offense only minutes after Virginia landed in New York. She was greeted there by Tom Slack, special investigator for the District Attorney of Los Angeles, and he walked with her into the Customs shed for the routine examination of her baggage. There was nothing visibly illegal in her luggage, but a Customs agent noticed a diamond ring on her finger.

"Did you buy that abroad?" he asked.

"No," she said. "Ben Siegel once gave me a watch in Los Angeles. I didn't like it, and I traded it for this ring at the Lackritz store in Beverly Hills."

"May I see it, please?"

She slipped the ring from her finger and handed it to the agent just as an incoming plane made a crash landing on the airstrip outside. Everyone rushed to the windows to stare at the wrecked plane, and when Virginia returned to the counter she said: "Where's my ring?"

"It was right here," the Customs man said. "I thought you had picked it up."

"Well, I didn't," she snapped. "C'mon, where is it?"

"I haven't got it," he said, flushing. "But it *must* be here somewhere."

He and other agents joined Virginia and Tom Slack, and they went over every inch of the floor and the long counters. But it was gone. Later, when Virginia complained to the Kefauver Committee about the loss, she was asked: "Did you make a claim against the Government for losing it while it was in their possession?"

"I didn't want to bother," she said testily. "I don't imagine the ring was worth more than five hundred dollars."

That same morning at the airport Virginia refused to discuss the Siegel murder with Agent Slack, and when he could not legally hold her there Virginia immediately left for her home in Miami Beach. Chick and Jerri were waiting for her. When Virginia learned they were man and wife she was purple with anger.

The tension in the house was aggravated by Virginia's strange new fear that she might be rubbed out by the same men who blasted Ben Siegel. Flood lights were installed, private eyes were put on duty, and Police Chief Short sat in his office hoping the bullets wouldn't perforate her there in an off-guard moment.

Several newspaper columnists printed teaser items that Virginia had really gone to Europe to beg Lucky Luciano for Siegel's life, that she had compiled an extensive dossier on her underworld activities, and had advised Chief Anderson where it could be found if she happened to be killed, and that Siegel had been slain because he wanted to take over the narcotics racket from Luciano. These items were columnist hokum, but Virginia read them, and alternately raged and wept. One evening Chick came home, saw Jerri in the living room and asked: "Where's Tab?"

"I don't know," his wife replied. "She hasn't been out of her room as far as I know."

Chick went to the bedroom, but the door was locked.

"Tab!" he called out. "Open the door."

He rapped his knuckles on the wood once or twice and then, getting no response, he kicked at the door until the lock broke. Virginia was flat on her back, still as death, with the familiar frightening color in her cheeks, and he shook her and slapped her face without result. "I pried her mouth open," he said, "and I found a handkerchief stuffed between her teeth. There was an empty pill bottle on the bed, and I knew she had done it again."

Minutes later Virginia was taken to the St. Francis Hospital in Miami Beach, and for the fourth time in as many months went through the unpleasant emergency treatment with the stomach pump. When Virginia regained consciousness, she gave reporters the usual explanation that she had been unable to sleep and took too many of the pills. Later, though, in a statement to Government agents, she accused Jerri of trying to kill her. She said she had taken three or four capsules, and that Chick's wife then urged her to swallow the others "just to make sure I would sleep."

In any case, the Florida suicide attempt was just the prologue to a frenzied journey covering thousands of miles—an aimless flight from pain and sorrow and the wreckage of her life with Ben Siegel. Chick was driving, Jerri sat beside him, Virginia's jewelry in a paper bag rested on the front seat. Virginia slumped in the back seat of the convertible, dragging on one cigarette after another. They went to Pensacola, where Chick and Virginia talked to one of their brothers, Robert "Tig" Hill. From there they sped to Point Clear, Alabama, and checked into the luxurious Grand Hotel as Mr. and Mrs. C. Hood and daughter, Betty." Chick put the jewelry into the hotel safe, and Virginia bought a .22 automatic in a pawnshop.

They stayed in Point Clear three days, drove through Biloxi, Mississippi, and across Louisiana and Texas into Arizona. They paused at the Grand Canyon, where Virginia refused to leave her room, and then swung northward into Salt Lake City. On September 24, again using aliases, the three wanderers checked into the Sky Lodge, a fashionable resort hotel on the shore of Swan Lake, far up in the northwest corner of Montana. Virginia soon made friends with Lee Brisey, owner of the Lodge, and his mother, Edith Brisey, and she made a nightly appearance in the bar. Occasionally she became bartender, standing behind the cash register in stockinged feet, and buying drinks for the house with a stack of twenty-dollar bills.

Amazingly, Virginia also organized a bear hunting expedition while she was in Montana, and paid two guides a total of $1270 for a three-day pack trip. Joe Epstein, who made the mistake of flying in from Chicago on the eve of this odd safari, was coaxed into joining the group. "Joe was out of shape," Virginia said later in her blunt fashion. "He made the first three miles on his ass, and then he sat down on a log and quit."

Shortly after Epstein returned to Chicago, having left behind his customary cash contribution, Virginia sopped up a dozen drinks, and invaded Chick's room, which adjoined hers, at four A.M. The aneurysm of her hate suddenly burst, and she cried: "Goddam you, Jerri, you tried to kill me in Miami. You wanted my jewels, and you couldn't get 'em with me alive!"

"Hey, Tab!" Chick protested. "Cut it out."

"Like hell I will!" Virginia screamed. "I'm going to kill the little bitch."

She jumped toward the bureau, where Chick kept his .38 in a top drawer, and found the gun. She crashed the butt against Jerri's skull. Once, twice. The blood ran down the young girl's neck, and she dropped screaming to the floor before Chick could grab Virginia's arm and get her out of the room. When he finally forced her into bed, her fury spent, Chick went back to his wife. They packed their luggage at once, and were hundreds of miles away before Virginia woke up and found them gone. Chick took Jerri to Pensacola, left her there, and told her he would get a quick divorce. "It's finished," he said. And it was.

Chick says he went to an attorney in a town near Pensacola—he can't remember which town it was—and paid $50 for a divorce. Jerri was not present for what was apparently a mere paper transaction, but he says he sent her a copy of the decree.

Jerri Mason Hill, though she has since remarried, cannot exorcise the devilish memories from her mind. I found her at home one morning, and her self-torture seems to have destroyed her. Here are some of the questions and answers from our interview, quoted verbatim:

A. She [Virginia] screwed up my life. To a point where I am a very sick girl. Do you realize that if I say anything I won't be living very long?

Q. You're not serious?

A. Yes, I am serious.

Q. Why would anybody do that?

A. Virginia Hill. Ben Siegel and I were very good friends, and Chick was also a good friend until his sister got ahold of him.

Q. I'm afraid this is a very painful subject.

A. It is more than painful. I have been trying to get it out of my mind. I just came from a psychiatrist. He gave me something to slow me down.

Q. Do you know who killed Ben Siegel?

A. Who killed Benny? Yes, Jerri knows. I don't even care if they kill me because I have come to the point where I don't care whether I live or not.

Q. But this was so long ago. I'm surprised it still bothers you.

A. It has bothered me. It has made me an alcoholic, and then I turned to sleeping pills because I have no peace of mind. I would like to get out of the country myself. I would be left alone. I am haunted, day in and day out.

Q. By what?

A. By this. It wasn't my fault. But I was there. I was married to Chick Hill, and I still would be now, but his sister turned him against me. He also thinks I know.

Q. Does anyone really know?

A. I was in the room when it happened. I ran downstairs to hear the last carbine shot. I saw the whole mess.

Q. Why did you quarrel with Virginia at Swan Lake?

A. Because she rejected my marriage to Chick. And she also objected to my drinking, and I wasn't drinking then.

Q. At that time?

A. No. I just came back from the psychiatrist right now. I didn't sleep all night. In fact, I tried to commit suicide myself, a week ago. And I almost succeeded.

Q. With sleeping pills?

A. Yes, I can get all I want.

Q. Why did Virginia want your marriage with Chick broken up?

A. Because I would not go into gambling, drinking, and carousing and sleeping with other men.

Q. She slept with everybody, I guess.

A. I don't think she missed one. They have all shoved me from part to part. I've been running—and running—and running and now I'm tired. It wouldn't surprise me if they used a carbine on me.

Q. You mean that?

A. Yes, I do. Because they're afraid of what I might tell.

Jerri would not explain what she knew about the murder, or why she thought she might also be killed. Chick Hill, who never saw her again after the mail-order divorce, is convinced that she has been seeing ghosts all these years. "Tab had nothing to do with breaking up the marriage," he said in Virginia's defense. "I felt sorry for Jerri after the shock she suffered that night, and that's why I married her. I was never in love with her. It was so long ago. She ought to forget it."

But at the moment the sound of bullets breaking glass, and the sight of Ben Siegel's bloody body are still in her brain, and seemingly cannot be erased. The psychiatrist talks to her, but it does not help.

At the Sky Lodge on Swan Lake shortly before Thanksgiving, 1947, the confetti of snow was swirling in the cold air. It was time to close the resort for the long winter, and it was time for Virginia to move on.

While she was packing her clothes, she selected a diamond ring, a pair of diamond earrings, and a bracelet studded with diamonds, rubies, and sapphires. She went down to the lobby and presented them to Edith Brisey. An attorney from Kalispell drew up a document stating that the gems—which were valued at $15,000—were given to Mrs. Brisey as a reward "for comfort given in time of need when all seemed lost."

None of the principals involved in this generous gift ever explained what was meant by "comfort in time of need," but the most likely answer is that Mrs. Brisey protected Virginia's anonymity at the resort, kept reporters out of her way, and somehow hushed up the pistol-whipping of Jerri Mason Hill. Mrs. Brisey, in fact, accompanied Virginia on a train journey to Spokane on November 9, stayed overnight with her in a hotel there, and hung around long enough to witness the arrival of Joe Epstein from Chicago. She said Epstein bought a whole new wardrobe for Virginia in Spokane, and that they went their separate ways on November 11.

It may have been disillusioning for Virginia to learn that Mrs. Brisey went by train to Beverly Hills and promptly sold the earrings and the bracelet to a shady diamond broker who, by coincidence, had been under surveillance for some time by Police Chief Anderson. The two baubles brought only $1000 to Mrs. Brisey, and the ring was subsequently sold to a Great Falls jeweler by Lee Brisey for $2000.

On November 24, two pretty women, a Mrs. Sylvia Nettler of Chicago and her friend, Mrs. Norma Hall of Timberline, Montana, checked in together at the fashionable Paradise Inn in Phoenix. Norma Hall, of course, was Virginia Hill. On the surface, Virginia looked chic and alluring in her new clothes, and her collection of mink and sable stoles caused talk even among women to whom costly fur coats were standard equipment. She had also cut down on her drinking, and seemed to be amusing herself in a mild flirtation with the young tennis pro at the resort.

But on December 12 she searched for death again. She was found unconscious in her room, and this time it took extreme measures by the doctors to get the barbiturates out of her system. She was in the Good Samaritan Hospital eight days, apparently eager to die, but when Chick came to deliver her Cadillac she had survived the ordeal.

On December 20 Virginia left the hospital, and drove off alone in her car. No newsmen witnessed her departure, and she vanished as instantly and as completely as though she had been killed and buried in a desert grave.

The investigation into the murder of Ben Siegel was brief and perfunctory.

In Washington, in an impassioned speech to the Associates of the FBI National Academy, J. Edgar Hoover talked about Siegel "and his criminal scum." He said:

> The glamor that surrounded his life in all its vile implications was shockingly disgusting. Siegel was a symbol. He fronted for more sinister and despicable characters—the "untouchables" who hire mercenaries to do their dirty work. I have no doubt of law enforcement's ability to cope with such characters, but I know that law enforcement is shocked by public indifference. Its fullest measure of protection cannot be given until every citizen not only recognizes his duty but has the courage to discharge his duty.

The FBI, of course, had no authority under law to work on the Siegel case. Chief Anderson, along with State and District Attorneys' investigators, spent weeks running down even the most insignificant clues, but it was like grasping for a cloud. An assessment of the investigation suggests that all concerned were relieved to have Siegel dead. No gangster in California history was more hated by the police than the vain and arrogant Bugsy.

But in Nevada the political leaders suddenly saw the Siegel murder as a threat to their growing gold mine—the gambling business that supplied the cash they couldn't get in taxes or any other way from the state's meager population, then about 140,000.

It was not just the killing that made them uneasy. It was the sudden realization that the big money was coming from the underworld, that they knew very little about the hoodlums in their midst, and that any homicidal thug like Siegel could get a gambling license merely by applying to city authorities.

So many complaints poured into the office of then Attorney General Alan Bible about the muscle tactics of Moe Sedway and Morris Rosen, and how they took over the Flamingo without court or other legal action, that he decided something must be done. Bible, now a United States Senator, studied the problem and authorized an opinion which stated that the Nevada Tax Commission, the board which controls gambling, could check the connections and backgrounds of all applicants before granting a casino license.

The legitimate operators said nothing, but the gamblers with syndicate backing cried persecution. Robbins Cahill, who was then secretary of the Commission, has since said that the members "figured that Rosen was bigger than Sedway. He was the guy we were really afraid of in connection with mob influence." Indeed, at a subsequent Commission hearing, with both Bible and Cahill present, Morris Rosen complained that his reputation was being ruined. He neglected to mention that he was a convicted burglar and bookmaker, among other things, but did say that his family was being harmed by the gossip. His son Jack was then in military school, and Rosen said the other pupils were avoiding him. (Jack Rosen would eventually marry and divorce Millicent Siegel, one of Bugsy's daughters.)

Some of the Las Vegas casino men chose to fight the Attorney General's ruling, but in the showdown the Nevada Legislature passed a law giving the State the right to approve or disapprove gambling license applicants in any city or county. The State thus got complete control of gambling and gambling taxes. In recent years Nevada's casinos have been winning more than $300,000,000 annually, and since the State collects 5.5 percent of the profits the importance of that law is plain.

In the spring of 1948, when Morris Rosen was the strong man behind the scenes at the Flamingo, the books showed that Sanford Adler was not filling up the bank vaults as fast as the stockholders hoped. The board took a vote, and fired Adler. The exmanager, convinced he was the innocent goat in a power struggle at the hotel, went to Carson City and formally asked support from the Tax Commission. He was so sure that the Commissioners were on his side that he drove happily back to Las Vegas, and as he walked up the steps into the Flamingo he encountered Rosen.

Anger blurred his natural caution, and he hit Rosen hard enough to drop him on the concrete steps. Adler got a sock in the eye in return, but the fight was broken up by other hotel officials. Adler, who thought he had won, soon discovered his error. He was told to leave town—or risk internment in the nearest crypt. Adler, who was described as "a weasel" by Ray Warren, Jr., then an investigator for the Tax Commission, gathered up his belongings and nearly broke a record for the long desert drive from Las Vegas to Beverly Hills.

There he went to police headquarters, and told Chief Anderson that the Vegas mob was going to knock him off. But when Anderson asked for details, Adler withdrew like a hermit crab. He sold out his Flamingo stock, moved to the Lake Tahoe area, where for some years he managed the Cal-Neva gambling casino, later temporarily taken over by Frank Sinatra. He is now an investment broker in Beverly Hills. He never returned to Las Vegas, and currently insists on having all questions about those bloody days put to him in writing; he then refuses to answer.

Having dumped Adler with their customary violent technique, Sedway and Rosen turned to Gus Greenbaum. Gus was shrewd and tough, but if he couldn't make the casino pay they faced the unhappy prospect of closing the doors. So Gus took over the management, and whatever the success formula was, he had it.

If there were cheating dealers he took them into a soundproof room and broke their hands or shoulder blades with a baseball bat. If there was a way to skim money off the top without having the Internal Revenue men snooping around, Gus could do it. If there were unwelcome visitors at the hotel—maverick hoodlums like Mickey Cohen—Gus would grab the seat of their pants and propel them to the nearest exit.

But for the so-called respectable citizens and the high rollers with class, Gus was as friendly and sincere as a Bible salesman. He knew the percentages of both gambling and public relations and he made them work. And after a year on the job, the Flamingo was out of the red and the books showed a $4,000,000 profit.

Greenbaum ran the Flamingo for seven years, with only one minor disturbance. Two small-time gunmen from Los Angeles, Tony Trombino and Tony Broncato, had the audacity to walk into the race book cashier's room at the hotel, and pull a stickup in which they and two other punks got a mere $3500—or so the police reports said. One of them left a fingerprint, and in August 1951, only three months after this foolish theft, the "Two Tonys," as they were known, got theirs in the accepted fashion. They were lured into a car in Los Angeles, and a hired gunman cut them down with eight bullets—four for each head.

Aside from this altercation there were no problems at the Flamingo, and the money was turning into a torrent. None of the heirs to Ben Siegel's desert marvel ever publicly gave him credit for the big dream. But they saw it take shape and grow, and soon there was a frantic scramble for land and money along the strip. During Gus Greenbaum's reign, from 1948 to 1955, millions of dollars, most of it mob money, went into the construction of the New Frontier, the Thunderbird, the Desert Inn, the Sands, the Sahara, the Riviera, the Dunes, and the Royal Nevada, each bigger and more luxurious than the last. In recent years, on land where the coyotes and rattlers and lizards once lay undisturbed in the sun, have also come the Stardust, the Tropicana, Caesar's Palace, and other castles towering into the sky.

Ben Siegel led them there; he was the man who invented Las Vegas.

The new faces come and go, most of them with the same gutter-animal habits and minds of a Ben Siegel. The guns don't roar as they did in the old days, the hoodlums are tailored and manicured and make their deals through well-known and expensive lawyers. But though they wear velvet gloves, the muscle still lies beneath, and one can believe that no sinner is ever very far from the gun or the knife.

Gus Greenbaum eventually got his. Old and sick, addicted to heroin, Gus quarreled with his masters, and retired to Phoenix. He was coaxed back to Las Vegas to manage the new Riviera. He was already in trouble with some of the Chicago mob, and during a lull in this deadly friction Gus went home for the Thanksgiving holidays.

On December 5, 1958, kill-for-pay boys flew in from Florida and used a butcher knife on Gus while he was asleep. They got most of his head off with one machete-like sweep, and they slashed his wife, Bess, with the same blade and then strangled her until they were sure she was dead.

Ben Siegel was taken fast by the gun and left life with somewhat more dignity, but Gus Greenbaum had a finer funeral than his old crony. Three hundred mourners—famous and infamous—came to see him off, and among them was United States Senator Barry Goldwater.

CHAPTER TWENTY-ONE

Chick Hill, who thought he was sitting on top of the world until the mob guns took Ben Siegel, was a lonely, frightened, and confused young man in the fall of 1948. Virginia was out of his life for the moment, and for the first time in years he had to make his own decisions and chart his own moves. Jerri had gone home weeping. He had nothing left but his clothes, his car, and—thanks to occasional pilfering from the Epstein money shipments—a wallet stuffed with cash.

He had one dubious talent, but perhaps he could make it pay. He remembered how he used to carry four dice in his pocket when he was a little boy, switching them around as he walked, and when Virginia was out he practiced throwing them on a blanket or a rug. "I was a blanket crap shooter," he said, "and I could make any number I wanted. Even with honest dice. I used to drive my brothers nuts. I could call a natural and—wham—there it was. They'd bet against a hard way eight, and out I'd come with the double fours. Oh, I was crooked as hell, and I figured I ought to cash in on it."

Chick and his brother Tig pooled their resources in Pensacola, and put up the graft to open two small gambling houses in the back rooms of restaurants. One was near the main gate of the Pensacola Naval Base, and on pay nights the sailors jammed their joint. In a few weeks the brothers filled up a small safe with $27,000 net winnings, and Chick got nervous about it.

"Tig," he said, "let's get this dough out of here. Some heist guy's gonna come in here some night and walk out with it."

"I'll take it out of here right now," Tig said.

He stuffed the cash into a chamois bag and walked to his auto, parked in a used car lot they owned a couple of blocks away. Chick found him there later with his skull split, and the money bag gone.

"The hell with it," Chick said days later, when Tig walked groggily out of the hospital. "I'm going to hit it for Mexico."

He drove across the border, and headed for Mexico City, where Virginia was waiting. She had sold her house in Miami, depositing the cash in the Banco Nationale de Mexico, and during the months Chick and Tig were in Pensacola she had made the whole Jet Set circuit—Acapulco, Cuernavaca, San Jose de Perua, and finally Mexico City under the alias of Miss Onie Brown.

There Virginia leased three floors of a five-story apartment building in an exclusive residential section, and for almost a year and a half she was hostess to an intriguing flow of men and women.

The guests often included Dr. "Mom" Chung, ostensibly a physician in San Francisco's Chinatown, but who actually had almost no practice there at all. For years Dr. Chung was one of San Francisco's distinguished citizens and during World War II she "adopted" many celebrated fighters into organizations called the "Beloved Sons and Daughters of the Fair Haired Bastards," "The Beloved Kiwis" (aviators), and "The Golden Dolphins" (submariners). Among those who carried membership cards in these honorary clubs were Commanding General Edward Morris of the Fourth Fighter Command; Vice-Admiral Bertram Rodgers; actor Glenn Ford, then a Marine sergeant; Admiral of the Fleet Chester Nimitz; Brigadier General Melvin Maas, and some 1500 others.

When she was stricken with a heart attack in 1958, Marie McDonald sent flowers daily, Sophie Tucker called her every evening, and Giorgio Tozzi of the Metropolitan Opera came to sing for her. At her death the San Francisco Board of Supervisors adjourned in her memory, and the mourners at the funeral included Mayor George Christopher, Admiral Nimitz, and Andre Kostelanetz.

But behind the publicity and the philanthropic facade, Mom Chung was a shadowy character who was just as intimate with Virginia Hill and the kings of the underworld, including Frank Costello, the Fischetti brothers, and Joey Adonis, as she was with the celebrities she was exploiting. Narcotic agents kept her under constant surveillance for years, but were never able to make an arrest. Other Federal agencies also kept an eye on her movements, and it is known now that she took large cash payments from Bugsy Siegel and Virginia. She delivered mysterious packages to Virginia in New Orleans, Las Vegas, New York, Chicago, and other cities, and during 1948 was Virginia's house guest many times in Mexico City. Chick never knew Mom Chung's exact role in the turbulent world of Virginia Hill. He thinks she may have been a mother to a girl who never really had one, and she may also have served as a money messenger. Some Federal agents are convinced she was trafficking in drugs, and at least one of the espionage arms of the government suspected her of subversive activities. But she certainly didn't accumulate great wealth doing any of these things, for when she died in 1959 her total estate, including a house in San Francisco, amounted to $47,164.

Virginia's regular guests in Mexico City also included the handsome young Major Luis Amezcua; politically powerful Chato Juarez; Pepe Romero, a Mexico City columnist; Valentio Quintara, a Mexican private detective, and Betty Goodrich Cromwell, a young American divorcee who chose to live in Mexico because it was cheap. There was only one link to Virginia's Las Vegas past—District Judge Frank McNamee, who is now Chief Justice of the Nevada State Supreme Court.

Chick Hill found that the *mañana* tempo of life in Mexico was not fast enough, and he probably would have returned to California if he had not renewed an acquaintance with Susan Cora, a lovely young Mexican movie actress he had met some years before. Susan was one of the regulars at Virginia's court, and, as Chick says, he was soon "crazy about this hot little tamale."

One day, when Virginia was busy with Major Amezcua, Chick took Susan to the nearest Catholic church and married her. He does not remember the name or address of the church, and he can barely recall the ceremony, which was in Spanish. Virginia took the news with surprising indifference, and as a wedding gift she presented them with a florist shop she had leased in the lobby of Mexico City's big Hotel Del Prado.

When Susan became pregnant, Virginia was piqued, and found

an excuse to pack up once more. She was also bored with many of her suitors who, like most Mexican men, were inclined to be imperious with their women. Perhaps she was a little homesick as well.

On June 28, 1949, she flew to Chicago and checked into the Sheraton Hotel. In mid-October Chicago newspapermen discovered that she was living there, and a series of interviews, with the inevitable "underworld Queen" tie-up, so embarrassed the management that she was formally asked to leave. Virginia was unusually docile about her eviction from the hotel, and promptly found an apartment at 215 East Chestnut Street. She bought a whole new wardrobe and gave her old clothes to her maid. She was soon back entertaining old friends in the mob, including Joe Fischetti and Joe Adonis, spending the evenings in two nightclubs, the Singapore and The Trade Winds, buying more jewelry, which she kept in a blue leather box, and going out to dinner now and then with Harry Jameson, a Chicago manufacturer, and his wife Dorothy.

One day in December she called her maid, Mrs. Delle Gordon, to her room and handed her six one-hundred dollar bills.

"Go to the Western Union office," she said, "and send this money to Major Amezcua in Mexico City. Here's the name and address written out."

Mrs. Gordon took the cash—it was the first of countless money orders she handled for Virginia—and a few days later the Mexican officer arrived in Chicago and moved into Virginia's apartment. Long afterward, when Kefauver investigators were trying to track down her money juggling, Virginia told a romantic story of how Major Amezcua, distraught with love for her, came to Chicago to propose marriage.

"I didn't want to marry him," she said. "But when he went back home he gave me a love gift of $15,000, and I used it to go to Sun Valley."

While she was weaving this sentimental fiction of unrequited love, Virginia neglected to mention that Major Amezcua never had as much as 15,000 pesos, and that the cash she wired him was to pay for his round trip flight to Chicago. Virginia pictured him to others as an ardent lover while she concealed her real motives. He would fix things in high places in Mexico, and she would need him for that.

It was true, though, as she told the Kefauver men, that she went to Sun Valley. The guests and employees who were at the luxurious lodge during January and February of 1950 are not likely to forget the six weeks of Virginia's bacchanalian fling. It was like an *au revoir* to the mournful days and the many suicide attempts that followed the murder of her secret husband, Ben Siegel. It was also *bon jour* to new horizons, and a kind of semirespectable living she had never had before.

From the moment she registered on January 4, when a wide-eyed bellboy saw her unpack bundles of currency from a suitcase, Virginia was the center of gossip. Her wardrobe was spectacular, her almost nightly parties were noisy and gay, and she herself gulped whiskey as though Prohibition was about to return. She was almost never alone. Her escorts included Billy Wilkerson; two Chicago slot machine manufacturers; a Los Angeles hoodlum, and a rich Chicago candy manufacturer.

And then there was Hans Hauser, a handsome Teutonic giant of a man who was the hotel's best ski instructor. Austrian by birth, Hauser was suspected of being a Nazi sympathizer during World War II, and was interned in an enemy alien camp for three years. But when the hostilities ended, he came back to Sun Valley with his dark good looks and his skiing talents unimpaired. On the snow-covered slopes he was a Wagnerian god pursued by every Brunhilde in the hotel, and Virginia, who used to think snow was something you took with a needle, suddenly became interested in the outdoor life.

She packed a lunch almost daily, rode to the top of the ski lift, and waited until Hauser showed up with one or more of his palpitating pupils. She managed to detain him long enough, sharing a sandwich and a glass of wine, to make him breathe harder than he ever had shooting down the mountains on his skis. When she discovered that one of Hauser's more favored students was Miss Ann Sothern of the movies, Virginia changed her strategy.

She pre-empted his instruction bookings—and his fees were expensive—to leave him no time for other students. She took him to her room and, as though by accident, popped open a suitcase and spilled thousands of dollars in cash on the spread. Mumbling an excuse about her carelessness, Virginia gathered up the pile of

$100 bills and stuffed them back into the bag. Hans Hauser needed no further prodding. He was hers alone for the rest of her stay.

The books at the lodge showed that Virginia spent $11,600 during her visit there—not counting the ski lessons, her purchases in the stores, or money she put out for Betty Cromwell. Mrs. Cromwell came to Sun Valley on a $200 money order sent to her by Virginia, and all her hotel expenses were paid for her. It was during this happy vacation that Virginia confessed to Mrs. Cromwell that she had married Bugsy Siegel in Mexico City.

"So you were his legal widow when he died?" Mrs. Cromwell said.

"Yes, I was," Virginia said. "But I was in no position to tell anyone. I could have claimed something out of the estate, but I wanted his two daughters to have whatever he had."

Betty Cromwell went back to Mexico before Virginia and Hans took a train to Glenwood Springs, Colorado, and registered at the Colorado Hotel as man and wife. They attended the ski races at Aspen and then moved on to Elko, Nevada. They stayed long enough to be married by a Justice of the Peace, and then went back to Sun Valley.

Virginia, always independent, took a train to Chicago, where the press really stirred up a storm on this new development in her life. The unfortunate publicity annoyed the executives of the Union Pacific Railroad, Hauser's employers, and he was immediately fired. Hauser was stunned by this disaster (his friends later said he had no idea Virginia was a gang moll) and was a dejected man when he left Sun Valley and joined her in Chicago. But the fallout that accompanied every explosive move made by his flamboyant wife was too much for this stolid and essentially simple mountain man. It was not just the publicity alone; Hauser also got the unnerving news that the Immigration Department was asking questions about his status.

He had a fear of being deported; the threat of it was always present, and despite his marriage to Virginia—which some people suggested was a cold-blooded scheme to avoid being sent back to Austria—he was vulnerable because of his wartime imprisonment.

Virginia knew his position was tenuous, and she begged Mom Chung to help Hans with her influential friends in Washington,

D.C. But Mom evidently lacked the connections in this crisis, and Hauser, on the verge of panic, left Chicago by train for a meeting with his attorneys in Spokane. By prearrangement, he got off the train at Pendleton, Oregon, and took a bus to a point some twenty-five miles from Spokane, where he was met by James Crick, Jr., a Spokane contractor and old friend. Hauser was carrying some $15,000 in cash in a sock—more money than he had ever seen in one bundle—and he handled it as gingerly as if it was a bottle of nitroglycerine. He asked Crick to take care of the cash, and the latter obligingly deposited it in his own bank account in Spokane.

The battle plan to save Virginia's husband from the immigration axe was well organized, and United States Senator Warren Magnuson, who was unaware of Virginia's relationship with the mobs, was asked to introduce a bill giving Hauser American citizenship. The drive was led by no less than the Girl Scouts of America of Spokane, through Executive Director Helen Bock who wrote a letter declaring that Hauser had enlisted 200 high school girls in a skiing program. "We have found that Mr. Hauser's integrity and sincere interest in assisting us in a wholesome outdoor program for girls is invaluable," Mrs. Bock said.

Senator Magnuson actually introduced two Senate bills on Hauser's behalf, but neither one passed. Hans Hauser was on borrowed time, and all the Girl Scouts in Spokane couldn't save him.

During 1950 and 1951, Hans and Virginia roamed around the United States—together or separately. They popped up in Pensacola and Miami, and from there Virginia flew to Havana, where she registered at the Sans Souci Hotel as Mrs. Onie V. Reid. She made another solo trip to New Orleans, where she was an incognito guest in the apartment of "Dandy Phil" Kastel, Frank Costello's Louisiana slot machine agent, at the Roosevelt Hotel. Some of Virginia's friends were puzzled by her seemingly purposeless tour, but she had a secret. Virginia Hill was pregnant. Perhaps it was a deliberate conception, for Virginia knew abortionists in every part of the country. Years later, she told a friend that Mrs. Crick, young wife of Hans's contractor friend, had urged her to "have a baby and settle down, and maybe that will cool you off." It was the first time in her life that Virginia had given a thought to the future.

In any case, Virginia did not want to be seen in public with the telltale swelling, and on June 15, 1950, she and Hans drove to Bar Harbor, Maine, and paid $1800 to rent a summer cottage called Eagle Cliff. She stayed out of sight there until October 15, when the lease was up, and moved to the Hotel Commander in Cambridge. When her child's birth seemed imminent, she went to St. Elizabeth's Hospital in Brighton—she was known there as Mrs. Ona Herman—and on November 20 her son, Peter Hauser, was born.

In December, strong enough to travel, Virginia and Hans took the baby and rented a suite at the Sulgrave Hotel on Park Avenue in New York. On January 19, they went to Spokane by train and paid $1000 a month to rent a house owned by a Mr. and Mrs. Howard Baker, Jr., at 4206 S. Latawah Street. When the Bakers returned from a vacation in Mexico, Hans and Virginia paid $31,000 for a house at 3905 Sky View Avenue. The view included a house across the street, owned by a pleasant couple named Mr. and Mrs. Clifford Rice, and if Virginia ever doubted the dark twists of fate she would be a believer soon. Cliff Rice was a special agent in the Intelligence Division of the Bureau of Internal Revenue.

In March 1951, Virginia went through her incredible comedy before the television cameras at the Kefauver Commission hearings. It was a *chef d'ouevre* of the thespian art, and confirmed the opinion of Lee Mortimer and others that she could have been a fine actress. All day long she was a female matador in a mink coat and a picture hat, dancing around the dangerous questions, parrying, and laughing at all of America, and at the end she had told them nothing.

There was one maneuver between Virginia and Rudolph Halley which seemed like an innocent exchange at the time. But she remembered it afterward and wished she had not been so flip.

"You don't seem to have taken the trouble to account to Uncle Sam the way the rest of us do," Halley said.

Virginia gave him a pleasant smile. "Well, then," she said, "he'll have to take care of that, won't he?"

"Uncle Sam?"

"Yes," she said.

"Well, maybe he will, Mrs. Hauser," Halley said grimly.

"Well, that's all right, sure," she nodded. "I don't blame him."

Uncle Sam was already very busy on the case, and it turned

out to be not all right with Virginia. Long after she left the stand that day, Senator Kefauver had an indelible portrait of her in his mind, and he said: "The strain of the life she led has taken its toll. The fading underworld queen is now a ravaged woman. . . . I imagine Miss Hill would think hard about whether the life she led was worth the price she has had to pay for having her name nationally famous. I would have preferred to spare her the ordeal."

Hans Hauser, an uneasy home owner still arguing his case with the Immigration Service, may have thought Virginia would stick around the house, caring for the baby and spending a little time in the kitchen on apple strudel and other German delights she knew how to cook. But she had a compulsion to move around, and during that spring she covered thousands of miles by plane, train, and car. She had already been in San Francisco, where she shared a St. Francis Hotel suite with Joe Epstein, and she joined him again in Minneapolis, Reno, Chicago, and Seattle. Presumably these meetings involved the usual cash pickups, plus some long-range plans for the future. Hauser had already been defeated in the final round of his long struggle to remain in America, and was given the choice of leaving voluntarily by September 1, or being forcibly ejected by the Government.

Virginia knew the cause was lost. And she also knew she was under the microscope at Internal Revenue offices, and she began accumulating cash for the threatened emergency.

At first there were regular shipments of money in the familiar shoe box marked RX-LOTION. Then came fat letters addressed to her maid, Delle Gordon, which Virginia grabbed and said they contained money from Epstein.

"You didn't ask me if you could use my name," Mrs. Gordon complained.

"You'll do what I say," Virginia said coldly.

"I don't like it a bit," Mrs. Gordon said.

Virginia suddenly slapped her maid's face so hard that the woman almost fell down. "Don't argue with me," she said, "unless you want another whack."

Thereafter Mrs. Gordon, whose sole income was $50 a week salary and who occasionally got some of Virginia's cast-off clothes, silently took Virginia's orders. At least twice there were Western

Union money orders—one for $1000 and another for $700—which were addressed to her and which she cashed for Virginia. In June, during a casual and friendly chat with her neighbor, Agent Rice, Virginia confided that Hans Hauser had decided to go to Chile where he could work as a ski instructor. Also, since few Chileans were applying for permission to emigrate to the United States, he could perhaps make the quota list, and thus come back. Virginia said she herself would remain in Spokane. She had already employed a nurse named Eva Beauchene to care for the baby.

One afternoon Virginia phoned Rice and asked if Hauser could take her new Cadillac when he started for Santiago in Chile. Rice knew the government was not prepared to file criminal charges against her, but the Internal Revenue was very much concerned with Virginia's tangible assets, and wanted to keep them in sight.

"I'm sorry," he said. "We can't let him take the car."

An hour later she called back, weeping and distraught. "Mr. Rice," she said, "Hans can sell that car in Chile for $20,000, and he needs the money. Can't you please let him take it?"

"There is just nothing I can do," he said. "The way things are my hands are tied."

That evening, returning from a dinner party, Rice and his wife saw the Cadillac in the garage of the Hausers' home and hooked up to it, extending into the driveway so the garage door could not be closed, was a new trailer. But the next morning the garage door was closed, and no one came when he rang the doorbell. Rice went to his office, and immediately set up a dragnet.

Customs and Immigration officers along the Mexican and Canadian borders were alerted, and teletype bulletins jumped along the wires to sheriffs and police officers in every western state. During the day, one highway patrol radioed a report that the big black car had gone through Missoula, Montana. Suddenly there was a strange atmospheric interference with radio transmission in the area, and by morning the quarry had disappeared.

The next day radio messages crackled across a dozen states, and by the merest chance the foreman of a railroad section gang near Palo Alto, the site of Stanford University, remembered seeing such a Cadillac emerging from the driveway of an estate owned by one of Hans Hauser's skiing companions. He reported his suspicions to the FBI, and the car was found in a Palo Alto garage where Hauser and his friend had put it in dead storage. But there was nothing left in it, not so much as a piece of paper or a map to suggest where Hans and Virginia might have gone. The Cadillac was subsequently sold by the Government for $3900, and later that year Internal Revenue agents found Virginia's Mercury station wagon in New York and sold it for $1900.

On July 4, a sharp-eyed Los Angeles police detective named G. L. Cruea spotted Hans Hauser, carrying his baby son, boarding a Pan-American plane headed for Santiago, Chile, via New Orleans. There was nothing he could do about it, because there were no warrants out for Hauser, and a quick search determined that Virginia was not aboard. Rice learned later that Hans, Virginia, and the baby had lived in the Clift Hotel in San Francisco, calling themselves Mr. and Mrs. Norman Hall. Indeed, Hauser had lunched with an old friend, Anthony Richter, who was *mâitre d'hôtel* at the Whitcomb Hotel, and had confided to him, for reasons that Richter never understood, that Virginia regularly got stacks of $100 bills in shoe boxes sent to her by Joe Epstein from Chicago.

Although Hauser was gone, Cliff Rice was convinced that Virginia was still in California, and would eventually try to scuttle across the border into Mexico. Ticket agents for all the airlines were given a description of her, and on the evening of July 5, Virginia walked alone into the San Francisco airport terminal and went to the Continental Air Lines counter. She had seven enormous suitcases with her, said her name was Harper and asked for a one-way ticket to El Paso.

Lilymae Ward, the girl making out the ticket, took a second look at this beautiful creature in her long mink coat, and recalled having seen her with Bugsy Siegel on a Western Air Lines flight out of Las Vegas four years before. The flight was already airborne when the girl alerted the FBI. When Virginia stepped out of the plane at El Paso, wearing one fur coat and carrying three others over her arm, she was stunned to be greeted by Government men.

In Spokane, meanwhile, Rice had obtained a jeopardy assessment against Virginia, and in order to keep her from crossing the border, Custom agents invoked a section of the Gold Act of 1934, which permits searching the luggage of anyone suspected of illegally taking gold out of the country. Virginia fumed and cursed, but there was no escape. Customs men opened her bags and found them stuffed with furs, jewelry, and other valuable personal things. When it filtered into her churning mind that her careful plans were ruined, she walked into the airport terminal and bought a ticket to Spokane. While she was waiting for the plane, Virginia battled two reporters who came asking questions about Hauser and the baby, and, lacking any other weapon, she hit both of them with one of her shoes.

She arrived in Spokane at seven the next morning, summoned a cab, and went directly to her house on Sky View Avenue. She fumbled for the key in her purse, and at that instant she saw the padlock on the front door, with a notice that the Government had put a lien on the house and its contents. She rattled the lock angrily, and looked inside through the living room window, where a guard sat in a chair keeping an eye on things.

"Open this door, goddamit!" she yelled at him.

The guard slowly got to his feet, and opened the door as far as a chain lock would permit. "This is my house!" Virginia cried. "You can't throw me out of here."

"I'm sorry," the watchman said. "The Internal Revenue has a lien on the place, and nobody comes in without their okay."

Virginia stood there a moment, then she ran down the street to the home of an attorney friend. In an hour or so she knew she had come to the end of the line in Spokane, or anywhere else in the United States. The assessment totaled $161,000, and she didn't have it. Joe Epstein didn't have it. Her two cars were gone. Her world was coming apart, and she was alone in the wreckage. Hans was in Chile with their baby. Bugsy Siegel was dead. Her underworld friends were either in jail, or having troubles of their own. The haze was finally dispersed, and the hopeless picture stood out in sharp perspective to Virginia.

Rice explained that the Internal Revenue Service would auction her house and her possessions there, and the proceeds would be credited to her delinquent account.

"I'll help all I can," she said. "I just want to get it over with so I can join Hans and the baby."

Toward the end of July, as Virginia began cataloging and

estimating the value of her things, she and Cliff Rice were almost like father and daughter. Once, when Rice was in the house making lists, Virginia came across the little book *Forever*. She told him the theme of the story, and she said: "Some day, somewhere, I'll see Ben again."

"You truly believe that, don't you?" Rice asked.

"Yes, I do," she said. "Not in this life. In another one. I would like to have you read the book, and then you'll understand."

"I can get a copy of it somewhere."

"No," she said quickly. "I want you to have mine. Here," she added, giving the volume to Mrs. Rice, "take it home with you. I'm giving it to you."

Mrs. Rice accepted the book and thanked Virginia. She and her husband have read it many times. They still have it in their library, and they understand. Colin and Julie. Ben and Virginia. Together. Forever. It was the only faith Virginia ever had.

On August 2, when the temperature in Spokane was touching 103°, more than 3000 men and women swarmed over the neat little lawn in front of the red brick ranch house for the sale by an auctioneer known as C. T. "Himself" Gregson. The inventory of her possessions, which the Spokane newspapers had publicized for three days in advance of the auction, included all her furs, some costume jewelry (her valuable gems had already been smuggled into Mexico and turned over to Susan Cora Hill), and enough china, silverware, rugs, furniture, and appliances for two houses. There was also her dazzling wardrobe—144 pairs of shoes, dozens of tailored suits, Howard Greer dresses and gowns, including the one which was torn in her fight with Lee Mortimer; gloves, purses, sports clothes, cashmere sweaters, and lingerie.

The sale began at ten A.M. and from any standpoint it was a disgraceful exhibition of human cruelty and greed. The customers not only came to scratch and claw for the bargain goods, but to look at a woman's heartbreak as she moved along the tables where people's hands were pawing her treasures.

One of the first items offered was a pair of plastic earrings, with a ring thrown in, and J. T. Gehrig, a Spokane insurance man, called out: "Ten dollars." There were no other bids, and Gehrig dubiously examined his purchase. The earrings were passable, but the ring was covered with soap and a white powder which turned out to be flour. An hour or so later Virginia heard about the sale to Gehrig, and immediately realized that they had sold her long-lost wedding ring. She told Rice she had been baking a cake, took it off while she was kneading the dough, and laid it in a soap dish on the kitchen window sill.

"I had never taken the ring off before," she said with tears in her eyes, "and I forgot it, and now they've sold it for a measly ten bucks. I want it back!"

The Government men at the auction were embarrassed when they heard Virginia's plaintive story, and they went through the crowd looking for Gehrig. He had come back and he said he had gone to a jeweler downtown where the ring was appraised at $450. They explained the error to him, and asked if he would return it.

"No," he said.

"Would you be willing to pay $350 for it?"

"No, I wouldn't," Gehrig said. "I bought it for ten dollars, and I have a receipt for it."

The Government agents checked with headquarters, and found that there was no legal way they could force Gehrig to return the ring, or pay what it was actually worth. Virginia, sick at heart because she had lost the last link to her murdered lover, spent the rest of that broiling day sipping iced tea with Rice and his wife in their home across the street. Subsequently, like a child eagerly telling her parents about her adventures, Virginia nostalgically recalled her love affair with Bugsy Siegel, her futile attempt to become a movie actress, the poverty of her Alabama childhood, and her endless wandering from one temporary home to another.

And she talked about her fear. It was not a fear she could analyze or trace to a source. It was a nameless dread that compelled her to buy a gun for the first time in her life. Once, when she saw Rice in his office, she asked him to keep the door open, and she sat with her back to the opposite wall. "Some day," she said, "I'll probably wind up in the gutter."

The auction yielded about $30,000 to the Government, including the equity in the house. Virginia's furs had a minimum appraised value of $23,200, but they brought in only $5280.

Virginia left Spokane with only the clothes she was wearing, and whatever the Government had not taken out of her suitcases, and she joined Chick and Billy Hill in Pensacola on August 17. On September 25, though government agents watching her were not aware of it, Virginia received Austrian passport No. VR-85-4239-127, issued to her in the name of Onie V. Hauser. She was next seen at the Shamrock Hotel in Houston, where she registered as Mrs. O. V. Hall and there, as she had planned, she was met by Joe Epstein and Major Luis Amezcua. Amezcua had diplomatic immunity, of course, and he arrived there in a new Chrysler sedan he had purchased at the factory in Detroit.

Virginia and the two men checked out on October 12, and Virginia casually mentioned to a Houston gambler named Al Cooper that she and her Mexican escort were driving to California. But the big car headed southward toward Laredo, and Government agents were powerless to intervene. Virginia did not look back when they crossed the Mexican border, and Amezcua drove her to the Hotel L'Escargot in Mexico City.

Thus, she closed the door on her native land.

"I will never come back to America," she said. "Why should I come back to be persecuted by those rats in Washington? They are the real gangsters in this world, and it is not in my heart to forgive those who have hurt me."

Bitterness and self pity, hate and loneliness, blindness to her own errors and sins—Virginia suffered from all these things. And at last, when she saw human frailties for what they were, and looked at the truth, she had no choice. Then, and only then, death could be a friend.

EPILOGUE

In the early days, when Bugsy Siegel was known as a "wealthy sportsman" in Hollywood, and was accepted without question by the big names of the motion picture world, a superstition passed from mouth to mouth that the handsome gangster was a jinx.

Chick Hill heard it, and called it "hogwash."

The Countess Dorothy DiFrasso was told by her friends that Ben Siegel could only give her a heartache, and she ignored the warning.

In the back rooms of restaurants where the mob men gathered, the rumors were kicked around that the Bug was a curse, and any of the informed hoods could rattle off a list of dead men and for each one add a fervent "God rest his soul."

A realist could laugh off these maledictions and say that people create their own damnations. But in the years since 1947 when Ben Siegel was put away in his crypt, the ledger shows a long list of significant entries.

There was Donald O. Bircher, for instance, the Internal Revenue agent who was working on the Siegel file and who was ready to bring the gangster to court when he was killed. Bircher retired from government service after twenty-three years as an agent, and opened a tax consultation service partnership with a man who represented Mickey Cohen and other racketeers. On March 8, 1961, Bircher went into the bathroom of his home, and put a bullet through his head.

In Beverly Hills Allen Smiley, who sat beside Siegel when he was slain, was convicted of falsely claiming American citizenship, and was sent to McNeil Island Penitentiary for a year. When he came out, and was just getting nicely started in a business, his $100,000 home burned down.

Mickey Cohen once told me that the best advice he ever had from Ben Siegel was: "Pay your taxes and don't fool around with the revenue guys." During his trial in 1951, Mickey tried to account for $25,000 in cash he got by swearing he borrowed it from Siegel. Siegel wasn't alive to deny it, but his brother, Dr. Maurice Siegel, testified that the gangster's estate had no record of any such loan. Mickey went to McNeil Island for four years, emerged cockier than ever, and immediately started cheating on his taxes again. This time he got fifteen years.

All of Siegel's intimate underworld lieutenants were murdered by one means or another—Krakower, Greenbaum, Reles, Big Greenie, Anastasia, Willie Moretti, Lepke, among others. Adonis and Luciano were deported, and Longy Zwillman hanged himself. Frankie Carbo, who twice avoided conviction in the Big Greenie murder, got a twenty-five-year term in an extortion case. Fred and Joe Sica, the dreaded Mafia brothers, were sent to prison.

The Countess DiFrasso died of a heart attack on a train to Los Angeles, and similar heart attacks killed Mark Hellinger, Lee Mortimer, Barney Ruditsky, Mom Chung, Little Moe Sedway, Tony Cornero, and Marino Bello.

George Raft tangled with the Intelligence unit of Internal Revenue, and pleaded guilty in Federal court to tax evasion. Supreme Court Justice Frank McNamee of Nevada was beaten savagely by a young punk named Philip Denning.

In October 1965, lovely Marie "The Body" McDonald, who had spent an occasional hour in Ben Siegel's bedroom at the Flamingo penthouse, was found dead in her San Fernando Valley home surrounded by bottles of sleeping pills. Medical investigators gave Marie the benefit of the doubt and said she had taken an overdose accidentally. Two weeks later her new husband, Donald F. Taylor, a movie producer, went into the same bedroom, wrote a farewell note, and killed himself with the same lethal Seconal she had used.

It is a formidable and frightening box score of men and women who are dead.

The curse of Ben Siegel? Perhaps.

By 1965 there were only two survivors of the original group —Chick and Virginia. Chick, who had divorced Susan Cora and married a pretty Los Angeles girl named Victoria Howe, was living under an assumed name when I found him operating a small business in central California. He was jittery and gun shy, and he had moved no less than six times in three years.

"Why are you running, Chick?" I asked.

"I don't know," he said. "I tried to burn up all the memories and shut the doors. But it stays with me day and night. I think of the mistakes I made, and the money I threw away, but that only makes it worse."

"Are you afraid?"

"Certainly I'm afraid. There are still some guys around. They think I know something. They think I'll talk. Goddamit—I don't know anything, and I don't want to know anything. I want to forget the whole lousy mess."

"And what about Virginia?"

"Well," he said, "I haven't seen Tab since I stayed with her in Switzerland—hell, it's almost ten years ago."

"Where would I find her now?"

"In Salzburg, in Austria," he said. "Why don't you write her a note?"

"I'll give it a try," I said.

Virginia's final erratic journey took her first to Santiago, then to a villa at Nina Del Mar, near Valparaiso, and when Hans could find no work there, they moved to Klosters, a ski resort in the Alps not far from Zurich.

Chick said this refuge was like being buried alive. He meant that there were no nightclubs or exotic restaurants, nor any newspapers anxious to give her a plug or a picture on page one. The streets were too narrow for Cadillacs, and instead of American whiskey most good burghers there drank kirchwasser or brandy.

She made news only once during the first two or three years when, on a visit to Hauser's relatives in Austria, she caught a photographer aiming his lens at her. She was playing tennis at the time, and with one mighty whack she used her racket to smash the man's camera. Another time, when writer Michael Stern called at the Chalet Primula in Klosters, where she had rented a floor, she called him a "no good bastard" and then, quixotically, invited him in for a drink.

The general impression in Chicago, Los Angeles, Las Vegas, and other places where hoodlums talk business was that Virginia had not only departed with a good deal of money, but that Government agents had reached a dead end trying to find her. The fact is there is not a wanted tax dodger anywhere in the world whose hiding place and daily movements are not known to the Intelligence Division of the Internal Revenue Service. The Government knew that Virginia was in Klosters, and was completely informed on the homey little details of her life in exile.

They knew she had made a round trip to Hong Kong, for instance. They had a chart of her trips to Naples, Paris, Venice, Vienna, and other cities. They knew she usually wore sweaters and blue jeans in Klosters, had a checking account in the Banque Privees des Grisons, drove a small Fiat sedan, and occasionally entertained such visiting American celebrities as movie director Howard Hawks and writer Irwin Shaw, and that she kept an apartment in Zurich.

While Virginia was killing time in Klosters, Cliff Rice and a score of other special agents were filling up their dossier. Virginia's financial wizardry was so bewildering that no single government agency could ever get all the figures. But there was enough. On June 23, 1954, United States Attorney Laughlin Waters gave the Federal Grand Jury in Los Angeles evidence that from 1944 to 1947 inclusive, Virginia claimed a total income of $68,870, and on that she paid income taxes of $21,398.64. Indeed, during one year Virginia applied for a tax refund, and actually got a check for $3100. She gave the money to Chick. The Grand Jury heard witnesses who testified that in the four year period Virginia had spent $195,727.13—which was perhaps a fifth of what she really scattered around—and that on the documented total she thus owed $119,961.98 income tax.

The jury returned a four count indictment and now, instead of being merely a delinquent tax payer, Virginia was a fugitive criminal. In December 1955, the Internal Revenue Service distributed hundreds of WANTED posters from coast to coast, with two pictures of her, both front view. Many of her friends and acquaintances took them off post office walls and mailed them to her. She was especially furious about the line that read: "Virginia Hill Hauser was formerly a paramour and associate of gangsters and racketeers."

Chick and Susan Cora Hill and their baby son, Carlos Eugenio Hill, Jr., went to Switzerland to live with Virginia for awhile, and they soon discovered that she was as hotheaded as ever. Virginia, moping about the WANTED posters, was drinking more liquor than she could handle, and she was so combustible that Chick said he avoided arguments and disagreements on every subject they discussed.

One cold winter evening, when the snow was piled high against the house, Virginia was on her tenth highball when Susan, who had been quarreling with Chick, accused him of using cocaine.

"Goddamit!" Virginia screamed. "You're a lying little bitch. Chick never took a shot of coke in his life, and you know it."

"He did, too!" Susan yelled back. "My brother saw him."

Virginia instantly sprang across the room and her right fist lifted Susan off her feet and dropped her to the floor. She tried rolling out of the way, but Virginia hit her again and again until she lost consciousness, and was a bloody heap in the corner of the room.

"Tab, for God's sake!" Chick cried. "Get away from her."

"You stay out of this!" Virginia snarled. She picked up a long knife and hurled it like a lance at her brother. He threw up his hand to protect his face, and the knife pierced his palm and stuck there. He pulled it out with a spurt of blood, and Virginia heard him grunting in pain.

"Oh, Chick!" she sobbed. "I'm sorry. I'm sorry. I didn't mean it. Here—let me fix it."

"Never mind me," Chick said. "Just beat it and leave us alone."

Virginia retreated to her room begging her brother's forgiveness as she went, but Chick was too busy trying to revive Susan. And within an hour, after patching up her bruises, Susan was packed and on her way to Paris. Government agents later heard that Susan Hill was in such a panic that she grabbed her baby and jumped from a second floor balcony into a cushion of deep snow. She took a taxi into Zurich, and Chick, in anxious pursuit, lost track of her there.

He did not see Susan again for eight months. He remained in Switzerland with Virginia. He now says that his wife left the chalet by the front door, not by a leap from the balcony, and took a train from Zurich to the Mexican Embassy in Paris. She borrowed money from friends there, and took a steamer back to the United States, and later obtained a divorce. When Chick finally went home, he also had to borrow money for passage on the French liner *Ile de France* in October 1957.

Virginia was once more alone. She was weary of living with Hans (she once told Chick he was "a clod") and she ached for the familiar sound of her own language. She knew she would never be anything but a stranger in a strange land, and she wanted to go home. Perhaps someone could arrange a deal. She remembered a conversation with Special Agent Rice, long before the Grand Jury indictment, when she had asked him how much time she would have to serve in prison if she were tried and convicted.

"I wouldn't want to make a guess," he said.

"But you must have a pretty good idea?" she persisted.

"Well," Rice said, "Frank Costello got five years. Adonis got three. They gave Mickey Cohen four, but he's out on appeal."

"I'm not Costello or Adonis or Cohen," she said sharply.

"I know. You're a woman. It would probably be less than three years. Maybe only one. You never know what a jury or a judge will do."

It would be worth it. One year in prison, perhaps less for good behavior. Anything was better than being exiled forever in Switzerland or Austria or anywhere else outside the United States. And it would be forever, because she could not be extradited on an income tax charge.

"I want to come home," she wrote to Chick. *I want to come home.* She sent a letter to Attorney Joe Ross in Beverly Hills, and he in turn sent the word to attorneys in Seattle and Spokane, and the wheels began to turn.

The Internal Revenue men had nothing personal against Virginia. It was their job to determine the taxes due in such cases and collect it if they could.

In Spokane, a Federal judge named Samuel Driver was known to be lenient in tax evasion cases because he felt that it was better for the Government to salvage unpaid taxes, if the culprits could raise the money, than to keep them behind bars and get nothing. The lawyers talked to Judge Driver and to the Internal Revenue men, and in 1958 an agreement was reached. Virginia would come back to Spokane via Hong Kong (U.S. Attorney Laughlin Waters in Los Angeles said he would not object to transferring the case) and would go directly to Judge Driver for a temporary release on bail. She did not want to be placed under arrest and jailed, and it was understood by all concerned that she would plead guilty and offer to pay up what she owed. In exchange she would get a year in prison and thereafter would be free. Free to live with her own kind, and free to stop running.

She began to pack her things for the long journey ahead. In September, Federal Judge Samuel Driver started on his annual vacation, driving south to California. He had a farm of his own in Pasco, Washington, and as he drove through the warm, inland Sacramento Valley near Woodland, he saw a great field of corn paralleling the road. He pulled to one side and told his wife he wanted a closer look at what seemed to be an unusually fine crop. He got out of the car, intent on the field, and did not see a car whizzing toward him. The machine hit him and threw him into the air. He died at the Woodland Clinic Hospital on September 12, and on that same day Virginia Hill Hauser died a little, too.

In April 1964, I sent a brief letter to Virginia at the Hotel Zistel Alm, a small *gasthaus* in Salzburg owned by Hans Hauser's family. There was no reply, but the following month I received from a Government source a copy of the following cablegram:

> ONIE VIRGINIA HAUSER (Maiden name Hill) Born 8-26-16, attempted suicide by taking sleeping pills in her lodgings at UNKEN/GFOLL District of Zell Am See, Austria. She was transported from UNKEN to the Provincial Hospital of Salzburg/ 1st Surgical side (Chirurgische Abteilung des Landeskrankenhauses Salzburg) on 4-20-65. When the officials questioned her she appeared to be extremely nervous and depressed. She said she wanted to commit suicide; that she had been ordered to return to the United States by JOE EPSTEIN, Hotel St. Clair, Chicago, Illinois, or her allowance would be stopped.

I showed the cable to Chick, and his eyes were wet, and for a moment he could not speak. "Oh, no!" he said presently. "Not again! She doesn't really want to die. She takes these damn pills, and she thinks she's strong enough to handle them."

"You really believe that?" I asked.

"Yes," he said, "You remember—I told you. She gets a mad on, and the damn pills work better than liquor."

"But this is the seventh time, Chick."

"Yeah, I know. Maybe she wanted to scare Joe, or she had a fight with Hans. I'm going to write her a letter right now, and give her hell. And I'll bet she doesn't even mention this thing."

Within a week Chick received an airmail letter from Virginia in which, as he predicted, she said nothing about being in the hospital. She said she was planning to take her son, Peter, and move to Mexico, and would leave as soon as she had the necessary visas. She said she would never return to the United States, and closed the brief note by warning Chick to stay away from Joe Epstein. "That dog got me into all this mess," she said, "and made my life a wreck, so don't let him around you."

On October 28, after Chick brought Virginia's note to my home, we placed an overseas call to her in Salzburg. Minutes later Chick was talking to his sister for the first time in ten years, and though the connection was poor he did learn that she had decided against Mexico, and was going to Havana instead. She begged him to telephone Harry and Dorothy Jameson in Beverly Hills (they had moved there from Chicago) and ask them to lend her $3000. Chick promised to phone the Jamesons, and the call was terminated.

He sat in my office shaking his head. "I lied to her," he said. "I'm not going to phone the Jamesons or anybody else and ask for money. Three thousand bucks! We used to blow that much on one lousy party. And she wants to go to Cuba! Why, those conniving thieves down there would steal her blind. She must be out of her head."

He heard nothing more from Virginia, but about a week later there was an airmail postcard from her son, sent from Prague where she was about to board an airliner for Havana. It read:

> Dear Uncle: We are probably coming back to the States now. I hope that you're OK. We were in Vienna in the USA Embassy,

and are waiting for a note from there now. We can talk to you again later. Merry Christmas.

Peter

Virginia was sure she had friends in Cuba. Men she had known in Mexico had told her that they would always be available if she needed help. Virginia had been in Havana often in the Bugsy Siegel days. The mob men had moved in there when Batista was in power, and their money was in the gambling halls. Even George Raft had invested $60,000 in the Capri Hotel, and was official greeter for the casino when the Americans came in at night.

Willie Moretti had been there, and Longy Zwillman, and Meyer Lansky. It was a good racket until Castro took over, and Virginia's friend George Raft suddenly found himself being hustled to the airport by bearded ruffians. He had to leave his $60,000 behind. They even took the last of his cash—$2500—out of his suitcase. They kept him off the plane and said he was going to face a firing squad for trying to smuggle money out, but at the last minute they let him go.

Virginia didn't know about that.

"They're friendly people," she wrote to Chick. "There's plenty to eat, and I've been promised a job."

Virginia spent the last of the money she had borrowed from Hans Hauser's family, and flew from Prague to Havana. Castro's representatives took one look at the name on her passport, and refused to let her leave the airport, or even make a phone call. "You have no visa," they said. "Go back to Prague."

Virginia returned to Hauser's hotel in Salzburg with her spirit broken. Her once lovely face was puffy and wrinkled, and the fire had died in her eyes. The winter snows were already caking the streets, and bending the boughs of the mountain pines. She and Peter had sold all their warm winter clothes, and she had no money to buy more.

She sat in her room, and wrote a plaintive letter to Chick. She asked him again to go to the Jamesons in Beverly Hills, and beg them for a loan, and she added: "I tried to get some money from Joey A. for the first time in my life, but he didn't even answer my letter so I see now he is no friend of mine. If you can do something, do it fast, as I want to get out of here."

Chick looked at his bank balance and he knew he could not help.

"Jesus," he said, "if Tab would only come home we could take care of her. Goddamit, this girl spent hundreds of thousands of dollars on people all over the country, and at least one of 'em might give her a lift."

I sent a long letter to Virginia that same day, and a week later I received this cable:

PLEASE CALL ME SALZBURG 74107
TAB

I placed the call immediately. Her voice was shrill and hysterical across the long miles of sea and air, and there was nothing but hate and fury against the world she had abandoned. I urged her to come home, and make peace with herself, because otherwise she would be running and hiding for the rest of her life, an outcast and exile.

"I wouldn't come back there for anything," she said. "Never. But if you've questions to ask me, write to me, or come over here. It's no good on the phone."

So I wrote to her again, and I told her what I knew about her life, and her vanished dreams and her feelings about Joe Epstein and the Government men. "Face the facts, Tab," I wrote. "You are the only one who can help yourself. The government didn't ruin you. You ruined yourself. Think it over, Tab."

In December there came one last convulsion from the volcano that seethed within her, and she chose to counterattack about the money I said she had spent and the taxes she had never paid. "As for the money you said I spent," she wrote, "I never said I didn't. I was kept by Eppy and he told me how much tax to pay, and I don't believe girls were paying tax when men kept them, so I know lots more who should be in the same fix."

I never heard from her again. In March 1966, at a time when Chick and I were both trying to reach her once more, she drove to a small mountain village called Koppl, not far from Salzburg. She walked into the deep woods, where the snow still lay like cotton on the limbs, and sat beside a brook. The water tumbled over the rocks as it flowed down from the craggy peaks above, and in a little pool she could see her face.

She was forty-nine years old; to her it seemed a thousand. She swallowed the first and second pills, cupping the icy water with her hands to get them down. And then came the others, one after another, twenty-eight in all. The sun sent the light down through the trees on golden cords, but her eyes were closed, and the darkness crept through her veins as she lay down on the wet ground.

Colin! Colin!
Oh, great Lord, we're dead, Julie.

This was Virginia's faith. Death and the resurrection. "This is forever," Julie had said. She and Ben Siegel would die, and they would be reborn, and be together again.